Media Law in Australia

Second Edition

Media Law in Australia

Second Edition

Mark Armstrong
Michael Blakeney
Ray Watterson

OXFORD
UNIVERSITY PRESS

Melbourne
Oxford Auckland New York

OXFORD UNIVERSITY PRESS AUSTRALIA
Oxford New York Toronto
Delhi Bombay Calcutta Madras Karachi
Petaling Jaya Singapore Hong Kong Tokyo
Nairobi Dar es Salaam Cape Town
Melbourne Auckland
and associated companies in
Beirut Berlin Ibadan Nicosia

OXFORD is a trade mark of Oxford University Press

© Mark Armstrong, Michael Blakeney and Ray Watterson 1983, 1988
First published 1983
Second edition 1988

This book is copyright. Apart from any fair
dealing for the purposes of private study,
research, criticism or review as permitted under
the Copyright Act, no part may be reproduced,
stored in a retrieval system, or transmitted, in
any form or by any means electronic, mechanical,
photocopying, recording, or otherwise without
prior written permission. Inquiries to be made
to Oxford University Press.

National Library of Australia
Cataloguing-in-Publication data:

Armstrong, Mark.
    Media law in Australia.

    Bibliography.
    Includes index.
    ISBN 0 19 554902 3

    1. Mass media–Law and legislation–
    Australia. I. Blakeney, Michael. II.
    Watterson, Ray. III. Title.

343.94'099

Typeset by Graphicraft Typesetters Ltd., Hong Kong
Printed by Impact Printing, Melbourne
Published by Oxford University Press, 253 Normanby Road,
South Melbourne, Australia
OXFORD is a trademark of Oxford University Press

CONTENTS

	Preface	vii
	Abbreviations	ix
1	Legal Context	1
2	Defamation	7
3	Defamation: Defences and Remedies	33
4	Protecting Business Reputation	61
5	Copyright	76
6	*Sub Judice* Publications	99
7	Courts and Parliaments: Criticizing and Reporting	129
8	Obscenity, Blasphemy and Sedition	145
9	Radio and Television	155
10	Access to Information	187
11	Press Regulation	204
12	Advertising	211
13	Sales Promotions	236
14	Competitions	244
	References	248
	Index	271

PREFACE

This book, the second edition, is for all those who work in the media, or deal with the media, or study them. Most chapters can be read on their own, but Chapter 1, which outlines the context of the legal system, should be read before any of the others, except by readers already familiar with the law.

The old concept of 'law for journalists' envisaged people of limited education working in the print media, who needed a few rules of thumb about defamation, copyright and contempt. This book recognizes the modern environment of the media by three departures from the old concept. First of all, the areas covered are much wider. Many of today's media workers are in advertising, radio, television, film, and public relations. Chapters on business reputation, electronic media, access to information, advertising, sales promotions and competitions recognize that. Secondly, we have given more attention to the principles on which the law is based. The media workers of today are better educated, even if their education has been less traditional. Our experience has been that they find it easier to understand and follow the law, even at the most practical level, if principles are explained through the reports of cases in which the law has been tested and applied to the complexity of real situations. We have avoided 'simple' rules of thumb, which often oversimplify dangerously, and are no substitute for actual understanding.

Legal colleagues are nevertheless asked to forgive us for some lack of precision and subtlety which cannot be escaped in a brief book about so wide a range of laws. With the encouragement of the publishers, we have forced ourselves to translate many safe, comfortable legal terms into English. The book is not a substitute for specialist legal texts, but it may serve lawyers as a quick index to the major sources of law and recent developments, particularly through the notes at the end.

This, the second edition, is based on the law in force at 1 January 1987, but we have incorporated several major developments which occurred after that date.

We sincerely thank Mark Aronson, Peter Banki, David Levine and Stephen Wilson for their expert comments on the drafts of particular chapters; Anne Armstrong for providing the index and improving the text by many valuable suggestions; and Sandra Cowling and Sue Pannowitz for a heroic typing effort under pressure.

ABBREVIATIONS

ABC	Australian Broadcasting Corporation
AC	Appeal Cases Law Reports
ACLD	Australian Current Law Digest
ACTR	Australian Capital Territory Reports
A-G	Attorney-General
ALJ	Australian Law Journal
ALJR	Australian Law Journal Reports
All ER	All England Reports
ALR	Australian Law Reports
AR (NSW)	Industrial Arbitration Reports (New South Wales)
ATPR	Australian Trade Practices Reporter
CJ	Chief Justice (or Chief Judge)
Ch	Chancery Reports
Ch D	Chancery Division Reports
CLR	Commonwealth Law Reports
Cth	Commonwealth of Australia
DLR	Dominion Law Reports
DPP	Director of Public Prosecutions
FLR	Federal Law Reports
FSR	Fleet Street Reports of Industrial Property Cases
J	Judge (or Justice)
JJ	Judges (or Justices)
KB	King's Bench Reports
LJ	Lord Justice
MCA	Media Council of Australia
MR	Master of the Rolls
NSWLR	New South Wales Law Reports
NSWR	New South Wales Reports
NZLR	New Zealand Law Reports
PC	Privy Council (UK)
QB	Queen's Bench Reports

Qd R	Queensland State Reports
R	The Queen (or King)
RPC	Reports of Patent Cases
SASR	South Australian State Reports
SBS	Special Broadcasting Service
SR (NSW)	New South Wales State Reports
St R Q	State Reports, Queensland
Tas S R	Tasmanian State Reports
Telecom Act	*Telecommunications Act* 1975 (Commonwealth)
TLR	Times Law Reports
VLR	Victorian Law Reports
VR	Victorian Reports
WAR	Western Australian Reports
WLR	Weekly Law Reports (UK)
WN (NSW)	New South Wales Weekly Notes

1
LEGAL CONTEXT

Mark Armstrong

There are a few points about the legal approach to problems and about legal institutions which can help people working in the media to understand the chapters which follow. Media people are used to boiling a whole issue down to a few paragraphs, a twenty-second clip, or even a one line advertising slogan. To them, the words of judges and Acts of parliament seem ponderous, circumlocutory, pedantic, abstract, archaic and overburdened with exceptions. The chapters in this book are shorter than the judgments in many of the hundreds of cases to which they refer.

On the other hand, lawyers are not always impressed by the work of media people. It is regarded as offensive and insulting to describe the writing of a legal colleague as 'journalism'. There are good reasons for the two groups to think differently: it is not just intolerance. The media live by communicating in a vital, concrete way to a diverse multitude. Lawyers and the courts live by getting the best result for individual people or companies. There is some truth in the statement that law sharpens the mind by narrowing it. Lawyers face daily the discipline of mastering every detail of a situation. If a document, a letter or judgment does that, nobody will care whether it makes good copy.

The sources of our law are Acts of parliament and decisions of the courts. When they lay down a general rule for human conduct, they are trying to cater for a vast range of different situations which strain the ingenuity of the best lawyer. It is not surprising that the result, an apparent forest of generalities, provisos and technicalities, would horrify a sub-editor. The nature of every society is reflected in its laws. Our society is complex, and that is reflected in our laws. They should be reformed and better expressed, but it is inevitable that they will continue to grow more complex as our society does. If our Acts of parliament were written by journalists, the result would make good reading; but anarchy would reign.

No introduction to the broad range of laws outlined in this book can fully reflect their complexity. The following chapters explain the basic principles in each area, and illustrate them by summaries of representative cases. In so few pages, it is impossible even to mention all the major cases, let alone proposals for reform. But we have not outlined the law uncritically, and the notes to chapters do mention the specialist texts and the cases which lead a researcher to the main body of the law. This text is, of course, no substitute for legal advice about particular legal problems which affect the media. It should help in preventing legal maladies and identifying symptoms, but as soon as an immediate problem is identified or foreseen, there is no alternative to consulting a qualified legal practitioner.

CASES

It is in the reports of cases most of all that the law reflects the complexity and diversity of human behaviour, and readers need to know something about the use of those reports. This book refers frequently to 'the common law'. In our context, the common law is the body of law made by the judges in deciding particular cases. In the Australian legal system, the judges are never asked to make laws, to legislate. Rather, they make statements about what the law is *incidentally*, in the course of deciding a dispute about something. They are not writing textbooks, let alone passing Acts of parliament. If the same dispute arises again, then the result will be that stated in the earlier case. But it is rare for exactly the same situation to arise more than once. When somebody asks what the law allows in a situation, the question is usually which of two or more cases already decided are most similar to that situation. It is then necessary to ask how the *principles* in the earlier cases are applicable, and also how far the *facts* of the case are comparable.

It is against that background that when discussing cases in this book we have often mentioned not only what a court said, but also what the facts were before it. The facts often qualify the statement. In the practice of law, it is necessary to master all the facts of a case reported in a judgment before using it as a precedent; and the summary of those facts may occupy many pages of the law reports.

COURTS

When case law is discussed, it is always important to bear in mind the degree of authority of the court which decided the case. The High Court of Australia is the most authoritative court in our legal system.

Even a passing remark by a justice of the High Court who was in the majority on the relevant point many sometimes carry more weight than a decision squarely on the same point by a state or territory Supreme Court. The authority of a Supreme Court is second only to that of the High Court, with several exceptions. There is also a Federal Court of Australia, which is superior to the Supreme Court of the ACT and the Supreme Court of the Northern Territory.

An appeal from a single judge of the Supreme Court of New South Wales is heard by the New South Wales Court of Appeal, consisting of three or more Supreme Court judges. In the other states, a similar function is performed by a Full Court of the Supreme Court. Similarly, a Full Court of the High Court of Australia hears appeals from a single justice. The degree of authority carried by decisions of a court corresponds with its place in the hierarchy of appeals. But there are a few judges such as Sir Frederick Jordan, Chief Justice of New South Wales from 1934 to 1949, whose reputation transcends their place in the hierarchy. There are many other Australian courts occupying places in the hierarchy below those mentioned, but they have not delivered many judgments charting the direction of the laws discussed in this book.

In the more traditional areas, such as defamation, contempt and copyright, many of the cases mentioned were decided by English courts. The modern Australian common law is based historically on the English common law. It is still very similar. Until recently, Australian courts were bound by decisions of the Appellate Committee of the House of Lords, commonly known as the House of Lords. It is the highest court in the United Kingdom. The High Court still considers decisions of the House of Lords carefully before departing from them. It was not until 1986 that appeals from state Supreme Courts to the Judicial Committee of the Privy Council in London were abolished. For that reason, there are many references to the Privy Council in the chapters which discuss traditional areas of law. Australian courts treat decisions of the English courts with respect. The main English courts mentioned in this book apart from the House of Lords and Privy Council are the (English) Court of Appeal and Queen's Bench.

FOREIGN LAW

Most of the judgments considered in Australia were delivered by Australian, English or New Zealand courts. Canadian cases are sometimes considered, because of the similarity of legal systems in the two countries. People who work in the media often find it hard to accept that the Australian legal system is not influenced by the United States as much as our media are. The US legal system is profoundly different from ours, and cases decided within it rarely have great legal relevance in Australia. In particular, US defamation, contempt and copyright laws are entirely different. US texts dealing with those areas are often of anthropological interest only. The Trade Practices Act and some other laws which affect advertising were partly copied from US models, so US advertising cases are often cited. US courts, so often represented in TV dramas, play a more pervasive social and political role than do Australian courts. That is more acceptable in a country where many judges are elected, and some campaign for election on the basis of the policies which they will pursue on the bench. One particular difference is that the US constitution places in the bench the trust which the Australian constitution places in the ballot box. Applying the US Bill of Rights, which includes a 'guarantee' of press freedom from government control, the Supreme Court in effect legislates about what the rights of the media should be from time to time.

PARLIAMENTS

Under the Australian constitution, it is for elected parliaments to decide what freedom the media should have. The common law developed by the courts is entirely subject to laws made by the parliaments. Responsibility for our laws rests with the federal and state parliaments. The courts have neither the mandate nor the research facilities to reform the laws. Any law making which they do is by default, applying the laws which parliaments have made to particular cases, or developing the common law in areas which a parliament has seen as unsuitable for legislation. Indeed, some of the most progressive judges are the most reluctant to change the law in the course of deciding cases, because of the implications for a democracy of laws made by those who are neither appointed by the community nor answerable to the community.

Which parliament makes laws for the media? The answer to that question lies in the notorious complexities of Australian federalism: it is that the federal and all the state parliaments make laws for the media, the exact combination varying from topic to topic. One reason for this difference is that the Australian constitution confers a limited list of powers on the federal parliament. The remaining powers are left to state parliaments. When the constitution was drafted in the 1890s, newspapers local to the separate Australian colonies were virtually the only media. No thought was given to national uniformity in media law. Today, the media are predominantly national in content and ownership, but the laws which govern them are not. So a nationally networked radio or TV programme is subject to eight bodies of defamation law, which include the laws of the Northern Territory and the ACT.

National advertisements are governed by nine sets of laws, since the federal parliament has passed the Trade Practices Act, but left state and territory advertising laws applying as well. Generally speaking, if the federal parliament has power to pass laws about a subject, it also has power to exclude the operation of state laws on that subject. Copyright law and radio and TV law are embodied in an exclusive federal Act, so those areas are uniform. Contempt of court is judge-made common law, so the ultimate authority of the High Court also makes that area nationally uniform.

TERMINOLOGY

This book follows the common legal conventions for referring to cases and judges. The cases are named after the parties to them, as in '*Hulton* v. *Jones*', which is referred to in speech as 'Hulton and Jones'. Criminal cases usually take the form of '*R* v. *Jones*', referred to in speech as 'the Queen against Jones'. It is a gaffe to pronounce the small 'v' between the parties as 'versus'. The abbreviation 'A-G' often found in case names refers to the Attorney-General. The names of most judges are followed by the letter 'J', which is usually translated into spoken English as 'Mr Justice' in the case of a man and 'Justice' in the case of a woman, although it is increasingly common to refer to men and women as 'Justice'. Judges of inferior courts are generally referred to as 'Judge' rather than 'Justice'. 'JJ' stands for 'Judges' and 'CJ' stands for Chief Justice. Abbreviations for the titles of English judges include 'LJ' for Lord Justice and 'MR' for Master of the Rolls. Other legal abbreviations, including those used in notes to the chapters, are set out in the table of abbreviations.

References to pages of judgments are not preceded by the letter 'p.', as is the practice in non-legal writing, and references usually include the page at which the report of a case starts as well as the specific page to which reference is made. For example, '*James* v. *Robinson* (1963) 109 CLR 593, 609 per Windeyer J' refers to page 609 of the judgment of Mr Justice Windeyer in the report of *James* v. *Robinson*, decided in 1963, which starts on page 593 of volume 109 of the *Commonwealth Law Reports*. Laws made by parliaments are known generically as legislation or statutes, and are properly called Acts. The three terms tend to be interchangeable in practice. The terms 'commonwealth' and 'federal' are also used fairly interchangeably among lawyers to refer to national laws and institutions.

Unfortunately, there are no adequate universal words to describe the media activities and occupations with which the law is most concerned. There is no adequate word for the activity of making something known to another person. The legal expression is usually to 'publish' even where the communication is by the electronic media. So those who work in radio, TV, film and advertising should not think that their activities are necessarily excluded from 'publishing'. For the divers products of the media, we have had to use stodgy terms like 'matter' and 'publication'. There are no universal legal terms for the area because there is no unified body of media law. As the following chapters show, most media law is the application of existing, wider categories of law to the special problems of the media.

2
DEFAMATION

Ray Watterson

SOCIAL PERSPECTIVE

Regardless of the audience, the medium employed or the technology adopted, Australia's media are affected by the law of defamation.[1] Thus an inventory of the media sources of litigated defamation claims would include: news reports, articles, entertainment reviews, letters to the editor, films, photographs, novels, poems, magazines, news and current affairs programmes on radio and television, talk-back radio, classified print advertisements, television advertisements, and even the packaging on consumer goods. The media are sometimes criticized for presenting information in a biased, unfair or inaccurate way, and for being sensational and intrusive. Media entertainment is sometimes claimed to be offensive; and its advertising is sometimes claimed to be misleading or exploitative. Some of these criticisms may attract sanctions under the Trade Practices Act, the Broadcasting Act or other laws discussed in later chapters; none of them will found a defamation action. Even a report which carries false information about a person will not necessarily provide the foundation for a defamation action.

Generally, the law of defamation may be invoked against the media only when an individual claims that a particular media publication adversely affects his or her reputation. Defamation is primarily a civil wrong which confers a right to claim money damages as compensation for impairment of reputation. In some cases, an injunction can be obtained to prevent publication of something which is clearly defamatory. Australian law still recognizes criminal defamation, but prosecution of the media for criminal defamation is such a rarity compared with the day-to-day reality of civil actions that only the latter will be examined here.

PROFILE OF DEFAMATION

The underlying principles of modern Australian defamation law were formulated in England over 400 years ago, against a background of limited forms of personal and social communication. Even during the nineteenth century, many Australian defamation cases appear to have been initiated by private individuals to protect their personal honour. Thus, the reported cases of that era include imputations of unchastity, illegitimacy and drunkenness. One Tasmanian case concerned a dispute between friends at a racecourse bar about who would pay for the drinks.[2]

In the 1980s, the processes of the law of defamation are still available to people seeking to preserve the esteem of friends and acquaintances from being lowered by private people or institutions other than the media. The nature of defamation litigation and the identity of those involved has changed, however, since the nineteenth century. From the Australian Law Reform Commission Report, *Unfair Publication: Defamation and Privacy*[3] emerges a profile of the modern defamation action as one initiated by a person whose career or prosperity depends on public reputation, and whose claim concerns a media publication related to public affairs. Typically, the person who sues will be a politician, public official, professional or business person or commercial organization.

Defamation and the Media

No satisfactory empirical studies about the practical effect of defamation law have been carried out. The clearest practical indications so far of the way in which the law of defamation operates on and affects the media in Australia have been provided by the *Unfair Publication* report. This is a summary of the more significant findings and conclusions of the Australian Law Reform Commission:

The overwhelming majority of reported defamation actions in Australia are against the media. Defamation is most likely to occur in a media coverage of news and current affairs. Newspapers are more commonly involved as litigants than television and radio stations. However, the recent growth of public access radio, through the development of 'talk-back' programmes on commerical radio and the establishment of public broadcasting stations, has created a fertile new field for defamation claims at the same time as it has opened up the airways to members of the public and community groups to express their views on contentious issues.

The cost to Australian newspaper companies of defamation claims appears

DEFAMATION 9

to be significant rather than crippling. The impact of the law does not appear to be critical to the financial survival of any major Australian newspaper organisation, however a small organisation (such as an independent suburban or regional newspaper, or a public broadcasting station operated on a volunteer basis) could conceivably be destroyed by a single high defamation verdict. Commercial rather than legal factors appear to be more influential in moulding the type of newspaper and media organisations that exist in Australia and their reporting style. Any inhibitions on the development of investigative journalism which exist in Australia could perhaps more convincingly be attributed to the reluctance of media management to make the high financial commitments which such journalism entails than to the law of defamation. However the present law of defamation unduly inhibits the publication of information by the media as a result of the sheer complexity of the law which generates uncertainty in the minds of editors and journalists (leading them to suppress rather than publish material which could in fact have been lawfully published) and of the inadequacy of the range of matters which may be safely reported under the defence of 'fair report'.[4]

SOURCES, STRUCTURE AND FUNCTION OF THE LAW

Sources of Law

The eight separate defamation laws of each state and territory can be grouped into three types: the common law; the codes; and the hybrid New South Wales system. They contain fundamental differences in such vital areas as the definition of defamation, defences and remedies. Victoria, South Australia, Western Australia and the territories operate under the common law, subject to some statutory modifications.[5] In Queensland the law is governed by a code.[6] The Queensland code has been adopted in Tasmania.[7] The Queensland code has also been adopted in Western Australia, but, in that state, it is primarily concerned with criminal defamation and applies only in part to civil claims.[8] From 1958 to 1974, New South Wales adopted the code, but the current *Defamation Act* 1974 returns some areas of the law to be determined according to the common law and makes others subject to special provisions which are contained in the Act itself. The New South Wales system of defamation law can thus be regarded as standing in a class of its own: a hybrid of common law and statute law.

In 1978 the Australian Law Reform Commission recommended the enactment of a new law of unfair publication, covering both defamation and privacy.[9] Its recommendations are mentioned at various points in this and the following chapter. They were intended, among other things, to replace the present eight separate defamation laws with a single law of defamation which would operate uniformly throughout Australia. After almost a decade the commission's recommendations have still not been implemented.

Libel and Slander

At common law, defamation is divided into the two actions of libel and slander.[10] Generally stated, defamatory matter is libel if it is in writing or some other permanent form, and it is slander if it is spoken or in some other transient form. In a libel case, a plaintiff does not have to prove that he or she suffered damage. The law assumes that some damage will flow from the publication of defamatory matter by the print media. Slander, on the other hand, generally requires proof of actual loss (for example, in income or profits) based on the social assumption that oral statements do less harm to reputation than written ones. Recognizing the weakness of the assumption and the power of the electronic media, s. 120 of the federal *Broadcasting Act* 1942 treats radio and TV as print media by deeming radio and TV transmissions to be 'publication in permanent form'. As a result, a plaintiff who brings a defamation action against a radio or television station is not required to prove that a broadcast of defamatory matter caused him tangible or financial loss.

Structure and Function of the Law

It is often said that the law of defamation has two basic and necessarily conflicting purposes: to enable the individual to protect his reputation and to preserve the right of free speech. By providing liability for the very act of communication, the protection of reputation necessarily entails limits on free speech. No modern democratic society has yet chosen to abandon legal liability for defamatory communications, or to refuse to accommodate the interests of free speech within a law of defamation.

The plaintiff in a defamation case must establish the elements of a cause of action in defamation: he must prove that material concerning him was published and that the material was defamatory of him. If he does so and no defence is proved, then the plaintiff is entitled to a remedy. The individual's interest in reputation is protected by affording him a right of action in defamation: the claim to free speech is supported by the range of defences which defeat and displace a plaintiff's claim to an untarnished reputation. The defences, though operating in differing ways, proceed on the general assumption that certain communications have a higher social value than the individual's claim to reputation. Australian law has not, generally speaking, developed special defences for the media based on the role of the media in Australian society. The mere publication of words defamatory of the plaintiff gives rise to a *prima facie* cause of action. In pressing his claim, a plaintiff has the benefit of the presumptions of falsity and of damage. He is not required to prove that the words are false: the law presumes in his favour that they are. The law also presumes that defamatory words cause harm. Thus it is not necessary for the plaintiff to produce witnesses to attest to the fact that they now think less of him, or to prove that he has suffered material or financial loss as a result of the publication. Furthermore, a plaintiff is not required to establish that the defendant *intended* to harm his reputation by the publication, or that such harm resulted from a lack of care or concern.

DEFAMATORY MATTER

As Lord Atkin conceded in *Sim* v. *Stretch*, 'Judges and textbook writers alike have found difficulty in defining with precision the word "defamatory".'[11] Classical judicial definitions which have helped to shape the law and continue to influence modern Australian cases include the following:

> A publication which is calculated to injure the reputation of another by exposing him to hatred, contempt or ridicule. *Parmiter* v. *Coupland* (1840) per Baron Parke.[12]

> A false statement about a man to his discredit. *Youssoupoff* v. *Metro-Goldwyn-Mayer* (1934) per Scrutton LJ.[13]

> A statement which would 'tend to lower the plaintiff in the estimation of right-thinking members of society generally'. *Sim* v. *Stretch* (1936) per Lord Atkin.[14]

> Matter is defamatory 'if it tends to make the plaintiff be shunned and avoided'. *Youssoupoff* v. *Metro-Goldwyn-Mayer* (1934) per Slesser LJ.[15]

The use of the expression 'calculated to injure' in the *Parmiter* v. *Coupland* formula is apt to create a false impression that intention to injure is a necessary element of defamation. As we have already noted, this is not the case. The test of injury to reputation in terms of 'hatred and contempt' was criticized for being too narrow by Lord Atkin in *Sim* v. *Stretch* and has been supplanted in practice by the more modern test suggested by him in that same case. Lord Atkin's test, however, has its own deficiencies: it does not clearly include a statement which may be defamatory of a person by injuring his professional or business reputation rather than tending to lower him personally in people's estimation. Moreover, the standard of the 'right-thinking' man is unsatisfactory. It has been displaced for most purposes in Australia by 'the ordinary citizen of fair average intelligence',[16] or its variant 'ordinary decent folk in the community'.[17]

The expression 'false statement' in Lord Justice Scrutton's definition may misleadingly suggest that falsehood is a necessary element of the cause of action. Even at common law, a true imputation may be defamatory, although its truth, if established, is a complete defence. In many Australian jurisdictions, truth alone is not a complete defence to a defamation action.

The code definition of defamation applying in Queensland and Tasmania is different in an important respect from the common law definition applying in all other states and the territories. For relevant purposes, the code defines a defamatory imputation as one 'concerning any person by which the reputation of that person is likely to be injured, or by which he is likely to be injured in his profession or trade, or by which other persons are likely to be induced to shun or avoid or ridicule or despise him'.[18] For the most part, the code merely embodies the elements in the common law definitions set out above. As we shall see later, the phrase 'by which he is likely to be injured in his profession or trade', however, has acquired a life of its own. It catches and includes as defamatory many statements which would not be defamatory at common law.

Though nowhere to be found succinctly stated in the modern case law, the following definition serves as a working summary of the modern common law position: 'A defamatory statement is one that tends to disparage a person's reputation or to display him in a ridiculous light or to make others shun and avoid him.' Each of the elements of this definition needs to be examined in turn.

Disparaging Personal Reputation

According to the Oxford English Dictionary, the word 'reputation' means 'what is generally said or believed about a person's character'. Statements which defame by alleging a fault or defect in a person's character are a time-honoured form of defamation. Thus it is defamatory to say that a person is dishonest, a hypocrite, a liar or a coward. The more serious character defects likely to elicit strong and universal condemnation are caught by the ancient formula of 'hatred and contempt'. The test of whether an imputation is capable of disparaging reputation currently employed by Australian courts, however, is whether that imputation is 'likely to cause ordinary decent people in the community, taken in general, to think the less'[19] of the person it concerns. This test takes into account both moral and social standards affecting community estimation of a person's character. It embraces a far broader field of character disparagement than the ancient formula. Thus it may be defamatory to say that a person has been disloyal or ungrateful, rude or intolerant in his personal relationships, egotistical or selfish, or a bad sport.

Disparaging Professional Reputation

Protection of reputation includes a person's reputation in his work, including all professions, occupations and offices other than illegal ones. Thus defamation actions have been successfully pursued by doctors, lawyers, manufacturers, traders, carpenters, station-masters, actors, journalists, jockeys, tennis players, prime ministers, public servants, aldermen and trade union officials.

Frequently, a statement reflecting on a work reputation will be disparaging and damaging to personal reputation. It has been held to be defamatory, for example, to accuse an alderman of abusing his position by securing preferential treatment for his own development applications; to say that a prime minister has engaged in dishonest practices in conducting political affairs; to accuse an author of plagiarism; to accuse the managing director of a company of defrauding the public; and to accuse a journalist of exploiting a close personal friendship to secure a story.

There are cases, however, where a statement may be injurious to the reputation of a professional person without reflecting on his personal character. A good example of the distinction is *Pratten v. The Labour Daily Limited.*[20] An article in *The Labour Daily* attacked Pratten, the then federal Minister for Customs, alleging that he had repudiated a government agreement with diary farmers for the export of butter. Pratten complained, among other things, that the article implied that he was unfit to hold ministerial office and injured his reputation as a minister.

The jury returned a verdict for *The Labour Daily* after the trial judge had directed them that:

the defamatory statement must be one which holds a man up to hatred, ridicule, contempt ... The nature of the charge has to be such as to invade his personal character, his reputation in the sense of reputation for honour, for honesty, for integrity ...[21]

On appeal, the Full Court of the Victorian Supreme Court directed a new trial on the ground that the trial judge's direction unduly limited the meaning of defamatory matter. The court observed that to rule otherwise would deny legal liability for a false statement of fact relating to the public conduct of a politician or public official which called into question his fitness for office, provided only that it cast no reflection on his personal character. Such an immunity would encourage reporting by those who took little or no trouble to verify facts and could not be supported on grounds of public policy.

An authoritative test of the defamatory character of an imputation concerning a person's work-related reputation is contained in *Drummond-Jackson* v. *British Medical Association*:

Words may be defamatory of a trader or businessman or professional man, although they do not impute any moral fault or defect of personal character. They may be defamatory of him if they impute lack of qualification, knowledge, skill, capacity, judgment or efficiency in the conduct of his trade or business or professional activity.[22]

In the *Drummond-Jackson* case, the court held that it was defamatory to say of a dental surgeon that he had developed and applied a dangerous anaesthetic technique. In a recent Australian case, *John Fairfax and Sons Ltd* v. *Punch*,[23] it was held to be defamatory to say of the leader of a political party that he had lost the confidence of the members of his party.

It has been suggested that it would be defamatory to say of a business person that he cannot pay his debts or delays in doing so, even in situations which are beyond his control.[24] But not every allegation of unfitness, or incapacity for calling or office, is defamatory. The courts insist that, at common law, mere injury to business, profession or calling by a false statement is insufficient to support a defamation action, although it may support an injurious falsehood action, as outlined in Chapter 4. To be defamatory of a person at common law an imputation must be disparaging of him or be likely to hold him up to ridicule or cause him to be shunned and avoided. In *Boyd* v. *Mirror Newspapers Ltd*,[25] the New South Wales Supreme Court, applying this test, held that an article in the sporting pages of the Sydney *Daily Mirror* which described a first-grade Rugby League footballer as unfit to play properly as a result of injury, and because he was fat and slow, was incapable of being defamatory. The article, while conceivably injurious to Boyd in his occupation as a professional footballer, did not disparage his personal character or his reputation as a professional footballer. It could be disparaging only if it said or suggested that Boyd himself was to blame; as a result, for example, of some failure or neglect by him in his training or preparation.

Likewise the following statements, though clearly likely to turn away customers and have a harmful impact on the businesses involved, do not disparage character or business reputation and have been held not defamatory at common law for that reason:

A newspaper item stating, incorrectly, that a named business had ceased to operate.[26]

A newspaper notice stating, incorrectly, that a named company had been the subject of a takeover.[27]

A short story in *Woman's Day* which identified a particular Arab airline and implied that potential travellers on it, through no fault of the airline, faced a serious risk of hijacking by Israelis.[28]

A front-page story in *Sunday*, claiming that a named thoroughbred stud was forced to close by reason of a highly contagious and dangerous virus, where there was no implication that closure was the result of carelessness or incompetence.[29]

A public notice incorrectly announcing that a musician was forced to cancel a concert through illness.[30]

A public notice incorrectly announcing that a race meeting had been abandoned.[31]

It is important to note that each of these statements could be defamatory under the codes applying in Queensland and Tasmania and under the definition of defamatory matter proposed by the Australian Law Reform Commission. The code definitions in these states and the commission's proposed definition abandon the common law reliance on the concept of disparagement of reputation, and treat as defamatory any statement concerning a person 'by which he is likely to be injured in his profession or trade'.[32] The High Court held that the above statements about the takeover and the airline were defamatory under the codes.

Ridicule

It may be defamatory to denigrate a person's character by suggesting, even in a humorous way, that he or she has undesirable personal traits, as demonstrated by the following extract from an article which appeared in the literary pages of the *Australian*. It described a couple who were regular patrons of the Sydney Journalists' Club:

> She is tall, slim, gloriously-waisted and with a bottom like a nectarine in jeans ... He is tall, hipless—I would like to say skinny, but he isn't. He is beautiful in the best sense of the word. Every Sunday about 7 they arrive. She in a blue jumper and blue slacks and with a face like Cleopatra's ... he in Yakker-Ds and a blue turtle-necked sweater. She is dark. He is fair. He has a beer. She has what looks like orange juice. Both have sandwiches and spend the rest of the evening watching television—Batman and all ... I would have thought that Beautiful People, specially as they don't appear to be married, would have better things to do on a Sunday night. Last Sunday one of them had. He fell asleep, sandwich in hand.

The essence of the case brought by the allegedly hipless sandwich-eater was that the article implied that there was something effeminate or less than manly about him; and that readers would regard him as ridiculous because 'having been with a beautiful girl he merely watches a juvenile television programme, eats a sandwich and while eating it, goes to sleep'. The court ruled that the article was capable of defaming him.[33]

The cases make it clear that an imputation that displays the plaintiff in a ridiculous light may be defamatory even if it would not be understood in a sense which disparaged the plaintiff's reputation. Thus, it is sufficient to support a defamation action if a person is depicted in a socially embarrassing situation which, through no fault of his own, makes him look absurd or a laughing stock. In an American case, *Burton v. Crowell Publishing Co.*,[34] the newspaper publication of a cigarette advertisement, which showed a jockey holding a saddle in front of his abdomen, made the saddlebag appear as if it were a part of his anatomy because of an accidental blurring of the photograph. A closer look at the photograph revealed that the object hanging between the jockey's legs belonged to the saddle and not to the jockey. But because it made him a laughing stock, a 'preposterously ridiculous spectacle', he was entitled to succeed.

The cases further insist that a distinction be drawn between merely exposing a person to good-natured humour and actually deriding a person with the use of humour. A newspaper item about a couple who were due to be married on the following day incorrectly indicated that they had been married on the day of the publication. Although that subjected the bridegroom to a certain amount of joking by his workmates during the morning of his actual wedding day, the court ruled that it had not exposed him to ridicule (as opposed to humour) and was not defamatory.[35]

It is not usually defamatory to publish candid photographs of people in humorous situations unless the photograph is likely to make its subject look ridiculous or the target of derision rather than good humour. Thus unauthorized publications of photographs and testimonials in newspaper advertisements which suggested that the plaintiff had smelly feet,[36] or constipation,[37] have been held to be defamatory.

The context of a humorous statement may be all-important in determining whether it bears a defamatory sense. Statements which might be treated or understood in a non-defamatory sense when first spoken to a limited audience may take on a defamatory meaning when removed from their context and reported in a newspaper or aired on a national television programme. It is possible for a story originally given airing by the plaintiff as a joke on himself to attract ridicule by 'outsiders' if given wider circulation in the media. In *Cook* v. *Ward*,[38] the plaintiff shared with a small group of friends a humorous incident in which he had been mistaken for a hangman. That incident exposed him to defamatory ridicule when repeated by a local newspaper.

There are few reported cases about defamation arising from cartoons or political caricatures. The leading practitioner's text says:

the limits of what is permissible in the way of cartoon and satire are undefined. Words obviously intended as a joke are not actionable but serious imputations of fact lying behind the superficially jocular may well be.[39]

In *Morosi* v. *Mirror Newspapers Ltd*,[40] the New South Wales Court of Appeal held that a cartoon published in the *Daily Telegraph* early in 1975 could be read as alleging that there was a politically embarrassing romantic attachment between the persons depicted in the cartoon, the then federal treasurer and his secretary. The court held that such an allegation was capable of defaming the secretary.

The paucity of reported cartoon cases may be the result of the politicians who are often the subject of them wishing to avoid adverse public attention, as well as to the reputed reluctance of juries to find defamation in cartoons. The politician plaintiffs in the political cartoon cases that appear in the law reports were unsuccessful.[41]

Shun and Avoid

In 1934 a Russian Princess sued MGM in relation to a film called *Rasputin, the Mad Monk*. She claimed that the film, which purported to deal with real life events, suggested that she had been raped by Rasputin. A jury awarded her £25 000 damages. MGM appealed on the ground, among others, that an allegation that a married woman has been the victim of a rape may not be actionable by her. MGM argued that the allegation could bring no moral discredit on her, being something beyond her control. The Court of Appeal rejected this argument. Drawing by analogy on cases where it had been held defamatory to allege that a person was insane or was suffering from a disease, Slesser LJ said:

> not only is the matter defamatory if it brings the plaintiff into hatred, ridicule or contempt by reason of some moral discredit on her part, but also if it tends to make the plaintiff be shunned and avoided and that without any moral discredit on her part.[42]

That ruling in the *Youssoupoff* case has been relied on by courts and commentators ever since as recognizing a separate category of defamatory matter, a category in which the test of the defamatory character of an imputation rests on its 'tendency to exclude the plaintiff from society rather than on (its) capacity to work an injury to reputation'.[43]

The test has a potential to extend the law of defamation to cover statements concerning a person which, although not affecting reputation, are capable of injuring business by deterring customers. Glass JA of the New South Wales Court of Appeal in the *Middle East Airlines* case[44] indicated that a statement that a particular airline faced a serious risk of hijacking could cause potential travellers to avoid it and might therefore be defamatory at common law, as a result of the application of the test in the *Youssoupoff* case. In more recent cases, however, the courts have refrained from extending the *Youssoupoff* test in this way, with the result that the only examples of its application are allegations of insanity, disease or rape.[45]

DISCOVERING THE MEANING OF WORDS

In any case, the words used may be open to differing interpretations. As Diplock LJ pointed out in *Slim* v. *Daily Telegraph Ltd*:

The same words may be understood by one man in a different meaning from that in which they are understood by another and both meanings may be different from that which the author of the words intended to convey.[46]

The basic test of the meaning of words on which the law operates is that which a 'hypothetical referee'[47] (the ordinary reader or viewer or listener) would ascribe to them. Neither the sense in which the words were intended by the author or publisher nor the sense in which they were understood by the audience to whom the material was published is relevant to the meaning.

Two Types of Meaning

The law recognizes two types of meanings: natural and ordinary meaning and innuendo or special meaning. For those who work in the media, it is important to understand the extent to which the courts will allow innuendoes to be read into superficially innocent statements.

The natural and ordinary meaning is that arrived at by having regard to the words themselves in the context in which they are published, and the general background at the time of publication. It includes not only the direct or literal meaning of the words themselves but also any implications or inferences which the ordinary reasonable reader would place upon or draw from the words.

The innuendo or special meaning is that arrived at when words are read in conjunction with extrinsic facts not generally known. An innuendo meaning is one which the ordinary reader 'acquainted with the extrinsic facts will ascribe to the matter complained of by reason of his knowledge of those facts because he will understand the words in the light of those facts'.[48]

The following statements will serve to illustrate the various meanings:

Statement A: 'The Reverend X is a regular client of prostitutes operating from premises in Young Street.'
Statement B: 'The Reverend X regularly visits prostitutes operating from premises in Young Street.'
Statement C: 'The Reverend X regularly visits certain premises at No. 15 Young Street.'

The literal meaning of *Statement A* is clear: the Reverend X avails himself of the services of prostitutes. Such a meaning, without more, is capable of defaming the Reverend X. Literally construed, *Statement B* does no more than say that Reverend X regularly visits prostitutes. He may do so for strictly moral purposes associated with the discharge of his ministry. The statement is open, however, to the inference in the mind of the ordinary person that he does so for immoral purposes and therefore is capable of defaming Reverend X in its ordinary and natural meaning.

The words in *Statement C* are of themselves incapable of any meaning defamatory of Reverend X. In the mind of a reader acquainted with the fact that No. 15 Young Street is a brothel, however, they may give rise to the derogatory *innuendo* that Reverend X visits No. 15 for immoral purposes.

Natural and Ordinary Meaning

The natural and ordinary meaning of words is the meaning which the words would convey to the mind of the ordinary reasonable reader drawing on his knowledge and experience of human affairs. The courts recognize that the meaning which words convey to the ordinary man is formed more as a matter of broad impression than as a result of a technical or critical process of analysis. As Lord Reid said in *Morgan* v. *Odhams Press Ltd* in relation to a report in a Sunday newspaper:

> If we are to take the ordinary man as our guide then we must accept a certain amount of loose thinking. The ordinary man does not formulate reasons in his own mind: he gets a general impression and one can expect him to look again before coming to a conclusion and acting on it. But formulated reasons are very often an afterthought. The publishers of newspapers must know the habits of mind of their readers and I see no injustice in holding them liable if readers, behaving as they normally do, honestly reach conclusions which they might be expected to reach. If one were to adopt a stricter standard it would be too easy for purveyors of gossip to disguise their defamatory matter ...[49]

In construing language for everyday purposes, the ordinary person may not only engage in 'a certain amount of loose thinking' but also 'read between the lines' and be guided by the maxim that 'where there is smoke there is fire'. In forming his impression, however, he is neither unduly suspicious nor avid for scandal nor prone to reaching damaging conclusions as a result of idiosyncratic beliefs and prejudices. Thus, the cases are clear that a media report which merely states that a person is being investigated by the police or has been arrested and charged with a criminal offence is capable only of bearing the imputation that the person is under suspicion and not that he is guilty or probably guilty. This is so because in the view of the courts:

the ordinary reasonable reader is mindful of the principle that a person charged with a crime is presumed innocent until it is proved that he is guilty. Although he knows that many persons charged with a criminal offence are ultimately convicted, he is also aware that guilt or innocence is a question to be determined by a court, generally by a jury, and that not infrequently the person charged is acquitted.[50]

Of course, a report of a criminal prosecution which goes further than simply narrating the facts of arrest and charge and suggests that the charge is well founded may defame the person charged by implying guilt.[51]

Defamatory Character of Words

Having discovered the meaning of the words used, a court must determine whether the imputation so discovered possesses a defamatory character. The same statement may have a different impact on different members of the community, lowering a person's reputation in the eyes of some people in the community, raising it in the eyes of others, and leaving it completely unaltered in the eyes of the remainder. This raises the problem of what segment of the community the media should look to in deciding what will be taken to be defamatory.

The classic resolution of this problem is provided by the words of Greer LJ in *Tolley* v. *Fry*:

Words are not defamatory however much they may damage a man in the eyes of a section of the community, unless they also amount to a disparagement of his reputation in the eyes of right-thinking men generally. To write or say of a man something that will disparage him in the eyes of a particular section of the community but will not affect his reputation in the eyes of the average right-thinking man is not actionable within the law of defamation.[52]

The term 'right-thinking' has been criticized for its ambiguity and for involving 'question begging assumptions and circuity of reasoning'.[53] It may be that it is likely to tempt judges resorting to it to substitute the standards and values which they believe ought to prevail in the community for those which in fact prevail. As mentioned previously, the phrase more often used in Australia is 'the ordinary citizen of fair average intelligence'[54] or its variant 'ordinary decent folk in the community'.[55]

Australian courts have followed the 'right-thinking' test in a limited class of case concerning police informers, represented by the English decision *Byrne* v. *Deane*.[56] In that case, the court held that an allegation that a member of a social club had informed the police about other members' illegal gambling activities at the club was not capable of harming his reputation.

The court refused to concede that many people (particularly fellow club members) would regard the member's action unfavourably. The judges insisted that any 'right-thinking' person would only think well of a person who did his duty by informing the police of a breach of the law, regardless of the surrounding facts and the nature of the law involved.

General rather than Sectional Standards

The second element of Lord Greer's test in *Tolley* v. *Fry* emphasizes that a statement will not be regarded as defamatory if it adversely affects a person's reputation only in the eyes of a limited group in the community. This element of the test needs no qualification: it is applied currently in Australia. It effectively excludes demonstrably anti-social values as well as those which are likely to be regarded as morally or socially eccentric. One example of the latter was a case where a press account of a motor accident incorrectly suggested that a passenger involved had a blood transfusion. Unbeknown to the reporter, the passenger was a Jehovah's Witness. Although the account would be capable of adversely affecting the standing of the Witness among the members of his own religion, it would not do so in the eyes of the general community. Accordingly the account would not be defamatory.[57]

On the other hand, the test does not exclude attitudes upon which there may be some differences of opinion in the community but which are shared by an appreciable section of the community. Thus in *Murphy* v. *Plasterers Society*,[58] the court said that it could be defamatory to call a unionist a 'scab': the average citizen, even one not a member of a trade union, would regard the word 'scab' as derogatory. In *Hepburn* v. *TCN Channel Nine Pty Ltd*,[59] a doctor sued in respect of an edition of a *60 Minutes* television programme which she claimed depicted her as an abortionist. The court acknowledged the existence of discrepant social attitudes on the issue of abortion in the community. It recognized that such a depiction might disparage the doctor in the estimation of those viewers who advocate the 'right to life' and raise her in the estimation of those who hold pro-abortion views. Nevertheless, the court held that the programme could be defamatory because the suggestion that she was an abortionist was capable of disparaging her in the estimation of 'an appreciable and reputable section of the community'.[60]

What is defamatory must be judged in the light of contemporary moral and social standards. The judgment is a matter for the jury in a particular case. It is a judgment which judges regard juries as especially suited to make and with which judges are reluctant to interfere. In *Cairns* v. *John Fairfax & Sons Ltd*,[61] the New South Wales Court of Appeal refused to set aside a jury verdict that an article in the *National Times* was not defamatory. The article referred to 'Cairns' girlfriend, Morosi'. Cairns was the federal treasurer. Ms Morosi was his secretary. Both Cairns and Morosi were married. The jury agreed that the article imputed that Cairns was sexually involved with his secretary but said that this imputation would not have been regarded as defamatory by community standards.

Context

The courts have recognized that the medium has an important influence on the message; and that the reading, listening and viewing habits of the ordinary person may vary with the medium involved. Thus a person may be expected to read a book more carefully than a newspaper. A TV viewer or radio listener gains an impression from a fleeting episode with no opportunity to hear the words again or to read and study them.[62]

The layout or presentation of the programme or article under consideration may affect its meaning. In a newspaper article, any prominence given to the words under consideration by their position in the newspaper as a whole or on the particular page as well as any emphasis given by the type and heading used will be significant. So too will be any accompanying graphics and photographs. In *Bickel* v. *John Fairfax & Sons Ltd*,[63] the author of a book on uranium and nuclear physics sued over a review in the *National Times*. He was able to rely not only on the words in the review but on the headline ('The Bomb Minus Morals') and an accompanying drawing (tombstones and a mushroom cloud) to support his claim that the review suggested that he lacked moral concern for the dangers of nuclear bombs and nuclear power.

By the same token, a plaintiff cannot detach the headline or a graphic from an article or a still from a film and complain of that alone. Similarly, a plaintiff is not entitled to succeed because some viewers or listeners might have left the room momentarily and thus missed parts of a broadcast which throw a different light on a programme as a whole.[64] The tone or style of a particular article or programme is also relevant. In *Morgan*

v. *Odhams Press Ltd*, Lord Pearson said of a report in a Sunday newspaper:

> I do not think the reasonable man—who can also be described as an ordinary sensible man—should be envisaged as reading this article carefully. Regard should be had to the character of the article: it is vague, sensational and allusive; it is evidently designed for entertainment rather than instruction or accurate information. The ordinary, sensible man, if he read the article at all, would be likely to skim through it casually and not to give it concentrated attention or a second reading. It is no part of his work to read this article, nor does he have to base any practical decision on what he reads there. The relevant impression is that which would be conveyed to an ordinary sensible man ... reading the article casually and not expecting a high degree of accuracy.[65]

In *Lloyd* v. *David Syme & Co. Ltd*[66] a jury awarded $100 000 damages to the captain of the West Indies cricket team for an article in the *Age* newspaper. The jury found that the article suggested that Lloyd and others had prearranged the results of a World Series Cricket match for financial gain. On appeal the publisher claimed that the jury had extracted an unreasonable meaning from the article. To defeat this claim, Lloyd relied on the language, structure and tone of the article and on a quotation with which the article commenced. The quotation (from F. Scott Fitzgerald's *The Great Gatsby*) included the words 'I remembered, of course, that the World's Series had been fixed in 1919 ... with the single mindedness of a burglar blowing a safe'. One judge on appeal pointed out that many readers of the article would read it 'without particular analysis and with the idea in mind, put there by the opening words of the quotation, that it was talking about the possibility of the Benson and Hedges World Cup Series being fixed in a similar way to the fixing of the World Series in 1919'.[67]

Circumstances

The natural and ordinary meaning to be attributed to a statement 'depends upon its terms, understood in the light of the circumstances generally known when the publications were made'.[68] This is illustrated by *John Fairfax & Sons Ltd* v. *Punch*.[69] A reporter wrote the report of a meeting before it took place. The events did not live up to the reporter's expectation. His report appeared in newspapers, including the *Sydney Morning Herald* and the *Newcastle Morning Herald*.

The report incorrectly said that a large number of members of the New South Wales Country Party had resigned and had called for the resignation of the then party leader, Mr Punch. The defendant newspapers submitted that the reported resignation call had suggested no more than a political tactic of opposition to a particular policy; and that no imputation reflecting personally on Mr Punch could be drawn from the report. The court rejected this view. As Brennan J observed:

> the election in which the respondent was leading his party was to take place a day or two after the articles were published, that is, on 1 May 1976. That was a fact of common knowledge at the time when the articles were published, and it places the reported demand for the respondent's resignation in a significant context ... A demand for the resignation of the respondent as Leader of the Country Party, made immediately before election day by a meeting of 250 members of his party, suggests that those members found his leadership gravely defective ... when a call for the leader's resignation is reported on the eve of an election, a reasonable reader not avid for scandal would readily infer that the respondent's personal qualities for leadership were defective.[70]

Innuendo

The law regards an innuendo (termed a true or legal innuendo) as a meaning which can be placed on words only by reference to some facts or circumstances which are outside the words themselves, and which are not generally known. A court will recognize as defamatory a meaning derived with the assistance of such facts. The plaintiff who seeks to derive such a meaning from the words, however, must, among other things, prove the existence of the facts, prove the knowledge of the facts by at least some of the people to whom the words were in fact published, and persuade a court that in the light of those facts the ordinary reasonable man would have given the publication a defamatory meaning.

The dangers for even the most cautious media of legal innuendo are obvious, since material may become defamatory in unlikely situations which could not be foreseen. This is illustrated by the famous English case of *Cassidy* v. *Daily Mirror Newspapers Ltd.*[71] At a race meeting, Michael Cassidy approached a photographer from the *Daily Mirror* and asked him to take a picture of him with his fiancée. Cassidy was a colourful character who owned racehorses and had apparently been a general in the Mexican Army. He sometimes used the name of Michael Dennis Corrigan. He gave that name to the photographer. A photograph of Cassidy with a woman on his arm appeared in the *Mirror* above the caption: 'Mr M. Corrigan, the racehorse owner, and Miss [X], whose engagement has been announced.'[72] Unknown to the *Mirror*, Cassidy was lawfully married to another woman, Anna Cassidy. She sued the *Mirror*, and her neighbours testified that they took the photograph and the caption to mean that she was not Cassidy's wife and that she had been deceiving them and was only his mistress. She succeeded and recovered substantial damages.

PUBLICATION

It is the publication, not the writing or creation of defamatory material which is the actionable wrong. Disparaging remarks communicated only to the person, the object of them, cannot injure that person's reputation. A man's reputation at law is not his pride or self-esteem but the estimation in which *others* hold him. Thus an author who shows his manuscript only to the person about whom it is written cannot be sued in defamation. There are no limitations on the form of publication which may convey defamatory matter, nor does the size of the audience matter for the purposes of founding an action. Newspapers, radio and television current affairs programmes are the most common carriers of defamatory material. But defamatory material can be communicated by more unusual forms, such as showering leaflets on a theatre audience, distributing a theatre programme, displaying a painting in a gallery, or portraying a person in street theatre.

Liability for Publication

Subject to limited qualifications mentioned in the next chapter, liability for publication of defamatory matter is strict. The intention of the author or publisher is irrelevant to liability. It matters not that the author did not understand the words in a defamatory sense or intend to harm the plaintiff. Nor does it matter that he exercised all reasonable care and caution in checking the material to avoid defamatory content.

The case which finally settled such a strict liability was *Hulton* v. *Jones*.[73] An article in the *Sunday Chronicle* contained a humorous description of the social scene at a motor festival at Dieppe. The article mentioned Artemus Jones, who was described as a married church warden of Peckham. It described his revelries and suggested that he was keeping a mistress.

Artemus Jones was a barrister who had formerly been a sub-editor of the *Sunday Chronicle*. He was not a church warden, he did not live at Peckham, and he was unmarried. He was well known, however, in the district in which the *Sunday Chronicle* circulated. A number of people who read the article testified that they believed it referred to him. At the trial, the writer, the *Sunday Chronicle's* Paris correspondent, maintained that he did not know and had never heard of the name Artemus Jones. He said he merely invented it. That explanation was accepted by the court. The jury returned a verdict for Jones, which was upheld by the House of Lords, whose decision is summed up in the words of Lord Loreburn: 'A person charged with libel cannot defend himself by showing that he intended in his own breast not to defame or that he intended not to defame the plaintiff if in fact he did both.'

The strict liability confirmed by *Hulton* v. *Jones* may arise from errors in typing, or layout, or in the captioning of photographs. The misplacement of a single comma, or a letter in a word has led to liability on some occasions. In one English case, the headline to a newspaper report of court proceedings read: 'Car Thief to Pay Wife £2,000'. Unfortunately, the item which followed was not a report of larceny proceedings but of divorce proceedings and the gentleman who had to pay the £2000 was not a car thief but the chairman of a well-known firm of car dealers. The compositor, seeing the headline written by a sub-editor as 'Car Chief to Pay Wife £2,000', thought that this was a mistake and changed the 'C' to a 'T'. The compositor's mistake cost the newspaper over £1000 in a settled defamation claim.[74]

Who is Liable for Publication?

For the purposes of imposing liability the law draws a distinction between primary participants (or 'originators') and secondary participants (or 'mechanical distributors'). In the case of defamation in a newspaper, the journalist who wrote the article, the editor and sub-editors involved in its preparation, the proprietor and even the printers are liable as primary participants. The liability of the proprietor and editor extends to matter published in their newspaper but contributed by outsiders, such as the writers of letters to the editor. Similarly, the corporation responsible for a radio or TV station will be liable not only for defamatory material broadcast by station announcers (whether paid or volunteer) but also for statements (impromptu or otherwise) made by interviewees, guest commentators, and members of the public who speak in talk-back programmes. People who play a more subordinate or mechanical role in distribution (such as newsagents, libraries and booksellers) are *prima facie* liable for publication but may escape liability if they can prove that they neither knew nor had reason to know or suspect that the material which they distributed contained defamatory matter.

Liability for publication extends to a person who makes a defamatory statement or furnishes defamatory information to the media knowing or intending it to be published and to the writer of a letter to the editor which contains defamatory material. Similarly, a person who invites reporters to a news conference to report a speech will be liable if the speech is defamatory.[75] It appears that a defamatory speaker who merely knows that reporters are present, however, will not be liable in respect of a subsequent media report of his speech.[76]

The Place of Publication and the Republication Rule

Publication occurs at the point where the matter complained of is seen or heard by the audience. Thus, a radio or television programme made in a studio in, say, Melbourne, and distributed nationally live or by delayed transmission is published in each state or territory in which it is received. A person claiming that a broadcast or newspaper distributed nationally defames him in practice brings a single action but pleads separate causes of action in respect of each of the states or territories in which the broadcast is received or the newspaper distributed.

Thus, *Gorton v. Australian Broadcasting Commission and Walsh*,[77] a case brought in the Australian Capital Territory, concerned an interview in a Canberra TV studio between Richard Carleton and Maximilian Walsh in an edition of the national programme *This Day Tonight*. It involved the application of the law of three different jurisdictions: the Australian Capital Territory, New South Wales and Victoria. As a result of differences between the laws in the various jurisdictions, Mr Gorton succeeded in respect of some jurisdictions and not in others. After considering a case involving the *Canberra Times*, which required that the law of six different jurisdictions be applied, Blackburn J said: 'It is an unpleasant feeling to know that one is lost; I am not sure that it is not equally unpleasant to be unsure whether one is lost or not.'[78] The same may be said for national media, which have the extra hardship of estimating *in advance* what a court in any one jurisdiction will say about the law in all the others.

Every person who repeats or republishes a defamatory communication faces liability for the defamation to the same extent as the original publisher. It is therefore no defence for a newspaper or broadcasting station to say that it has named the original maker of a statement or named a source of information, which it is repeating without endorsement. The truth of any defamatory charges which it has repeated must be proved, or else some other defence must be established.

IDENTIFICATION

To succeed in a defamation action, the plaintiff must prove that he was the person defamed by a statement. The most straightforward case is when the plaintiff is actually named, but a reference to his address, office or occupation, physical characteristics or even his social habits may be sufficient. It has been said that no 'mysterious principle of law' is involved here. 'It is ordinary plain common sense that a hurtful statement may be made concerning a person though his name is not given.'[79]

The result of *Hulton* v. *Jones*, already mentioned, is that any person identified as the subject of a defamatory article by a reasonable reader possessed of special facts may sue. *Lee* v. *Wilson*[80] starkly demonstrates one of the logical outcomes of the *Hulton* v. *Jones* principle: even a newspaper article which identifies a person by name carries the risk that another person who also bears that name may sue. The fact that words were intended to refer to X and are true of X does not afford a defence in an action brought by Y if the words could coincidentally lead reasonable persons to understand that the words referred to Y. The facts of *Lee*'s case were that during a public inquiry into charges of bribery in the Victorian police force a witness gave evidence that 'First Constable Lee of the Motor Registration Branch' had accepted a bribe. The *Star* newspaper reported the witness as having said that 'Detective Lee' had accepted a bribe. A reporter had originally taken that evidence down correctly in shorthand and then carelessly altered 'First Constable' to 'Detective'. There were three police officers named Lee in the Melbourne force: one in the Motor Registration Branch and two who were detectives attached to the Criminal Investigation

Branch. Each of the two detectives brought an action against the newspaper and each succeeded.

The risk of coincidental identification, such as that in *Hulton and Lee*, may be reduced by avoiding the use of 'fictitious' names and by the use of care and particularity in the use of names in reports.

More difficult for the media to avoid are cases where *circumstances* connect the person defamed to a publication. That was what happened in *Steele* v. *Mirror Newspapers*.[81] A news item appeared in the defendant's newspaper late in 1971 about a police investigation of the suspected theft of a large quantity of wheat from temporary storage sites in western New South Wales. It said that police investigations in the Newcastle and Quirindi areas indicated that large public road carriers were being used to transport the stolen wheat which was then being sold to pig and chicken farmers in outer Sydney. There was no express reference to Ms Steele in the report. She was a woman with a criminal past, having been convicted of a number of crimes of dishonesty between 1952 and 1968 in or near Newcastle. Since 1969 she had been running a business involving large-scale carting and wheat-cleaning operations, including the transport of surplus wheat from New South Wales Grain Elevators Board silos to temporary storage in the western districts. Cleaned wheat from her operations was available as chicken and pig feed. A number of witnesses gave evidence that they understood the article to refer to her, and had inferred that she was suspected by the police of being involved in the thefts. They did so, essentially, because they knew of her past, the present nature and scale of her operations, and her connections with the Grain Elevators Board. She was awarded $45 000 damages. By a majority, the New South Wales Court of Appeal held that the report was capable of being understood by the reasonable reader, possessed of the facts relating to Steele's past and her present operations, as referring to her.

The courts have adopted the view that newspaper readers skim-read without a great deal of concentration and care (particularly in the case of reports which are put together in a similar fashion), gloss over minor discrepancies between facts relating to the person they know and the facts as they appear in a report, and are prepared to reach far-fetched inferences. The standard of reasonableness attributed to the mass media audience is not high, and has permitted identifying inferences, sufficient to support a defamation action, which the courts themselves have described as 'not sensible' and 'nothing short of far-fetched'.[82]

Group Defamation

A class of people cannot be defamed as a class. A statement defaming 'the government', 'Italians living in Sydney' or 'Parramatta football fans' does not afford a right of action to the group concerned or to a representative of that group. In some circumstances, however, a statement denigrating a group or class of persons may give rise to a cause of action by an individual who is a member of that group. The individual must be able to establish that the words would be reasonably understood to refer to him or her in particular.

The relevant test is indicated in the following statement of Lord Porter in *Knuppfer* v. *London Express Newspapers Ltd*:

> In deciding this question the size of the class, the generality of the charge and the extravagance of the accusation may all be elements to be taken into consideration, but none of them is conclusive. Each case must be considered according to its own circumstances. I can imagine it being said that each member of a body, however large, was defamed where the libel consisted in the assertion that not one of the members of a community was elected as a member unless he had committed a murder.[83]

The size of the class appears to have been a significant factor in the court's decision in *Knuppfer*'s case, where it was held that a newspaper article which attacked the 'Young Russia Party', a political group with an international membership of some 2000 people, could not be taken to refer to the plaintiff, a member of the British branch of that party.

Similarly in *David Syme* v. *Canavan*,[84] the High Court held that a report in a newspaper of a public meeting at which a speaker attacked the members of a returned soldier's association was incapable of personally defaming the plaintiff, who was one of the thousand members of that association.

In *Healy* v. *Askin*,[85] the leader of the Liberal Party in New South Wales authorized a television advertisement to be shown on the eve of a general election in 1974. The advertisement depicted a woman who had migrated to Australia from Estonia saying, in broken English, among other things, 'Today I can see that the Labor is disguised socialist. But for me it is disguised communist.' The Labor Party candidate for a Sydney electorate began an action against Askin, alleging that he had been defamed by the television broadcast and seeking an injunction restraining further televising of the advertisement. The court held that the advertisement could only reasonably be regarded as referring to the ALP itself and not to any individual member.

Who may be Defamed?

The general rule is that any person may sue in respect of defamatory material published about himself. 'Person' in this context includes any organization with a legal personality. Thus a company, a local council, or a trade union may bring an action but unincorporated associations, such as many clubs and societies, may not.

The legal personality of corporations, councils and trade unions limits the nature of an action that may be brought. A corporation cannot have 'personal' reputation and can therefore sue only in respect of allegations relating to its business operations, including, for example, allegations that it conducts its affairs dishonestly or unfairly or without a proper sense of business ethics or that it is in financial difficulties. Thus the BBC was successfully sued in respect of a radio programme in which two speakers attacked the plaintiff company for having operated a computer school as 'a financial racket where the aptitude test is bogus to begin with, where the certificate at the end is bogus'.[86]

In *Bargold Pty Ltd* v. *Mirror Newspapers Ltd*,[87] the New South Wales Supreme Court recognized the right of an investment company to take action in respect of an article in the financial section of the *Weekend Australian* which, it alleged, conveyed the imputation that the company was financially unsound and likely to collapse. Similarly, a local council may sue to vindicate its governing reputation, and a trade union may sue to vindicate its financial or its governing reputation.[88]

Only a living person may be defamed. There is no liability for 'defamation of the dead'.[89] Distress caused to relatives or friends or injury to their feelings will not support an action by them nor may the legal personal representatives of a deceased person sue to vindicate his reputation and recover damages for his estate. For a statement about a deceased person to be defamatory it must contain an imputation reflecting adversely on a living person. Thus, a statement that the deceased Mr X was never lawfully married would support an action at the suit of Mrs X, his now widowed, lawful wife.[90]

3

DEFAMATION:
Defences and Remedies

Ray Watterson

JUSTIFICATION

What a layperson would call the defence of truth, the law calls 'justification'. A person who complains that a report published in the media defames him has a distinct advantage if he wishes to take legal action. The law presumes that the media report is false. The defendant carries the burden of proving that the report is true, or of establishing some other defence in relation to it. If he can establish the truth at common law operating in Victoria, South Australia, the Northern Territory and Western Australia, he has a complete defence. If he relies on the defence of truth and fails in his attempt to establish it, then he not only loses the case, but may also aggravate the damages which may be awarded against him.

The burden of establishing truth has enormous practical significance for the operations of the media. It is not enough to believe strongly in the truth of a defamatory report, no matter how reliable the source of information may be. To rely on the truth of their publications, the media must be able to prove it in court by legally admissible evidence. It is not always easy to do so. Information included in a report which has been obtained from secondary sources is inadmissible (as hearsay) unless that source materializes, in the form of properly obtained documents or of a witness with direct knowledge of the events or circumstances described in the report, and who is prepared to testify. Sources of information who will not allow their identity to be revealed, no matter how well placed to know the facts, are no help in court. The difficulty of legally proving truth constitutes 'a powerful brake on public debate and the flow of information by underscoring the wisdom of caution and self-censorship'.[1]

Such censorship may stop not only false or inaccurate publications, but also true publications.

What the Defendant Must Prove

The defence must prove the truth of all imputations expressly or impliedly contained in the challenged material, as well as imputations which arise by innuendo. The allegation that 'Dr X treats his patients badly' may be understood to mean that he treats them discourteously or uncivilly. That would have to be established by proving habitually poor bedside manner, not by proving he had been discourteous to a patient on one or two occasions. The statement may also imply that his medical treatment of his patients is habitually neglectful or substandard. That imputation also would have to be proved true. It would not be sufficient to defend this imputation to show that he was remiss on one occasion.

Although the standard of accuracy demanded by the law is high, it is not beyond reach. It is sufficient if an imputation is true in substance. It is not necessary to prove the truth of every last detail in a statement provided the substance or gist is proved to be correct and provided minor inaccuracies do not aggravate the defamation. In an old English case, a railway notice listed the plaintiff as having been convicted of travelling on a train without a ticket, and also as having been fined (with three weeks' imprisonment in default of payment). He had been convicted and the defendant established this; the offence for which he was convicted, however, carried the sentence of a fine with two weeks' imprisonment in default of payment. Nevertheless the defence succeeded.[2]

If the matter complained of consists of several distinct defamatory imputations, then the substance of each must be proved to be true. If the defendant fails to establish the truth of one of a number of imputations in a statement, the whole defence fails. The plaintiff is entitled to recover damages and would normally be awarded his legal costs notwithstanding the fact that the false imputation may have caused no significant damage to his reputation when viewed in the light of the true charges. In one case, the defendant alleged that the plaintiff had been guilty of a variety of acts of cruelty to a horse, and of knocking out its eye. The defendant proved all the acts of cruelty against the horse apart from that of knocking out its eye. The court held that the defence of justification had not been made out and the plaintiff was entitled to succeed.[3] In New South Wales and Tasmania, the defamation Acts now seek to avoid such a result.[4] The New South Wales provision requires the court to consider the whole of the publication which is the subject of the action, and to measure the relative worth of the allegations proved true by the defence against the allegations not proven. The court must then ask whether, on the whole, any significant injury has been done to the plaintiff's reputation.[5]

Public Interest

If a defendant can overcome the difficulties canvassed above and establish the truth of allegations made against the plaintiff, that is a complete defence at common law. Legislation in Queensland, Tasmania, the ACT and New South Wales, however, has incorporated individual privacy protection into defamation law.[6] The legislation requires that defamatory matter justifiable on the ground of truth should also be published 'for the public benefit'[7] or should relate to 'a matter of public interest'.[8] Despite the potential of the added requirements to curb the legitimate public role of the media, there are few reported cases which turn on whether a defamatory publication was 'for the public benefit' or in the 'public interest'. It is not always clear whether disclosure of embarrassing but true private facts will be justifiable. It seems, however, that topics in which the public is interested (in the sense of being curious about), such as personality gossip and inside stories on the domestic lives of public men and women, will not be equated with 'public interest' by the courts.

One case which offers some guidance is *Mutch* v. *Sleeman*.[9] The plaintiff, Tom Mutch, was a minister of the crown who attacked a newspaper in parliament under the benefit of privilege. The minister adopted a high moral posture and criticized the salacious pictures and lewd writing which he said appeared in the newspaper. In a stinging editorial response to the minister's attack, the newspaper sought to expose his own moral standards. It accused him of having 'ratted' on his own party; having betrayed his leader; and of being drunk and using foul language. For good measure it added:

> then again that divorce of yours, the evidence of your wife was that you struck her, that you were nothing but a brutal wife-basher ... If Young Australia, Tom Mutch, models itself on a wife-beating example, will Young Australia not be on the road to corruption and degradation?[10]

Mutch sued the newspaper for defamation. The newspaper claimed justification. The court ruled that the defence was not available to the newspaper as it would be impossible for any reasonable man to say in the circumstances that it was 'a matter of public benefit that something that took place between (the Minister) and his wife three or four years before should be published to the world, even if the facts were truly stated'.

ABSOLUTE PRIVILEGE

There are certain limited occasions when the law allows people and institutions to speak or write unfettered by the prospect of a defamation action. On occasions of absolute privilege, the interests of society in free communication are considered of such importance that they justify displacing completely the individual's interest in the protection of his reputation. Absolute privilege provides complete immunity from liability, regardless of the motives of the speaker or the accuracy of his statements.[11] Generally, it is available only for the legislative, executive and judicial functions of government.

Statements made in the course of proceedings in parliaments and courts and documents presented in them or published under their authority receive the benefit of absolute privilege. The privilege attaches to the institutions themselves, and does not extend to republishers such as the media. What a politician says during debate in parliament attracts absolute privilege. The same statement made in a 'kerbside' press conference outside the parliament attracts no absolute privilege for the media or for him.

QUALIFIED PRIVILEGE

The common law applying in New South Wales, Victoria, South Australia, Western Australia, the ACT and the Northern Territory recognizes limited occasions of qualified privilege on which a person is allowed to make defamatory statements about another regardless of whether they are true or false. Examples are a character reference concerning an employee provided by a former employer to a prospective one, and a statement made to the police in response to their inquiries into the commission of a crime. Unlike absolute privilege, qualified privilege is lost if it is abused for some improper purpose or if the publisher is actuated by ill will. The rationale for sacrificing individual reputation to social demands has been stated as follows:

It may be unfortunate that a person against whom a charge that is not true is made should have no redress, but it would be contrary to public policy and the general interest of business and society that persons should be hampered in the discharge of their duty or the exercise of their rights by constant fear of actions for slander.[12]

Whether or not a particular occasion is a privileged one is a question of law. If a person can bring himself as a matter of law within the protection of qualified privilege, it is for the plaintiff to prove as a matter of fact that the person abused the privilege.

A communication attracts qualified privilege at common law if it is made on:

an occasion where the person who makes a communication has an interest or a duty, legal, social, or moral to make it to the person to whom it is made, and the person to whom it is so made has a corresponding interest or duty to receive it. This reciprocity [of both interest and duty] is essential.[13]

The privilege was designed for interpersonal, one-to-one communications such as a reference for an employee communicated between employer and prospective employer. The open-ended nature of the formula quoted above, however, has encouraged the mass media to attempt to persuade the courts to bring them within its protection. The news media have argued without success that the public interest function they perform and the special nature of their relationship with their audience justify that kind of immunity from defamation actions.

The position of journalists and media commentators was laid down by the Privy Council in 1914:

The freedom of the journalist is an ordinary part of the freedom of the subject, and to whatever lengths the subject in general may go, so also may the journalist, but, apart from statute-law, his privilege is no other and no higher. The responsibilities which attach to his power in the dissemination of printed matter may, and in the case of a conscientious journalist do, make him more careful; but the range of his assertions, his criticisms, or his comments is as wide as, and no wider than, that of any other subject. No privilege attaches to his position.[14]

The position has been forcefully restated more recently in Australia by the New South Wales Court of Appeal in *Morosi* v. *Mirror Newspapers Ltd*.[15] The case arose out of a cartoon and various articles published in the *Daily Mirror*, *Daily Telegraph*, *Sunday Telegraph* and the *Australian* during 1974 and 1975. Morosi was at that time private secretary to the then treasurer, Dr Cairns. She claimed that the publications suggested that she was promiscuous, romantically attached to Dr Cairns, and an embarrassment for the Labor government in general. Mirror Newspapers contended that Morosi's fitness and suitability to hold the position of private secretary to the treasurer was a matter of public interest. It pointed to the fact that the subject had been debated in parliament and otherwise publicly aired by politicians. They claimed, among other things, that the publications were protected by qualified privilege at common law. In rejecting the newspapers' claim, the court said:

We do not think that there is any need to adapt the law of privilege, so that it will extend to publications of kinds we have been considering. Newspapers play an important role in our society, but that role does not call for an unrestricted licence to defame people, simply because it can be shown that the defamatory material was part of an article or other form of publication on a matter of public interest, and that the publication was not malicious. Defamatory publications on matters of public interest are protected under the common law, and by statute, in various ways, but something more than mere public interest is required. It may be truth; or it may be reasonableness, in all the circumstances, of the conduct of the publisher in making the publication; or it may be some other requirement. To establish its claim of privilege the [newspaper] must satisfy us that it had a duty or interest to publish the articles and the cartoon. We can see no occasion to establish or to recognize such a duty or interest.[16]

Although the broad ground of public interest will not yield a privilege for media publications, more restricted forms of privilege are available. The media have the qualified privilege which belongs to a fair and accurate report of the proceedings of legislative and other public bodies. This will be dealt with later. They may also have the qualified privilege which the law grants to statements made in reply to an attack.

Reply to Attack

A person has qualified privilege to reply to an attack on his character, conduct or business or property interests. The editor of a newspaper is entitled to respond in its pages to a public attack on his newspaper's reputation. More usually, however, qualified privilege will be granted to the media when they provide a public vehicle for a person who is responding to a public attack against himself. In *Adam* v. *Ward*,[17] a member of parliament, Adam, made a speech in parliament falsely accusing an army officer of misconduct in the course of his duty. The officer was precluded from answering the charge publicly and referred it to the army council. The army council conducted an inquiry, concluded that Adam's charge was unfounded and issued a statement to the press on the matter for publication. Adam sued the secretary of the council, claiming that the press release contained statements defamatory of himself. The House of Lords held that the press release was privileged. Lord Atkinson said:

I think it may be laid down as a general proposition that where a man, through the medium of Hansard's reports of the proceedings in Parliament, publishes to the world vile slanders of a civil, naval, or military servant of the crown in relation to the discharge by that servant of the duties of his office he selects the world as his audience, and that it is the duty of the heads of the service to which the servant belongs, if on investigation they find the imputation against him groundless, to publish his vindication to the same audience to which his traducer has addressed himself.[18]

The right to respond to parliamentary attack on character in the council's press release in *Adam* v. *Ward* would also have protected any media which published the release.

The right of the media to publish a reply to a public attack was in issue in *Loveday* v. *Sun Newspapers*.[19] Loveday was a member of an unemployed workers' organization. He had been a relief worker with Canterbury Municipal Council for about sixteen months and then had been denied relief work. The workers' organization took up his case. It sent a deputation to see the Town Clerk, who was responsible for employing council workers and allocating relief work. Dissatisfied with the clerk's response, the organization decided to go to the press. The secretary of the organization, with the knowledge and consent of Loveday, sent a letter to the *Sun* complaining that Loveday had been victimized because of his role in the organization. The *Sun* published an article about this allegation, which included the Twon Clerk's reply to it. The article reported the Town Clerk as saying that Loveday had been refused relief work because of his general unsatisfactory conduct, which included abuse of gangers and the spreading of restlessness among his fellow employees. The High Court held that the reply in the *Sun* was covered by qualified privilege. As Latham CJ said: 'The plaintiff himself had chosen the public press for the purpose of giving publicity to his complaint and he cannot complain if the defendant uses the same medium for reply.'[20]

There are limits to this right of self-defence. The law allows a defendant to justify himself to those who heard the charge against him. Thus, an original charge levelled at a social gathering cannot provide the basis for a privileged response on the front page of a newspaper. Moreover, a person who goes beyond defending himself by making counter-charges against the original attacker unconnected with the substance of the original attack will lose the privilege. So will the medium which carries the excessive counter-attack.

Abuse of Privilege

Qualified privilege may also be forfeited by an abuse of the occasion for which the privilege was granted. Privilege will be lost if the defendant takes advantage of the occasion by making statements which he does not believe to be true, or for the purpose of venting his spite on the plaintiff or for some other improper purpose. Moreover, the malice of a reporter may be imputed to exist in the mind of the media company that employs him. 'Malice' in this context means that the author bore ill will or some other personal animosity to the subject of his article and that a desire to indulge that animosity and injure his subject was the dominant motive for publishing the article. So it is not enough to establish malice to prove that the defendant published a statement that was unreasonable, unfair or even untrue. A plaintiff who seeks to demonstrate malice must go further and show, for example, that the defendant published the statement knowing that it was false.[21]

The courts have said that when a matter is published on a privileged occasion they should not be quick to find evidence of malice because to do so would defeat the protection which the law confers. It is especially uncommon for an allegation of malice or other abuse of privilege to succeed in a media case. In *Pinniger* v. *John Fairfax & Sons Ltd*,[22] an entertainer who used the name 'Madame Lash' appeared as a guest on a television show conducted by Mike Walsh. In the course of the show, Madame Lash accidentally struck Walsh with a stock whip. The blow left a bruise on Walsh's face and caused a ringing in one of his ears for which he sought medical attention. The *Sun* reported the incident as follows:

Walsh still has a flea in his ear.

Mike Walsh will see a specialist this week. Walsh still has a 'ring' in his one good ear after being badly slashed with a stockwhip by Madame Lash during last Thursday's Mike Walsh Show.

The incident happened after Walsh accidentally broke the strap on one of Madame's platform shoes.

Most of the swelling on Walsh's face went down over the weekend.

But when he went back on air today he still had to use make-up covering a welt on the right side of his face.

Walsh hopes the ringing in his good ear—the other has only 20 per cent hearing—is only the result of temporary inflammation.

But his doctor has referred him to an ear, nose and throat specialist.

In the meantime Channel 10 has vowed to be more careful in future.

Madame Lash claimed the article depicted her as vicious and ill tempered and sued the *Sun*. The *Sun* claimed privilege for the publication and the trial judge left the matter to the jury on the basis that there was evidence of malice in the publication of the article. The jury returned a verdict for Madame Lash. The *Sun* appealed. Madame Lash sought to rely on the 'exaggerated' and 'sensational' style and language of the article as evidence of malice. The High Court held that there was no evidence to support the jury's verdict, however, and set it aside. Barwick CJ said:

> Exaggeration which the use of the word 'badly' is said grossly to exhibit and the resort to such argot as 'a flea in the ear' are stressed ... but these are a commonplace in journalism of the kind in which sensation seemingly is prized above truth. Lack of care for the consequences of exuberant reporting is not the equivalent of malice: nor is it in this case ... evidence of malice.[23]

New South Wales Statutory Modifications

Section 22 of the New South Wales Defamation Act introduces an additional defence of qualified privilege, which is quite important for the media. A media defendant in a particular case can use either or both common law qualified privilege and the privilege contained in s. 22. The section applies where the recipient has an interest or apparent interest in having information on some subject; the matter is published to the recipient in the course of giving him information on that subject; and the conduct of the publisher in publishing that matter is reasonable in the circumstances.

Section 22 was designed to enlarge the protection afforded by the common law principles and might have been expected to provide a greater degree of latitude to media reporting. The New South Wales Court of Appeal has ruled, however, that s. 22:

> gives no carte blanche to newspapers to publish defamatory matter because the public has an interest in receiving information on the relevant subject. What the section does is to substitute reasonableness in the circumstances for the duty or interest which the common law principles of privilege require to be established.[24]

If a media defendant wishes to use the provisions in relation to a report the truth of which he is unable to prove, it will not be sufficient merely to show that the topic of the report was a matter of public interest. He will need to go further and establish circumstances or point to proven circumstances which make it reasonable to publish the defamatory matter to the world at large.

In deciding whether a publication was reasonable, the courts consider the circumstances leading up to and surrounding the publication, including: the manner and extent of publication; the steps taken to check the accuracy of the publication and whether or not the author held an honest belief in the truth of what was published. The media defendant bears the onus of establishing that the publication was reasonable. As a result of the approach adopted by the courts on this issue, it has been difficult for the media to establish the defence of privilege contained in s. 22. The courts' approach is illustrated by the following cases.

In *Wright* v. *Australian Broadcasting Commission*,[25] a political commentator, Richard Carleton, before appearing on the television programme *This Day Tonight*, interviewed Senator Wright on the topic of a secret ballot which had been held to elect a president of the Senate. The Senate was evenly divided between Labor and Liberal, and there were two independent senators. The ballot resulted in the election of the Labor nominee. In an effort to unravel the secret voting, Carleton asked Senator Wright, a Liberal, whether or not he had voted for the Liberal nominee. Wright refused to answer the question and rebuked Carleton, saying that the question was improper and insulting as implying that he betrayed his party.

During a broadcast of *This Day Tonight* later on the day of the interview, Carleton outlined the circumstances surrounding the ballot. Discounting the possibility that both independent senators had voted for the Labor nominee, he turned his attention to Liberal and Country Party senators and said, according to the transcript:

> Now there are no options, there are no possibilities. It must it must be this, that in the er in the vernacular of politics, someone in the Liberal or Country Party ratted. Now, who did it? Now there er are possibly three or four men that er one could er one could suggest er er as er having an inclination towards er not voting for their party nominee, Mr Magnus Cormack. And each one of those men I went up to today and asked them ah in reasonably direct terms how they voted. Even though it was a secret ballot ah and, to a man, they told me that they supported the party candidate, to a man, that is, except Senator Reg Wright, the rebel Liberal or one-time rebel Liberal from Tasmania, and ah when I went to Senator Wright's office in Parliament House today, this evening, and asked him the very direct question, he said to me that is a preposterous question to ask, I should be ashamed of myself for asking the question, so really one can only guess where that one vote came from—who was the rat.

Wright sued the ABC, claiming that Carleton's commentary defamed him by suggesting that he was the one who had betrayed his party and voted against it under the cloak of a secret ballot. The ABC called no evidence to attempt to establish that broadcasting Carleton's commentary was reasonable in the circumstances. It relied solely on the commentary itself.

The Court of Appeal found that the commentary was defamatory and that its general topic was a matter of public interest. The court held, however, that the ABC could not shelter under the umbrella of the public interest. Section 22 required the court to assess the reasonableness of the broadcast. In the absence of any evidence from the ABC explaining the circumstances behind the broadcast, the court looked to the content of the commentary to determine whether its broadcast was reasonable. The court concluded that Carleton's defamatory suggestion, that Senator Wright had 'ratted', was nothing more than a guess and that it was unreasonable to broadcast such a serious defamatory allegation supported only by guesswork.

In *Austin* v. *Mirror Newspapers Ltd*,[26] the trainer of the Manly Rugby League Team, Reg Austin, sued the *Daily Mirror* for an article by columnist Ron Casey. Casey's article said that Austin was training the team to the point of exhaustion three times a week. The article described Austin as a fitness fanatic, claimed that his training methods had contributed to the team's poor match performance and ended with the advice that Austin should be sacked.

The jury found that the article was defamatory and untrue and awarded Austin $60 000 damages. The trial judge, however, decided that the *Daily Mirror* was entitled to rely on the defence of qualified privilege under s. 22. Austin appealed to the Privy Council. It set aside the trial judge's decision and restored the jury's award of damages to Austin. The Privy Council found that Casey did not take reasonable care to check his facts before he wrote the article and that the *Daily Mirror* had therefore failed to establish that publication of the article was reasonable.

Qualified Privilege under the Codes

The codes which apply in Queensland and Tasmania set out a list of cases in which there is qualified protection. Of special relevance to the media is the defence which arises if a publication is made 'in good faith in the course of, or for the purposes of, the discussion of some subject of public interest, the public discussion of which is for the public benefit . . .'[27] As a result, a media defendant in Queensland or Tasmania may escape liability for the publication of defamatory, untrue statements if it can persuade a court that the purpose of the publication was to give information to the public on a matter of public importance; and if the plaintiff is unable to prove that the defendant was actuated by ill will or other improper motive.[28] The media defendant will not have to prove the truth of the damaging statement. This result contrasts not only with the common law but also with the position under s. 22 of the *Defamation Act* 1974 (NSW) where, as we have seen, it is necessary for a media defendant to establish that the publication of material, the truth of which he is unable to prove, is reasonable in the circumstances.

The contrast between the code position and that of the common law is demonstrated in *Gorton* v. *Australian Broadcasting Commission*,[29] a case mentioned in Chapter 2. Mr Gorton, the then Prime Minister of Australia, sued the ABC in relation to a television interview on *This Day Tonight* between Richard Carleton and Maximilian Walsh. The action was taken in respect of the broadcast of the programme in the ACT, New South Wales and Victoria. At the time of the broadcast (1971) the *Defamation Act* 1958 was in force in New South Wales. That Act included a provision identical to the provision of the Queensland and Tasmanian code quoted above. Gorton complained, among other things, that a statement made by Walsh in the interview falsely suggested that he had instructed one of his ministers to issue a false denial of a story that he knew to be true. The court found that such a suggestion did arise from the interview and that it was defamatory and untrue. It held that Gorton was entitled to succeed in the ACT and Victoria. In relation to the broadcast in those places, the ABC had claimed justification but had been unable to prove the truth of the suggestion. The court held that in New South Wales, however, the code defence of publication in good faith in the course of discussion of a subject of public interest was entitled to succeed. The court pointed out that the subject of the interview, the political conduct of the Prime Minister, was a matter of public interest and that for the ABC to succeed under the code defence it was not necessary to establish the truth of the defamatory suggestions made in the course of the interview.[30]

FAIR COMMENT

It is a defence to a defamation action to prove that the words complained of were published as fair comment on a matter of public interest.[31] The defence, which protects expressions of opinion on any matter of public interest, is regarded as 'one of the essential elements that go to make up our freedom of speech'.[32] If a matter is one of public interest, a commentator is free to express an opinion on it. As long as the opinion is honestly held and the commentator gets his basic facts right, his right of free speech is not forfeited merely because he employs an acid tongue. *Silkin* v. *Beaverbrook Newspapers Ltd*[33] arose from the following *Sunday Express* article:

> Sugar for Silkin. From these humble Tories I turn to a lordly Socialist. Forward, the first Baron Silkin. Observe the return to Britain of the Heinkels. Not in the skies, but on the rolling roads. These economical little runabouts are selling briskly in the petrol famine. They are seen everywhere—even in New Palace Yard, Westminster, where M.P.'s park their cars. What has this to do with Lord Silkin? Why he is chairman of Noble Motors, who market the Heinkels in Britain. And his son, former Socialist candidate Mr John Silkin, is a director. Oh, the eloquence that solemn portly Lord Silkin has churned out in the House of Lords against arming the Germans. He has said that part of his case is 'emotional'. 'I feel it is wrong that, so soon after the events of the war, we should join hands with them today for the purpose of combining our forces'. Of course, when Lord Silkin joins hands with the Germans now, he represses his emotion. It is just good solid business. From which, no doubt, he makes a fine profit.

Lord Silkin sued the *Sunday Express* claiming that the last three sentences of the article accused him of being a hypocrite who was prepared to sacrifice his principles for personal profit. The *Sunday Express* responded that the facts throughout the article were true and that the conclusions of the last three sentences were fair comment on a matter of public interest. The newspaper's contention was upheld.

The defence of fair comment has a wide scope and is particularly important to the media in the treatment of current affairs, the coverage of sport and public entertainment and the criticism of theatre, art and literature. The main ingredients of fair comment are that the comment must be recognizable as comment; the comment must be based on fact; the comment must be 'fair'; and the comment must be on a matter of public interest. A comment is 'something which is or can reasonably be inferred to be a deduction, inference, conclusion, criticism, judgment, remark or observation' as distinct from a 'direct statement concerning or description of a subject'.[34]

Comment Recognizable as Comment

The test of whether matter is comment or an assertion of fact is the impression it creates in the mind of the ordinary reader or viewer: would he or she understand the matter to be a statement of fact or merely an expression of opinion? Much depends on context. If the facts of a matter are set out or referred to by a commentator and he then goes on to express an opinion on those facts or to draw a conclusion or inference from them, then that opinion, conclusion or inference will be taken as his own comment. On the other hand, generalized allegations or claims without reference to the facts on which they are based will usually be classified as assertions of fact:

> To say that a man's conduct was dishonourable is not comment: it is a statement of fact. To say that he did certain specific things and that his conduct was dishonourable is a statement of fact coupled with a comment.[35]

Bald assertions may be taken by the reader as founded on unrevealed facts known to the commentator; and the reader or listener may be inclined to treat the assertion itself as one of fact. In *Bamberger* v. *Mirror Newspapers*,[36] Freddie Bamberger, a television entertainer, sued a newspaper for an article which claimed that during his performance in a television show Bamberger 'came out and plonked out an atrocious solo—Rhapsody in Blue. Then, with gags the same colour he visited France and leered at the chorines' legs'. The jury found that the statement that the 'gags' were 'blue' was defamatory—it suggested that Bamberger had used his television show to retail dirty jokes—and that it was a statement of fact and not a mere expression of opinion. The High Court held that it was open to the jury to reach that conclusion.

A commentary or report which mingles statements of fact with statements of opinion runs the risk of creating a total impression in the mind of the ordinary reader that the whole of the commentary or report consists of assertions of fact. A commentary or report whose format clearly separates facts from comment is less likely to meet this difficulty. In *Hunt* v. *Star Newspaper Co. Ltd*, Fletcher Moulton LJ said:

> Comment in order to be justifiable as fair comment must appear as comment and must not be so mixed up with facts that the reader cannot distinguish between what is report and what is comment. Any matter which does not indicate with a reasonable clearness that it purports to be comment and not statement of fact, cannot be protected by the plea of fair comment.[37]

O'Shaughnessy v. *Mirror Newspapers Ltd*[38] arose from a performance of 'Othello' in which Peter O'Shaughnessy played the lead and directed the performance. A review by theatre critic Katharine Brisbane appeared in the *Australian*. The review headed 'What a Tragedy' said, in part:

> Stupidity and lack of talent are forgivable; brave failures are deserving of praise—these are every-day human failings. But the waste and dishonesty of this production, or rather recitation, make me very angry indeed ... I suspect the liveliness of John Norman's athletic, romantic Cassio and the lifelessness of Rob Inglis' Iago had something to do with the fact that Othello is seldom on stage with the former and almost always with the latter. Mr Inglis' Iago is most elaborately boring. Mr O'Shaughnessy in his programme note 'flatly rejects' the Leavis view that Iago is 'not much more than a necessary piece of dramatic mechanism' but that is exactly what he makes of Mr Inglis. In short the performance is a disaster which has all the making of a fine production. All it needs is a producer with a little humanity, who understands that the actors on stage are people and the audience are people too. As it was the only fellow feeling I had with the stage on Tuesday was with Miss Thody's (Desdemona) expression at curtain-call. She looked as if she had had enough for one evening, and so had I.

O'Shaughnessy sued the *Australian* claiming that the review suggested that he had directed the play dishonestly, suppressing the performance of the other actors in order to enhance his own role in the play. The *Australian* claimed that the whole of the review was merely comment upon and evaluation of the production of the play itself.

The High Court said that the passages (quoted above):

> could fairly have been regarded by the jury as going beyond criticism of the production and attributing a dishonourable motive to the plaintiff as a statement of fact. This is one of those cases where the critic, in making her evaluation that the production was a disaster—which, of course, she was entitled to do—did not plainly confine herself to commenting upon facts truly stated; she wrote what could, we think, have been regarded as amounting to a defamatory statement of fact, viz. that the producer dishonestly suppressed the roles of other players to highlight his own role. It is not that the writer merely failed to preface what she had to say about the production with some formula such as 'it seemed to me'; it is rather that the jury could have found that an imputation of dishonesty was levelled against the plaintiff as the writer's explanation of what she asserted to be a waste of talent.[39]

The form of the expression provides no clear guide. The use of such common phrases as 'it appears to me', 'in my opinion', 'I believe', while undoubtedly intended by the author or speaker to signal that what follows is opinion, may or may not lead the reader or listener to comprehend the content of the statement which follows as an expression of opinion. Such phrases are not decisive and cannot automatically convert everything that precedes or follows them into a statement which will be recognized as an expression of opinion. As Lord Oaksey said in *Turner* v. *MGM*,[40] 'a statement which is plainly one of fact cannot be transformed into a statement of opinion merely by prefacing it with the words "in our judgement"'.

Newspaper headlines and posters are more likely to be understood to be assertions of fact than inferences. In *Smith's Newspapers Ltd* v. *Becker*,[41] a German doctor who practised in South Australia without being registered as a medical practitioner sued *Smith's Weekly* over an article headlined 'German Quack runs riot on the Murray Flats'. It claimed that the doctor had negligently prescribed and administered a dangerous drug which had caused the death of many of his patients. The High Court rejected a plea of fair comment in relation to the article, on the ground that the ordinary reader would take it as asserting that the description of the doctor as a 'quack' was an allegation of fact rather than merely the opinion of *Smith's Weekly*. Evatt J pointed to the difficulties which a sensational headline can place in the way of a successful claim of fair comment by a newspaper:

So fortunate an avenue of escape, via fair comment will seldom, if ever, be open to a newspaper which uses defamatory headlines or headings, without making it quite clear that a mere expression of opinion is being announced to the world, upon the basis of the facts to be stated in a sub-joined article. Streamer headlines, the intermingling of facts with actual or possible expressions of opinion and screaming posters are features of this age of industrialism, and praise or blame is no concern of ours. But the legal defence of fair comment will very rarely protect defamatory matter contained in such journalism, not because the motives of the proprietors are mercenary ... but because of the impossibility of achieving sensations, and still effecting a clear separation of the facts from the defamatory expressions of opinion.[42]

Comment Based on Facts

There are two aspects of this requirement. Firstly, it is an essential ingredient of fair comment that the comment must be based on facts which are either stated by the commentator or indicated by him with sufficient clarity to permit the reader or listener to know the matter on which the comment is being made.[43] The inclusion of (or reference to) the facts on which the comment is based in the statement containing the comment enables the reader or listener to judge for himself the value of the commentator's opinion. In the case of a book review, for example, the reader is given the opportunity to judge the value of the critic's comments if the critic simply makes a clear reference to the particular book he is reviewing. It is not necessary to set out the entire text of the book or even passages from it in the review. A comment cannot be fair, however, if it is based on facts that are misstated, or invented. There must be a sufficient basis or foundation of true fact to support the comment. Thus, if a critic in reviewing a book or play misquotes from it or misdescribes its contents, the defence may fail. Similarly, if a reporter states that A was convicted of a serious crime and goes on to comment adversely on the fact, but omits to mention that the conviction was set aside on appeal, his report cannot be defended as fair comment.

This does not mean that the commentator will always be required to establish the truth of the facts. If the facts are protected by privilege, expressions of opinion about those facts may be protected as fair comment even though the facts turn out to be false.[44] So, if a television current affairs programme accurately reports evidence given in court proceedings and then comments on the evidence, the defence of fair comment will protect the station despite the fact that matters stated in the evidence cannot be proved to be true.

Comment Must be Fair

The word 'fair' can mislead. The test is honesty, not fairness in the sense of reasonableness. Comment is 'fair' if it is one that any honest person could have expressed on the facts as proved, provided that the comment represented the commentator's real opinion and was not distorted by malice in the sense that malice had warped his judgment.[45]

Lord Diplock J summed the matter up to a jury in a defamation case, *Silkin* v. *Beaverbrook Newspapers Ltd,* in this way:

> The expression 'fair comment' is a little misleading. It may give the impression that you, the jury, have to decide whether you think that it is fair. If that were the question which you had to decide, you realise that the limits of freedom which the law allows would be greatly curtailed. People are entitled to hold and to express freely on matters of public interest strong views, views which some of you, or indeed all of you, may think are exaggerated, obstinate, or prejudiced, provided—and this is the important thing—that they are views which they honestly hold. The basis of our public life is that the crank, the enthusiast, may say what he honestly thinks just as much as the reasonable man or woman who sits on a jury ...[46]

As a result of the adoption of the test of 'honestly' held belief rather than reasonably held belief, the scope of the defence is quite broad. The courts have taken the view that:

> in the case of criticism in matters of art, whether music, painting, literature or drama, where the private character of the person criticised is not involved, the freer the criticism is the better it will be for the aesthetic welfare of the public.[47]

Comment on a Matter of Public Interest

The courts have also been liberal in specifying this element of the 'fair comment' defence. As Lord Denning said in *London Artists Ltd* v. *Litter*:

> There is no definition in the books as to what is a matter of public interest. All we are given is a list of examples, coupled with the statement that it is for the judge and not the jury. I would not myself confine it within narrow limits. Whenever a matter is such as to affect people at large, so that they may be legitimately interested in, or concerned at, what is going on, or what may happen to them or others; then it is a matter of public interest on which everyone is entitled to make fair comment.[48]

The defence has been successfully pleaded in connection with national, state and local government affairs; public administration; the administration of justice; the public affairs of private professions, institutions and corporations. It also covers sporting commentary and criticism of books, plays, films and other works which are placed in the public arena.

The defence will not be available, however, to protect criticism which deals with the purely private affairs of people, even of public figures, notwithstanding the fact that such matters attract public curiosity.[49] Thus in *Mutch* v. *Sleeman*, outlined above, a newspaper allegation that a politician was a 'wife-basher' was denied the defence of fair comment on the ground that:

> the mere fact that a man is a politician, or is engaged in some occupation which brings him into public notice, is not of itself enough to make his private life a matter of public interest, so as to justify the kind of defamatory comment to which, so far as his public activities are concerned, he must submit as one of the incidents of his position.[50]

PROTECTED REPORTS

The republication rule (examined in Chapter 2) makes a person liable in defamation simply for repeating what someone else has said. If unmitigated, the rule would seriously restrict the free flow of information on public affairs. There are, however, important exceptions to the rule. A fair and accurate report of certain official proceedings receives protection from the law. This protection arises from the common law relating to qualified privilege and a host of special statutory provisions.[51] In New South Wales, Victoria, South Australia, Western Australia, the ACT and the Northern Territory, a report may seek protection from either or both the common law of privilege and the statutory provisions of the jurisdiction. In Queensland and Tasmania, the code excludes the common law. Marked variation exists between jurisdictions in relation to the subject matter and scope of the statutory protection afforded. The law of protected reports in Australia has only one unifying principle: no question of protection arises unless the report contains a fair and accurate account of its subject matter.[52]

Fair and Accurate Report

The requirement of a fair and accurate report takes account of the way in which modern printed and electronic media reports are compiled, the exigencies of time and space, and the demands of the public for selective and concentrated summaries of public proceedings. Protection is therefore not confined to verbatim or lengthy accounts but extends to summaries and sketches of official proceedings and documents, provided that they are fair and accurate.[53] Defamation law is very similar to the contempt law discussed in Chapter 6 in this respect. The requirement of fairness and accuracy is to be judged by the standard of the ordinary reader rather than by that of a trained lawyer, so not every insignificant slip will deprive a report of protection. Nevertheless, the requirements of accuracy demanded by the courts are substantial. The following statement of the New South Wales Court of Appeal in *Allen* v. *John Fairfax & Sons Ltd* (made in relation to court proceedings) summarizes those requirements:

> An abridged or condensed report of judicial proceedings must be fair, not garbled so as to produce misrepresentation nor by suppression of some portion of the proceedings giving an entirely false and unjust impression to the prejudice of the plaintiff.[54]

The requirements will not be met if a reporter makes significant errors or, while reporting correctly a part of a protected proceeding or document, leaves out other parts and so gives a different and prejudicial complexion to the whole matter. *Bunker* v. *James and Downland Publications Ltd*[55] illustrates these principles. The following misleading report appeared in *Truth*:

Woman—My Rape Ordeal

A WOMAN has claimed that a naked man hit her about the head and body before and after raping her in a suburban flat.

Contractor Acquitted

The woman said the man gritted his teeth, snarled and frothed at the mouth during a bedroom ordeal she claimed lasted from the early hours to mid-morning.

52 MEDIA LAW IN AUSTRALIA

At one stage, the woman alleged, she told the man: 'Take what you want, you animal, and get out.'
Bunker pleaded not guilty to a charge of having raped the woman at Essendon on July 2.
A jury found Bunker not guilty.
A woman in her mid-thirties told Judge Byrne and the jury in Melbourne County Court that Bunker arrived at her flat on July 2. Bunker had hit her several times, pushed her towards her bedroom and said: 'Get in here and get your gear off.'
She said Bunker pushed her on to a bed and then 'man-handled' her. He then started ripping her clothes off.
Bunker was naked and started having intercourse with her, she told the jury.
She said: 'I started to scream and that's when he started to hit me. It wasn't hits, it was punches.'

Night

She said Bunker had struck her about 100 times during the night and morning.
Bunker told the jury from the witness box that the woman's rape claim was a lie.
He said he hit her several times, but only to force her to spit out some sleeping tablets.
He said: 'I suggested she go and sleep it off. I sat in a chair and fell asleep'.[56]

Bunker sued *Truth* for defamation. *Truth* claimed, among other things, that the report was privileged as a fair and accurate report of court proceedings. The report was of a Melbourne County Court trial for rape. The trial lasted seven days and produced over 200 pages of transcript. The court held that the report did not cease to be fair and accurate because it was in an abbreviated form, because it did not set out the prosecution and defence cases in detail, or because it gave prominence to sensational features of the woman's evidence. It could not be said that the report failed to make clear that the plaintiff was acquitted of the charge. The court did not hold that the report was not a fair and accurate one because what was printed was wrong. In fact what was printed was correct. The court held, however, that the report was not fair and accurate because it was too one-sided. Practically all of the report was devoted to the woman's allegations, and only three very short staccato paragraphs at the end dealt with Bunker's defence. By omitting to mention that his defence included a denial of sexual intercourse, the report could have given readers the misleading impression that he had admitted intercourse and only pleaded consent. The report also failed to mention other significant features of his case: that he was at the flat at the woman's invitation; that for a time there had been another person present; and that he had grappled with the woman in an attempt to prevent her taking an overdose of sleeping pills. He was awarded $4500 damages.

Loss of Protection

A report of a protected category of proceedings or statements which is fair and accurate may lose the protection provided by common law privilege or by statute. The protection of common law privilege will be lost if a report is actuated by malice. Statutory protection is lost where a report is not made in 'good faith'.[57] Absence of good faith is not the same as malice. As we have seen, a publication protected by qualified privilege is malicious and loses that protection if its publisher did not have an honest belief in the truth of what was published. However, a reporter need not have an honest belief in the truth of matter reported under statutory protection. Provided such a report is an accurate one, absence of good faith cannot be established and statutory protection lost merely by showing that the reporter knew that what he reported was false.[58]

Categories of Protected Reports

Parliamentary proceedings and papers

A fair and accurate report of a debate or proceedings in parliament[59] is entitled to qualified privilege at common law. In most Australian jurisdictions, such a report is also granted statutory protection.[60] Statutory protection is also given to a copy of or extract from or abstract of any paper published by order or under the authority of parliament.[61]

Judicial proceedings

Fair and accurate reports of public judicial proceedings receive qualified privilege at common law and are also protected by statute.[62] Protection does not extend, however, to affidavits and other documents filed but not brought up in open court.[63] At common law, reports of foreign legal proceedings do not automatically qualify for protection; the particular matter before the foreign court must be of significant enough local concern before the privilege arises. In *Thompson* v. *Australian Consolidated Press Ltd*,[64] a Sydney newspaper report of a New York trial of Australians indicted on charges of importing heroin into America from Sydney was held to attract the privilege. The argument that state courts are 'foreign' in the context of the law of protected reports was raised in *Bunker* v. *James and Downland Publications Ltd.*[65] That case, already discussed, concerned a newspaper report published in South Australia of a rape trial in Victoria. The *Wrongs Act* 1936 (SA) s. 6 provides protection, relevantly, for 'a fair and accurate report in any newspaper of proceedings publicly heard before any court ...' Remarking that 'what goes on in one State of Australia is of interest to another State' and that 'we are all part of a community of Australians',[66] the South Australian Supreme Court rejected the submission that the word 'court' in the South Australian Act was limited to a South Australian court and held that the report could attract privilege.

In all Australian jurisdictions, protection has been granted by statute to the publication of a fair and accurate report of the proceedings of an inquiry (such as a royal commission) held under legislative or executive authority and to a fair extract from or abstract of the proceedings or official report of any such inquiry.[67] Such reports have also been held to be privileged at common law but only where the nature of the tribunal, the interests of the public in the proceedings, and the duty of the tribunal towards the public justify the publication.[68] The common law test, while easily satisfied in the case of royal commissions and other governmental inquiries, may not be satisfied by the proceedings of 'domestic tribunals'. So, for example, a report of the disciplinary proceedings of a sporting association may not be protected by the common law. In *Chapman* v. *Lord Ellesmere*,[69] the court held that a report in *The Times* of the findings of Jockey Club stewards that a trainer had been 'warned off' for administering a drug to a horse was not privileged. A report of the disciplinary proceedings of a professional, business or sporting association receives statutory protection only in New South Wales.[70]

Official notices
A notice or report which is issued for the information of the public by a government department, or office, or any of its officers and published by their request is accorded statutory protection.[71] This covers a large range of matters, including such things as police notices about suspected criminals and missing persons, but only when the actual words in substantially the same form in which they were issued in the notice are

repeated. The text of the notice or report is protected, and not some paraphrase composed for publication in what may be regarded as a more attractive form from a journalistic point of view.[72] It is important to distinguish between such notices which can properly be described as an official release and 'mere interesting gossip supplied to journalists by the publicity officer of a Minister for the purpose of keeping his Minister and his Minister's department prominently in the public eye'.[73] Press releases for political publicity not clearly within the objective of the statutory provision may not be protected by them. Similarly, not all statements made by a minister of the crown are privileged simply because he is a minister. Neither privilege nor statutory protection attaches to statements made by a minister of the crown simply because it is made by him on matters falling within his portfolio.

In *Brooks* v. *Muldoon*,[74] the New Zealand government had established a committee to recommend a suitable appointee to a statutory post. The committee recommended Brooks, but the government decided he was unsuitable. In answer to persistent questioning from press and television reporters at a news conference, Muldoon, who was then Minister for Finance, suggested that Brooks was biased and in other ways unfit for the job. Brooks sued the minister, who attempted to set up a claim of privilege. The New Zealand Supreme Court rejected the claim and held that a public statement could not be protected by qualified privilege simply because it was a statement made by a minister.

Public meetings
At common law, reports of the proceedings of a public meeting, however bona fide lawfully convened for a lawful purpose, and for the public benefit, are not privileged.[75] When dealing with topics of public interest, however, public meetings are accorded statutory protection in all jurisdictions except Victoria and the ACT.[76] Likewise, reports of meetings of local councils and other local authorities have not been accorded privilege at common law but have been given statutory protection in all jurisdictions.[77] Finally, a report of a company meeting carries no common law privilege but is protected by statute in South Australia and the Northern Territory.[78]

Public records
The common law, operating in Victoria, South Australia, Western Australia, the ACT and the Northern Territory, grants

privilege to a fair and accurate extract from a public record kept under the authority of a law and to which the public have access. Such an extract has been given statutory protection in New South Wales.[79] So, for example, an extract from a Companies Act register or a register of court judgments is protected. A reporter using protected public records must be careful to ensure that the extract he or she relies on accords accurately with the material on the primary record. If he or she relies on an extract which has been incorrectly copied from the primary record, the protection is lost. This applies even where the reporter has been supplied with an incorrect copy by a public official.[80]

OTHER DEFENCES

Statutory Defence of Innocent Publication

Under the common law, a publisher may be liable for defamation even though he took reasonable care in the preparation and publication of his material, did not intend the matter to be defamatory, and did not know of the circumstances which made the statement defamatory. Statutory reforms, however, offer some relief to a publisher under these circumstances. The New South Wales *Defamation Act* 1974, for example, provides a procedure for a person who publishes material in the circumstances outlined above to make an offer of amends (including publication of an apology and correction) to a person who claims to be defamed by the article.[81] If the offer is accepted by the offeree, he is by statute barred from future defamation proceedings in respect of the matter. If an offer made under the statutory procedures is not accepted, then the publisher has a defence in a subsequent action if he can establish, among other things, that the publication was innocent, and that he acted promptly on becoming aware of the defamatory matter. The procedure, which must be followed strictly, is cumbersome and has not been extensively used.[82]

Consent

It is a defence at common law to prove that the plaintiff assented to or acquiesced in the publication complained of.[83] The evidence must demonstrate, however, more than mere knowledge of publication on the part of the plaintiff. It must go further and clearly establish that the plaintiff authorized the publication by the defendant. Thus a consent to be interviewed does not necessarily mean that the interviewee consents to the whole of the subject of the interview being published. A person will be deemed to have consented to publication of false information which he feeds to the media. Thus Mr Cassidy in *Cassidy*'s case (mentioned in Chapter 2) could hardly complain that the photograph whose publication he procured suggested that he was about to commit bigamy.

The time-honoured challenge to a speaker to repeat his allegations outside parliament or in front of witnesses must be distinguished from consent. Such a challenge is simply an indication of a preparedness to bring an action on the words if repeated, rather than a consent to their repetition.

Triviality

At common law the nature of a statement is taken into account in determining whether it would tend to affect adversely the reputation of a person. The cases have recognized that statements which subject a person to 'mere abuse' as distinct from a real possibility of harm, injure pride but not reputation, or expose a person to harmless joking as opposed to ridicule are not defamatory.[84] New South Wales, Queensland, Tasmania and the ACT have each provided for a separate defence which permits the circumstances surrounding the publication of a statement to be taken into account as well as the nature of the statement itself. Thus Queensland and Tasmania provide a defence 'that the publication was made on an occasion and under circumstances where the person defamed was not likely to be injured thereby'.[85] In New South Wales, s. 13 of the *Defamation Act* 1974 provides that 'it is a defence that the circumstances of the publication of the matter complained of were such that the person defamed was not likely to suffer harm'. Such defences are particularly applicable to cases arising from limited social contexts where the range of publication is limited: for example, where a mildly defamatory statement is made in a jocular way to a few people in a private home. The defence will be less frequently available to media publications. In *Morosi*'s case, the court held that s. 13 could not be applied to widely published newspaper allegations concerning Morosi's private character.[86] In *Australian Consolidated Press Ltd* v. *Bond* the court refused to apply the defence to an ABC television programme which defamed businessman Kerry Packer to a 'vast audience'.[87]

REMEDIES

Damages

The main purpose of defamation actions is to compensate a person for harm to his or her reputation. As Windeyer J said, however, in *Uren* v. *John Fairfax & Sons Ltd*:

> It seems to me that, properly speaking, a man defamed does not get compensation *for* his damaged reputation. He gets damages *because* he was injured in his reputation, that is simply because he was publicly defamed. For this reason, compensation by damages operates in two ways—as a vindication of the plaintiff to the public and as consolation to him for a wrong done. Compensation is here a solatium rather than a monetary recompense for harm measurable in money.[88]

Compensation is provided by an award of damages, a specific lump sum of money. Where a jury is involved in the hearing of an action, the amount of money is determined by the jury.

The factors which the jury may take into account when fixing the amount of damages that are appropriate to compensate for harm to reputation include:

- The nature of the defamatory matter and the circumstances in which it was published, including the manner and extent of publication. So a higher sum would be awarded for an allegation of evasion of income tax by the filing of a false return than for an allegation of failure to pay tax through the careless omission to file a return. A national newspaper or a television programme which is networked nationally may expect to face a higher award of damages than a suburban weekly with a limited circulation or a small community radio station.
- Injury to personal feelings. As we have seen, there is no action in defamation for a publication merely because it injures a person's feelings; but once it has been established that the publication harms his reputation, the jury is entitled to take into account the psychological and emotional impact of the statement on the plaintiff. So distress, loss of self-confidence and self-esteem, and even fear of diminished prospects in employment or professional or business opportunities, may be considered.

- Financial loss suffered or likely to be suffered by the plaintiff, for example, the prospect that career advancement or business profits have been put in jeopardy.
- The position and standing of the plaintiff; whether or not the defendant published a retraction or apology; the conduct of the defendant from the time of the publication to the handing down of the verdict, including the conduct by the defendant or his legal representatives at the trial.
- Mitigating factors such as the publication of a retraction or apology; the fact (if established) that the plaintiff already had a generally bad reputation.

If the harm to the plaintiff is regarded as being exacerbated by the very nature of the publication or by the publisher's conduct, the jury may include a component of 'aggravated damages' as part of the compensatory damages it awards to a plaintiff. In some jurisdictions, the jury may award 'punitive damages', not to compensate the plaintiff but to punish the defendant. To justify such an award, however, there must be evidence that the defendant was high-handed, insolent, vindictive or malicious or in some other way exhibited contemptuous disregard of the plaintiff's rights.[89] Finally, where the matter complained of is of a trivial nature or the plaintiff has suffered no real or appreciable damage, the jury may award nominal damages.

The Australian Law Reform Commission has criticized the preoccupation of the present law with money damages and has recommended that the courts should have power to order publication of a correction of a false, defamatory statement as a remedy additional to damages. The commission envisages that a speedily available alternative legal remedy of correction would not only provide defamed people with more effective redress but also improve the flow of accurate information to the public.[90] As mentioned previously, the commission's recommendations have not been acted upon by government.

Injunction

An interlocutory injunction may be granted by a judge at any time after the issue of the writ which claims that a publication is defamatory. Such an injunction may even be granted in the absence of the defendant. An interlocutory injunction restrains the defendant from publishing until a full trial can be held to hear and determine the matter. The courts have developed a special approach which restricts the availability of interlocutory injunctions in defamation cases. They have done so from a reluctance to restrict freedom of speech and an anxiety to avoid usurping the jury's function of determining whether the matter is defamatory and, if so, defensible. No injunction will be granted if there is any real room for debate on whether the statements complained of are defamatory or if, on the evidence before the judge, there is any real ground for a defence.[91]

In addition to an interlocutory injunction, the court has the power, after trial of an action in which a verdict has been returned for the plaintiff, to grant a permanent injunction restraining a defendant from future publication of the defamatory matter. A court will grant such an injunction only if it is satisfied that the defendant is likely to repeat the defamatory publication.

4
PROTECTING BUSINESS REPUTATION

Michael Blakeney

Not only is business reputation protected by the tort of defamation, but also the valuable reputation of the goods or services offered by a business is protected from unfair disparagement by the tort of injurious falsehood. Disparagement in advertisements is regulated by the voluntary advertising codes of the various media industry self-regulation bodies. The wrongful appropriation of another's business reputation creates liability in the tort of passing off. Finally, unfair disparagement or passing off may fall foul of the Trade Practices Act.

DEFAMATION

It is beyond question that a company will be defamed by statements 'such as to lead people of ordinary sense to the opinion that they conduct their businesses badly and inefficiently'.[1] Thus to use the example of the judge in the most recent New South Wales Supreme Court decision on corporate defamation, the attribution in a newspaper of the closure of a breeding stud because of a highly contagious virus to the carelessness and incompetence of the owners or managers will be defamatory.[2]

The possibility of defamatory statements also being considered to be misleading or deceptive and in breach of the Trade Practices Act was accepted by the Federal Court in *Global Sportsman Pty Ltd* v. *Mirror Newspaper Ltd*.[3] That case concerned an allegation of disloyalty on the part of Australian test cricketers to the former captain Kim Hughes. The principle was extended to business reputation in *Australian Ocean Line* v. *West Australian Newspapers Ltd*.[4] That case concerned untrue newspaper reports about a cruise undertaken by a tourist vessel operated by the plaintiff. The court ruled that these news reports were both defamatory and in breach of s. 52 of the Trade Practices Act.

Media concern that the Trade Practices Act, without the traditional defences to defamation actions, would entirely replace defamation caused s. 65A to be inserted into the Act in late 1984. That section prevents the relevant sections of the Act applying to information providers such as the news media.

INJURIOUS FALSEHOOD

Injurious falsehood or slander of goods, as it is sometimes called, consists of a disparaging statement about a trader's business which is false and which causes damage to the business. The tort embraces attacks on the quality of a person's 'goods, services, employees, customers and place of business or house'.[5] An example of the sort of statement likely to cause media liability for injurious falsehood is illustrated by *Sungravure Pty Ltd* v. *Middle East Airlines Airliban SAL*.[6] That case, mentioned in Chapter 2, was brought under s. 5 of the New South Wales *Defamation Act* 1958 which, until its repeal in 1974, included imputations concerning a person and likely to injure him in his trade within the definition of defamation. The case concerned a short story in the *Woman's Day* called 'Dateline Masada' about a fictitious hijacking of a number of the airline's aircraft by a pro-Israeli organization. The High Court agreed with the airline that the story raised the inference that travellers with Middle East Airlines were at risk of being hijacked. The court held, by a majority, that such an inference was defamatory of the airline, according to s. 5, because it was likely to injure its trade.

Injurious falsehood differs from defamation in that for it to be established, falsity, malice and actual damage to the business of the plaintiff must all be demonstrated, whereas in defamation actions these elements are more easily assumed by the courts. The jealousy with which the law protects freedom of speech is said to explain the difficulty in establishing injurious falsehood, since unlike defamation, there is no countervailing principle that individuals' privacy be protected.[7]

The courts allow puffery, or exaggeration, as a defence to injurious falsehood. A distinction is drawn between statements which make unflattering comparisons and those which involve positive disparagement of a competitor's business. The former are considered to be unobjectionable puffery and the latter to be actionable. This distinction is often difficult to make, as Walton J explained in *De Beers Abrasive Products Ltd* v. *International Electric Co. of New York Ltd*.[8] He observed:

> In the kind of situation where one expects, as a matter of ordinary common experience, a person to use a certain amount of hyperbole in the description of goods, property or services, the courts will do what any ordinary reasonable man would do, namely, take it with a large pinch of salt.
>
> Where, however, the situation is not that the trader is puffing his own goods, but turns to denigrate those of his rival, then, in my opinion, the situation is not so clear cut. Obviously the statement: 'My goods are better than X's' is only a more dramatic presentation of what is implicit in the statement: 'My goods are the best in the world'. Accordingly, I do not think that such a statement would be actionable. At the other end of the scale, if what is said is: 'My goods are better than X's because X's are absolute rubbish,' then ... the statement would be actionable.
>
> Between these two kinds of statements there is obviously still an extremely wide field; and it appears to me that, in order to draw the line, one must apply this test, namely, whether a reasonable man would take the claim being made as being a serious claim or not.[9]

An alternative approach adopted by the courts to distinguish between permissible vaunting of one's own products and statements involving actual disparagement of those of a trade rival is to ask whether the statement makes some specific allegation about some factual aspect of a trader's business. Thus in *White* v. *Mellin*,[10] the endorsement of 'Dr Vance's prepared food for invalids and infants' described as being 'far more nutritious and healthful than any other preparation yet offered' was not actionable. Statements by advertisers that a competitor's products contained an undesirable ingredient[11] or had not undergone some secret process of manufacture,[12] or that they wore out quickly[13] have been held to be specific enough to be disparaging. Similarly, it was actionable for a defendant to claim that his paper had a circulation twenty times greater than any rival.[14] Where a specific allegation about a trader's business is made in sufficiently vituperative a manner as not seriously to be believed by a reasonable man, however, it may simply be regarded as unobjectionable vaunting. In the *De Beers* case, Walton J said of a hypothetical claim by the manufacturer of an amphibious car that it floated while a Rolls-Royce car would not, 'although this would be a specific enough criticism of the Rolls, nobody would take it seriously'.[15]

The remedies available to a trader complaining of injurious falsehood include damages and the entitlement to an injunction to restrain dissemination of the falsehood. In considering whether to grant interim relief, the courts apply the defamation principle that the importance of leaving free speech unfettered is a strong reason for dealing most cautiously with the granting of an injunction.[16]

MEDIA INDUSTRY CODES ON DISPARAGEMENT

Disparagement in advertising a person's business activities or products is the subject of a number of prohibitions contained in various codes of media industry organizations. The general application of these codes to advertising is discussed in Chapter 12. The Media Council of Australia, which is a voluntary association representing commercial print and electronic media, provides in clause 15 of its Advertising Code of Ethics that 'Advertisements shall not disparage identifiable products, services or advertisers in an unfair or misleading way'. In a guide to advertisers explaining this clause, the Media Council stressed that 'the intent and connotation of ads should be to inform and never to discredit or unfairly attack competitors, competing products or services' and that where a competitive product was named 'it should be one that exists in the marketplace as significant competition'.

Section 38(i) of the Television Programme Standards, administered by the Australian Broadcasting Tribunal, provides that 'advertisements should contain no claims intended to disparage competing advertisers or their products or services, or other industries, professions or institutions'. The Commercials Acceptance Division of the Federation of Australian Commercial Television Stations (FACTS), to which most TV commercials have to be sent for approval before they can be broadcast, applies the Media Council guide on disparaging advertising.[17] The guide has been applied in some interesting ways. In December 1981, FACTS refused approval to commercials for an anti-smoking game because the game was disparaging of cigarette companies, presumably in the same way as is the health warning on cigarette packets. Similarly, 'healthy lifestyle' advertisements prepared by the Health Commission of New South Wales were initially approved by FACTS; but an appeal committee suspended them because, among other things, they were disparaging of butter and dairy products. The Australian Broadcasting Tribunal did not share this view.[18] The decision by FACTS to prohibit a commercial depicting Richard Nixon endorsing cassette tapes, however, was upheld by the tribunal because, among other things, it was disparaging of the US presidency.[19] As this last decision indicates, the prohibitions against disparagement overlap with prohibitions of advertisements lacking in taste and decency contained in the Television Programme Standards. These standards are discussed in Chapter 9. This decision may explain the FACTS refusal to allow a commercial for mineral water to be broadcast in which the presenter was an actress resembling the then Lady Diana Spencer. The commercial was held to be either lacking in taste, deceptive, or disparaging of the Prince of Wales.

The Federation of Australian Radio Broadcasters (FARB) similarly observes the Media Council's Advertising Code of Ethics. The Australian Broadcasting Tribunal's Broadcasting Advertising Standards 1981 contain no prohibition against disparagement although these standards, as administered by FARB, implicitly prohibit matter lacking in taste and decency.

FACTS, FARB and the Australian Publishers' Bureau (APB), which represents the commercial print media, all enforce the Therapeutic Advertising Code which regulates the advertising of medicines and therapeutic appliances. Clause 14 of the code provides: 'an advertisement relating to goods for therapeutic use shall not contain claims intended to disparage other medicines or the medical or allied professions'. Some anti-smoking newspaper advertisements prepared by the Health Commission of New South Wales were suspended by the APB, because they were construed as advertisements for therapeutic services and had not been approved by the APB.

A Joint Committee for Disparaging Copy was established in 1954 to deal with complaints in the advertising industry made by advertisers or their agencies about advertisements that were considered unreasonable or unnecessarily critical. The committee consists of seven members drawn from television, radio, press, national advertisers and agencies. It is empowered to veto an advertisement which 'contains a specific and identifiable disparagement of a particular product or service advertised by a rival'. Of 589 complaints made to the committee between 1954 and 1980, 181 were upheld, 84 were considered to be outside the jurisdiction of the committee, 41 were withdrawn, and 282 were not sustained.[20] As with most of the industry associations, the determinations of the committee have been criticized as lacking in consistency. An allegation by Colgate-Palmolive that the advertising by Rexona of its 'Aim' toothpaste was unfairly disparaging of Colgate-Palmolive was ducked by the committee as being too technical, although

Colgate-Palmolive was able to make its claim in the Federal Court.[21] On the other hand, the claim by Moccona that its coffee had been unfairly disparaged by Andronicus was sustained by the committee after having been rejected by the Federal Court.[22]

PASSING OFF

The main tort protecting business reputation is the tort of passing off. The tort prohibits a person using names, marks, letters or other signs by which he may induce consumers to believe that the goods or services he is supplying are the manufacture of another person. A plaintiff must prove that he has established a reputation upon which the defendant is trading. This reputation may exist in the name of the trader or his products, their get-up or appearance, the trade marks he uses or the style in which his products are advertised. That reputation must be such that the conduct of another will cause confusion among consumers and deception of them. Media industries have been the source of a large number of passing off actions.

Names

The classic case of passing off is where the name of a company or of its products bears very close resemblance to the name used by another. In a mid-nineteenth-century case, for example, a magazine called *Bell's Life* successfully prevented another magazine using the name *Penny Bell's Life*,[23] and recently the proprietor of a Hong Kong television station, on which a Chinese language programme *New Looks of Women* was broadcast, obtained an injunction preventing a women's magazine from adopting the same name.[24]

In establishing passing off, a plaintiff must be able to establish that the name he uses is considered distinctive by relevant consumers. Where the name is invented, this task will be easier than where the name is also descriptive. As Gibbs J explained in ruling the name 'Budget Rent A Car' to be distinctive:

> It is clear law that a name composed of descriptive words may become distinctive of the business of an ordinary person, and if a plaintiff shows that the name in fact distinguishes his business and that the use of the name by the defendant is calculated to deceive persons into supposing that the business carried on by the defendant is that of the plaintiff, and is likely to cause damage to the plaintiff's business, he will be entitled to relief.[25]

On the other hand, in *South Australian Telecasters Ltd* v. *Southern Television Corporation Limited*,[26] Waters J held that 'New Faces' as the name for a television programme had become merely descriptive of talent quests throughout Australia.[27]

In the United Kingdom, the descriptive names *Belgravia*,[28] *London Evening News*,[29] *Punch*,[30] *Morning Post* and *Evening Post*[31] have been held to be distinctive of newspapers and thus protected against passing off, whereas the name *Today* was held to be insufficiently distinctive of a plaintiff's magazine.[32] Reluctant to grant monopolies in descriptive names, the courts accept slight differences as distinguishing similar names.[33] And a name originally considered distinctive of a person's business may become so well known that it loses its secondary association with its original user. 'Gramophone', for example, was held in 1910 to have lost its originally distinctive association with the British Gramophone Co.[34]

The tort of passing off not only protects the name of a trader or his product, but also protects, in the media context, the name of a play: 'The New Car';[35] a television programme: 'It's Academic';[36] an invented television character: 'Alvin Purple';[37] and the journalistic *noms de plume*: 'Pierpont'[38] and 'Mary Delane'.[39]

Get-up

The way in which a product is 'got up' for sale may become distinctive of the manufacturer and protected from imitation by passing off. In successful cases, the deceptively similar get-ups are invariably associated with a similar name. A recent case, *News Group Newspapers Ltd* v. *The Rocket Record Company Limited*,[40] illustrates this. The defendant was the producer of a record which contained a song entitled 'Page Three'. The sleeve of the record contained a photograph of a partially clad girl similar to the photographs carried on page 3 of the London *Sun*. The lyrics of the song reproduced on the cover also referred to 'page 3'. The publisher of the *Sun* attributed the fact of its having the biggest circulation in the United Kingdom to the distinctive female photograph it carried on its third page; and successfully prevented the record company from using the name.

Confusion

To establish passing off, it must be demonstrated that the impugned imitation is likely to be confusing to the relevant customers of the person claiming to be damaged. A recent illustration is the failure of the producers of the 'Miss World' contest to prevent the release of a film entitled 'Miss Alternative World'.[41] The *London Financial Times* described the film in this way:

> A film record ... in which contestants of all shapes, sizes and sexes, clad in *outre* dress or undress, trod the dais under such names as Miss Carriage, Miss Misanthropic and Miss Winscale Nuclear Reactor. The appalling apparel ranges from alien chic—a spike-studded costume with reptilian face-covering —to leather beach-wear, and the oversize cherry on the camp cake is America's drag supremo 'Divine' lording it over the evening with woozy and wobbly charisma as the show's leopard-skinned compere.[42]

Lord Denning confessed his inability to render this description into English but found that the similarity in names was not likely to confuse the patrons of the 'genuine' 'Miss World' contest.

In the United Kingdom, the courts have insisted that the parties to an action be engaged in a 'common field of activity' before passing off can be established. In *McCulloch* v. *Lewis A. May (Produce Distributors) Ltd*,[43] 'Uncle Mac', the host of a children's radio programme, was unable to obtain an injunction to restrain the manufacturers of breakfast cereals from selling puffed wheat as 'Uncle Mac's', because the parties were not engaged in the same business. Similarly, the inventor of the name of the mythical 'Wombles' characters who picked up garbage from Wimbledon Common was unable to prevent the use of the name by a commercial garbage collector,[44] and the proprietors of the 'Kojak' television show were unable to prevent the sale of lollipops under the name 'Kojak lollies'.[45]

In *Radio Corporation Pty Ltd* v. *Henderson*,[46] the Supreme Court of New South Wales declined to follow the United Kingdom approach in insisting upon the requirement of a common field of activity and allowed two ballroom dancers to prevent the use of their photograph on a record of dance music. The Supreme Court of Victoria followed *Henderson*'s case in allowing the Totalizator Agency Board to prevent the publication of a race-tipping newspaper under the name 'TAB'.[47] In its most recent passing off decision, *Children's Television Workshops Inc.* v. *Woolworths Limited*,[48] the Supreme Court of New South Wales seemed to take the view that the question of the common field of activity is relevant to whether the relevant consumers are likely to be confused. That likelihood is obviously greatest where the parties are engaged in the same business, but it will not be absent where the enterprises are different. Helsham CJ found that the unauthorized reproduction of the 'Muppet' characters, 'Big Bird', 'Oscar the Grouch' and the 'Cookie Monster' by Woolworths, in the form of plush toys, was likely to confuse members of the public into believing that there was a business association between the parties.

Reputation—Subsistence

An issue which has been critical to the success or failure of a number of recent passing off cases is whether the person establishing the passing off has been able to demonstrate a reputation among the public and, in particular, a reputation in the geographic area where the passing off is said to have occurred. The recent Privy Council decision in *Cadbury Schweppes Pty Ltd v. Pub Squash Co. Pty Ltd*[49] is an illustration of the difficulty of establishing the requisite reputation. That case concerned the launch by Cadbury Schweppes in 1974 of a new product to compete with Coca Cola. A lemon squash was selected, which the trial judge described as 'a type of soft drink commonly accepted in hotels and licensed clubs and restaurants as an occasional alternative to beer'.[50] The advertising campaign on both radio and television stressed the masculinity of the product with references to the sort of squash made in the past by hotels and bars. In April 1975, the respondent launched a product called 'Pub Squash' with a television campaign described as 'heroically masculine' in which the hero, after his endeavours, hastily consumed a Pub Lemon Soda Squash with an audio which evoked the memory of pub squashes of the past. The defendant's soft drink was got up in cans of the same greenish-yellow colour as the plaintiff's with a similar medallion-type label, but the Privy Council refused to find that a passing off had occurred. It explained:

Competition is safeguarded by the necessity for the plaintiff to prove that he has built up an 'intangible property right' in the advertised descriptions of his products: or, in other words, that he has succeeded by such methods in giving his product a distinctive character accepted by the market. A defendant, however, does no wrong by entering a market created by another and there competing with its creator. The line may be difficult to draw; but unless it is drawn, competition will be stifled.[51]

It appears from this decision that the line is only likely to be crossed where in addition to similarity in advertising and in get-up, there is a deceptive similarity in names.

Reputation—Location

To succeed in a passing off action, a trader must establish a reputation in the eyes of the public in the area where the passing off allegedly occurs. A number of passing off actions have failed because a trader, although enjoying a considerable reputation in one area, was unable to demonstrate the existence of that reputation in the area where imitation occurred. In *A. Bernadin et Cie* v. *Pavilion Properties Ltd*,[52] for example, the Parisian 'Crazy Horse' restaurant was unable to complain of the use of that name by a London restaurant because it could not demonstrate a public reputation in London. A similar result was reached in *Taco Company of Australia Inc. and Anor* v. *Taco Bell Pty Ltd*,[53] in which the American Taco Bell chain was unable to use the 'Taco Bell' name in Sydney because of its previous use by a local trader who had copied the American name.

The cases offer no clear help on what a trader must do to earn a protectable reputation in a particular geographic area. The *Crazy Horse* case was thought to suggest a rule that actual trading was required. In a directly contradictory later case, *Maxim's Ltd* v. *Dye*,[54] the Parisian restaurant 'Maxim's' was able to restrain a restaurant in Norwich from using that name. Similarly, in *Sheraton Corporation of America* v. *Sheraton Motels Limited*,[55] the American hotel chain which had no hotel in England was able to restrain the use of its name by an English hotel. Admittedly, there was some evidence that Sheraton accepted bookings for its hotels in England.

It has been suggested that the *Crazy Horse* principle is too doctrinaire for Australia as it requires a trader to establish a reputation in each state before national protection can be obtained. *Fletcher Challenge Ltd* v. *Fletcher Challenge Pty Ltd and Others*,[56] a recent decision of the Supreme Court of New South Wales, appears to endorse that perception. The case arose out of the reorganization of a number of New Zealand companies which was announced in the Australian financial press on 22 August 1980. On the same day, the newly adopted company name 'Fletcher Challenge' was reserved by two people at the Sydney Corporate Affairs Commission. Powell J allowed the New Zealanders to prevent the registration by the Sydney company, finding that a reputation had arisen in Sydney on the publication of the announcement of the reorganization. In the United Kingdom and Australia, however, there appears to have been a reversion to the strict *Crazy Horse* approach. In *The Athlete's Foot Marketing Associates Inc.* v. *Cobra Sports Ltd and Another*,[57] an American company was unable to protect the name 'Athlete's Foot' in England even though it had entered into a number of franchise agreements with English traders, and in the *Taco Bell* case the Federal Court unequivocally endorsed the *Athlete's Foot* decision.

A practical result of the application of the narrow approach to the subsistence of reputation is that traders who have successfully established a reputation in one state may find that others are able to imitate them in other states before they can establish a reputation in them. In *Dairy Vale Metro Cooperative Ltd. v. Brownes Dairy Ltd*,[58] for example, Toohey J refused to consider deceptive the promotion and sale of the defendant's 'Temptation' yoghurt in Western Australia, even though he conceded that the defendant was inspired by the success of the plaintiff's 'Eve' yoghurt in South Australia. This was despite his Honour's observation that:

In the context of containers in which the general get up is much the same, especially the way in which the fruit is depicted, there is an overall impression of likeness. The resemblances between the television advertisements are even more striking. The general presentation, the background music of heavy strings, the use of a naked woman and seductive tones of the announcer make the differences of minimal importance.[59]

An almost identical case was *Dairy Industry Marketing Authority v. Southern Farmers Cooperative Ltd*,[60] in which a New South Wales company which had established a reputation in that state in its product, 'Good One Malt & Honey', was unable to prevent the marketing in South Australia of 'Malt N Honey' by a South Australian company. The manufacturer of the 'Good One' product had started a television promotion in South Australia with a view to launching its product in February 1982. The South Australian competitor launched its product in January of that year. Despite the similarity in product names, packaging, advertising theme and television commercials, Lockhart J was not prepared to find that the reputation of the Sydney corporation protected it in South Australia.

THE TRADE PRACTICES ACT

The traditional legal protection of business reputation through the torts of defamation, injurious falsehood and passing off has been supplemented by the remedies provided in s. 52 of the Trade Practices Act to restrain misleading or deceptive conduct. This section is discussed in Chapter 12 in terms of its application to advertising. The High Court recently held that trade practices actions can be brought simultaneously with these traditional actions, provided they all arise out of a common sub-stratum of facts.[61] In *Hanimex Pty Ltd v. Kodak (Australasia) Pty Ltd*,[62] for example, Lockhart J allowed an action brought by Hanimex to prevent advertising by Kodak.

Hanimex alleged that the advertising was defamatory, constituted injurious falsehood and was misleading or deceptive, in breach of the Trade Practices Act. Kodak had produced a television commercial in which the purchaser of a film in a bright green box was castigated for not having purchased Kodak film in its typical yellow box. Hanimex submitted that the advertisement conveyed the meaning that anyone who purchased Hanimex (which was customarily sold in a green box) was so lacking in judgment that he or she deserved rebuke 'and that Hanimex's products are of such shoddy quality that any sensible person would be ashamed to accept them even as a gift'.[63] Lockhart J accepted that the advertisement could be construed as defamatory and involving injurious falsehood, and that the suggestion of superiority of the Kodak product went beyond puffery and was possibly deceptive.

Names and Affiliations

The first High Court decision under s. 52 of the Act involved the suggestion by the Sydney Building Information Centre Ltd that the adoption by another company of the name Hornsby Building Information Centre Pty Ltd was an attempt to mislead the public into believing that there was a business relationship between the two enterprises.[64] The High Court rejected this suggestion, ruling that the words 'building information centre' were merely descriptive of a type of business. A similar case in the media area was *United Telecasters Sydney Ltd* v. *Pan Hotels International Pty Ltd*,[65] which was brought by the producers of a television programme 'Thank God it's Friday at the Zoo', suggested by the CBS film 'Thank God it's Friday', and shot at the 'Zoo' discotheque in Los Angeles, which sought to prevent a Sydney discotheque from being called 'the Zoo'. Franki J denied the television company an injunction because it would have been tantamount to granting a monopoly in this essentially descriptive name.

The principle that there can be no deception in descriptive names which have acquired no secondary association with a particular trader has produced some interesting decisions. In *McWilliam's Wines Pty Ltd* v. *McDonald's System of Australia Pty Ltd*,[66] McDonald's, despite saturation advertising for their 'Big Mac' hamburger, were unable to prevent McWilliam's from using the same name for a wine cask. In the Federal Court's view, 'Big Mac' was a descriptive name. On the other hand, the Federal Court was not prepared to accept that the name 'Popular Mechanics' was descriptive, when granting an Australian rock group with that name an injunction to restrain a New Zealand group with the same name from using it in Sydney or Canberra.[67]

In addition to actions brought to restrain the use of names which suggest an erroneous affiliation between the trader of repute and the imitator, a number of actions have been brought under s. 52 of the Act to restrain the use of other indicia of affiliation. The Rolls-Royce company, for example, successfully prevented a motor car manufacturer from using the distinctive Rolls-Royce emblem and radiator grille,[68] and a hotel in Noumea successfully prevented an Australian travel agency from imitating its distinctive advertising logo.[69] In *Mundine* v. *Layton Taylor Promotions Pty Ltd*,[70] the heavyweight boxing champion of Australia was able to prevent a fight from being promoted in Brisbane as the 'Australian heavyweight championship' since he was not a participant, and in *Michael Edgley Pty Ltd* v. *Ashton's Nominees Pty Ltd*,[71] the promoters in Australia of the 'Monte Carlo Circus' were able to prevent a local circus from being promoted under the same name, and from being represented as enjoying the patronage of 'Prince Rainer' (*sic*) and 'Princess Grace and their family'.

Get-up

Following the approach of courts in passing off cases, very few actions alleging deception in relation to the similar appearance of goods have succeeded under s. 52 of the Act. In *The Terrace Times Pty Ltd* v. *Brock*,[72] for example, the trial judge had found that two cookery books were 'strikingly similar' since they had identical sizes and bindings, were similarly decorated with patterns of iron lace, contained line illustrations of old buildings, with historical notes, and contained similar price tags. The appeal court declared, however, that 'we consider it would be extremely difficult to establish the requisite degree of distinctiveness based on the shape and size of a book',[73] despite the court's conceding that the defendant's book 'drew its inspiration' from the plaintiff's book. In *Stuart Alexander & Co (Interstate) Pty Ltd* v. *Blenders Pty Ltd*,[74] Lockhart J was reluctant to find that consumers would be misled or deceived by Andronicus imitating the apothecary jars used by Moccona in bottling its coffee. Mention has already been made of the *Flavoured Milk*[75] and *Yoghurt*[76] cases in which virtually identical packages and advertising campaigns were held not to be passing off or deception under s. 52 of the Act. In *Parkdale Custom Built Furniture Pty Ltd* v. *Puxu Pty Ltd*,[77] its most recent decision under s. 52 of the Act, the High Court refused to consider deceptive the imitation of the plaintiff's characteristic 'Post and Rail' furniture by the defendant.

As with passing off cases, a similar get-up may breach the Act where it is combined with a similar product name. Thus, in *Bradmill Industries Ltd* v. *B. & S. Products Pty Ltd*,[78] the imitation of the distinctive Bradmill packaging was considered to breach s. 52 when a rival's bed linen was sold under the name 'Bart Mills'. In the *Rolls-Royce* case,[79] the imitation of the appearance of the famous English car was held to be deceptive when an Australian company called its product the 'Phaeton' which was similar to Rolls-Royce's 'Phantom'.

Deception

As with passing off cases, a successful action under s. 52 depends on a trader establishing that the conduct of another has deceived the relevant members of the public. The courts under s. 52 are not prepared to find confusion where the parties are not engaged in common fields of business. In the *Big Mac* case,[80] for example, the Federal Court observed that intending purchasers of wine would not expect to receive a hamburger when ordering a cask of 'Big Mac'. Similarly, in *Lego Australia Pty Ltd* v. *Paul's (Merchants) Pty Ltd*,[81] the manufacturer of the children's toy 'Lego' could not complain of the use of that name by a manufacturer of irrigation equipment.

The propensity of a name to mislead or deceive within the meaning of s. 52 has been held to depend on the sophistication of the relevant target audience. In *Weitmann* v. *Katies Ltd*,[82] for example, a manufacturer of women's garments which he sold under the name 'Saint Germain' alleged that the imitation of that name by Katies was deceptive of consumers. He produced a number of witnesses from the rag trade as well as fashion writers and boutique customers who testified to being deceived. Franki J rejected this evidence, declaring that the relevant audience were 'those likely to be buying shirts from a Katies retail store'; he described a person from such an audience as 'likely to be a fairly typical member of the community who is not seeking to purchase a particularly high-fashion article but seeking what might be described as good value for money'.[83] This audience, he ruled, would have been oblivious to the secondary connotations of the 'Saint Germain' name. On the other hand, Sheppard J found in *Emrik Sporting Goods Ltd* v. *Stellar International Sporting Goods Ltd*[84] that the name 'Supergraph' had come to indicate to members of the tennis-playing public a particular source of supply of racquets.

Reputation—Location

Cases brought under s. 52 of the Act apply passing off principles in establishing the geographic extent of reputation. The *Taco Bell* case[85] is the Federal Court's most recent expression of the view that reputation is invariably linked with the location of the person claiming the reputation. In *Snoid* v. *CBS Records Australia Ltd*,[86] the court would allow a pop group to protect its name only in the two cities in which it had performed, even though it had Australia-wide record sales. In the *Zoo Discotheque* case,[87] the court was not prepared to concede an Australian reputation for an American film which had been released here. Finally, as we have seen, the courts have not been prepared to concede traders' reputations in the states outside which they trade.

5

COPYRIGHT

Michael Blakeney

WHAT IS COPYRIGHT?

In general terms, copyright is the exclusive right given by the *Copyright Act* 1968 to reproduce, publish, perform, broadcast and adapt a work. This exclusive right may be assigned or licensed to others and the duration of protection is usually for the life of the creator of the work plus fifty years. Copyright does not exist apart from the Act. It vests in the creator as soon as a work is created and does not require registration. The Act lists the works in which copyright can subsist and describes the exclusive rights of the copyright owner. One of the most important of these is the right to stop infringement of the copyright. The Act protects the copyright of Australian citizens and of people in Australia during the creation of their work. It is supplemented by the protection given by international conventions to which Australia is a signatory.

IN WHAT MAY COPYRIGHT SUBSIST?

The Act lists as the subject matter of copyright literary, dramatic, musical or artistic works and certain new applications of technology. These applications include radio, television, film and sound recordings. The latter include sound recordings, 'cinematograph' films, television and sound broadcasts and published editions of works. A work does not exist until it can be said to be an ordered expression of thought.[1] Thus copyright will not subsist in ideas, opinions or information but will subsist only after the application of skill or labour by the creator. The *Daily Telegraph*, for example, was restrained from reproducing the style and sequence of the birth and death notices carried by the *Sydney Morning Herald* but was allowed to publish the same information in an altered arrangement because no protection existed for the factual information contained in such advertisements.[2] Copyright will not subsist in a work until it is reduced to some tangible or material form. Hence copyright will not exist in a speech declaimed extempore which is not recorded in any way. Finally, the work, to be the subject of copyright protection, must be original. Probably the best definition of originality is that of Lord Devlin in *Ladbroke (Football) Limited* v. *William Hill (Football) Ltd*,[3] where he explained that 'the requirement of originality means that the product must originate from the author in the sense that it is the result of a substantial degree of skill, industry or experience employed by him'.[4] These criteria of order, form and originality will have slightly different emphasis in each of the following subjects of copyright.

Literary Works

The Act does not give a comprehensive definition of literary work, but merely provides in s. 10 that 'literary work includes a written table or compilation' and that 'writing' means a mode of representing or reproducing words, figures or symbols in a visible form and 'written' has a corresponding meaning. The expression 'literary' is very broadly interpreted, it is not confined to works of high literature but, in the words of Peterson J, 'seems to be used in a sense somewhat similar to the use of the word "literature" in political or electioneering literature, and refers to written or printed matter'.[5] The term 'literary work' has been held to apply to articles in a newspaper,[6] advertisements,[7] a race programme,[8] a racing information service,[9] chronological lists of football match fixtures,[10] and a compilation of horses and weights accepted for races at Canterbury on a particular day.[11]

Some of these decisions are difficult to explain, given that the criterion of originality requires that a modicum of skill or labour is required in the creation of a literary work, and given that similar facts have produced opposite results. In *Hotten* v. *Arthur*, Vice-Chancellor Page Wood declared that copyright could not subsist in 'a mere dry list of names like a postal directory, Court guide or anything of that sort',[12] whereas copyright has been held to subsist in a railway guide,[13] business directory[14] and in a price list.[15] The critical feature in each case is whether the court thinks that the relevant compilation is a commonplace selection or whether it evinces a degree of literary labour.

Even where there has been a substantial application of labour, the result may be too insubstantial to justify the description 'literary work'. For example, in the recent case *Exxon Corporation* v. *Exxon Insurance Consultants International Ltd*,[16] the plaintiff was refused copyright in its name, which it had adopted after the lengthy and expensive deliberations of a committee it had set up to devise an appropriate name. The judge was not prepared to allow that a single word could be an original literary work. Similarly, the Privy Council in *Francis Day and Hunter Ltd.* v. *Twentieth Century Fox Corporation Ltd*[17] ruled that the title 'The Man Who Broke the Bank at Monte Carlo' did not breach the copyright of the owners of the song of the same name because of the insubstantiality of this collocation of words. Lord Hodson subsequently commented that this case does not 'support the proposition that, as a matter of law, copyright cannot subsist in titles'.[18] The suggestion has been made that copyright may subsist in the title of the English version of the Peter Weiss play 'The Persecution and Assassination of Marat as Performed by the Inmates of the Asylum of Charenton under the Direction of the Marquis de Sade'.[19]

Dramatic Works

A dramatic work is defined in s. 10 of the Act as including '(a) a choreographic show or other dumb show if described in writing in the form in which the show is to be presented; and (b) a scenario or script for a cinematographic film. The definition does not include a cinematographic film as distinct from the scenario or script for a cinematograph film.' The criterion of form requires that there be something to which the copyright can attach. Obviously there is no problem with the script of a play published in book form; but scenic effects, dramatic incidents or devices will not be protected unless recorded in some visible form. In the case of ballet and dance, the use of Blenisch or Laban notations will allow the protection of choreography.

Musical Works

As with drama, copyright will subsist in the notation of sounds or other material form in which music is reproduced. Music will include tapes, cassettes and sound tracks. There is no copyright in improvised music but, where a performance is taped by an unauthorized person, the copyright in that tape will belong to the performer. Finally, copyright may subsist in arrangements of copyright or non-copyright works.[20]

Artistic Works

Section 10 of the Act defines an artistic work as meaning (a) a painting, sculpture, drawing, engraving or photograph, whether the work is of artistic quality or not; (b) a building or a model of a building, whether the building or model is of artistic quality or not; or (c) a work of artistic craftsmanship to which neither (a) nor (b) applies. As with literary works, artistic works do not have to be the products of aesthetic quality to be the subject of protection. Thus, the design on a confectionery tin was held to be an artistic work in *Tavener Rutledge Ltd.* v. *Specters Ltd.*[21] Copyright law will protect the various forms of modern art where the court considers that sufficient skill has been extended in production. This may involve an aesthetic judgment where a collage of empty cans or other refuse has been 'arranged'. It is worth noting the comments of Pape J in *Cuisenaire* v. *Reed*,[22] where he refused copyright protection for coloured rods used in the teaching of mathematics because 'It is obvious that no special skill or training is required to cut strips of wood into predetermined lengths and then to colour them in different colours, and in my view, it cannot be said that any craftsmanship was involved in their production'.[23]

Sound Recordings, Cinematograph Films, Television, Sound Broadcasts and Published Editions of Works

These categories are not referred to as 'works' in the Act. Thus there is no requirement that their subject matter be original to be protected. The copyright in recording media subsists independently of the copyright in the works recorded by them.

Sound recordings

A 'sound recording' is defined as 'the aggregate of sounds embodied in a record'. The Act defines 'record' as meaning a disc, tape, paper or other device in which sounds are embodied. A sound recording is deemed to have been made at the time when the first record was produced. The copyright owner is the person who owned the record at that time, not the artist or recording engineer.[24]

Cinematographic films

Section 10 of the Act defines 'cinematograph film' as the aggregate of visual images embodied in an article or thing capable of being shown as a moving picture; or of being embodied in another article or thing. It includes the aggregate of the sounds embodied in a sound track associated with visual images. Videotapes probably fall within this definition as embodying something which can be shown as a visual picture.[25]

Copyright exists in a film made before the beginning of the Act (1 May 1969) where it can be defined as an original dramatic work. The same rule applies to photographs made before that date.

Television and sound broadcasts

'Broadcast' is defined by s. 10 of the Act to mean a broadcast by wireless telegraphy, that is, 'the emitting or receiving, otherwise than over a path that is provided by a material substance, of electromagnetic energy'. A 'television broadcast' is defined as visual images broadcast by way of television together with any sounds broadcast for reception along with those images. A 'sound broadcast' means sounds broadcast otherwise than as part of a television broadcast. The requirement in the definition of broadcast that transmission of signals be over a non-material path seems to suggest that cable TV and other wire diffusion services are not broadcasting[26] and are thus not protected by copyright. Copyright does not subsist in broadcasts made before 1 May 1969 or in broadcasts which are repetitions of broadcasts made before that date.[27]

The copyright owners of radio and television broadcasts are either the ABC or SBS, the holder of a commercial or public radio or television licence under the Broadcasting and Television Act, or the holder of a licence under the Wireless Telegraphy Act. Following the decision of the High Court in *Victoria Park Racing Club* v. *Taylor*,[28] which held that a racing club had no remedy when a radio station set up a stand outside a racecourse in order to broadcast descriptions of the races to its listeners, s. 115 was inserted into the Broadcasting and Television Act. That section limits television transmissions from outside places such as sporting grounds. With other special restrictions on television and radio, it is outlined in Chapter 9.

Computer programs

The question whether copyright exists in computer programs was inconclusively answered by the Federal Court in *Apple Computer Inc.* v. *Computer Edge Pty Ltd*.[29] That case concerned the imitation of micro-chips. The trial judge ruled that micro-chips could not be the subject of copyright protection. The appeal court disagreed with this decision, declaring that micro-chips were adaptations or translations of original works. This matter was put beyond doubt by the *Copyright Amendment Act* 1984 which expands the definition of 'literary work' in the Act to include computer programs.

Published editions of works
From the beginning of the Act on 1 May 1969, copyright exists in a published edition of a literary, dramatic, musical or artistic work, or two or more of such works.[30] The copyright subsists in the typographical arrangement of the printed pages and not in the works themselves. Thus copyright may subsist in an edition of the works of William Shakespeare although the content of those works is in the public domain.

Copyright in news
It is often said that there is 'no copyright in news'. This is substantially correct and follows from the principle that there is no copyright in information. Copyright does, however, exist in the mode of expression. Although a news medium may borrow the substance of a news item from a competitor,[31] the item needs to be re-expressed in a significantly different way. In *Walter* v. *Steinkopff*,[32] for example, the 'lifting' of about two-fifths of an article by Kipling was held to be actionable since the passages copied were characteristic of that author. It is believed by some journalists that reproduction with acknowledgement is permissible, but this is an erroneous belief. There is no such legal principle.[33] Finally, if news is stolen from confidential sources the news medium may be liable in damages for breach of confidence.[34]

DURATION OF COPYRIGHT

The general rule is that copyright protection lasts throughout the life of the creator of the work and for fifty years thereafter.[35] This rule was varied on the beginning of the Act on 1 May 1969 in the special cases listed.

Literary, Dramatic and Musical Works
If before the death of an author, the work or an adaptation of it has not been published, performed in public, broadcast or

offered or exposed for sale to the public, any copyright subsisting in the work will continue to subsist until the expiration of fifty years after any one of those events happening.[36] The effect of this rule is that copyright in an unpublished literary, dramatic or musical work can subsist in perpetuity.

Artistic Works

In the case of artistic works, excluding photographs and engravings, copyright will expire fifty years after the death of the creator of the work, irrespective of whether it was published during the lifetime of the creator.[37]

Photographs

In the case of photographs taken before the beginning of the Act, copyright expires fifty years after the calendar year in which the photograph was taken. Copyright in photographs taken after the starting date will expire fifty years after the calendar year in which the photograph was first published. In other words copyright may exist in perpetuity in photographs only if they were taken after the beginning of the Act.

Engravings

The term of copyright protection for engravings is the same as for literary works. So where an engraving is published during the lifetime of its creator, protection lasts for another fifty years. Where an engraving is not published during its creator's lifetime, it is protected for fifty years after the time of its first publication.[38]

Sound Recordings

In the case of records made before the beginning of the Act, protection will subsist until fifty years after the calendar year in which the recording was first made.[39] If it was made after that date, protection will expire fifty years after the calendar year in which the record was first published.[40]

Films

There is no copyright protection for films made before the Act, although protection would exist if the film were an original dramatic work, and any photographs used in a film would have been given the protection for photographs discussed above. Since the beginning of the Act, films are protected for fifty years after the expiration of the calendar year in which they are first published.[41]

Television and Sound Broadcasts

As with films, no copyright subsists in broadcasts made before the beginning of the Act, and there is no protection for broadcasts which merely repeat broadcasts made before this date.[42] Copyright protection for broadcasts made after that date expires fifty years after the calendar year in which the broadcast was made.[43]

Published Editions

There is no copyright in published editions published before the beginning of the Act,[44] but in editions published after that date copyright continues until twenty-five years after the calendar year of publication.[45]

Anonymous and Pseudonymous Works

Copyright in works where the author is not known expires fifty years after the year in which the work was first published.[46] Where, however, the identity of the author can be ascertained by reasonable inquiry before the expiration of this time, the standard time calculated from the death of the author will apply.[47] These provisions apply to all literary, dramatic, musical and artistic works, with the exception of photographs.

Works of Joint Authorship

A work of joint authorship, defined as a work produced by the collaboration of two or more authors in which the work of each author is not separate from the contribution of other authors,[48] remains protected until fifty years after the death of the last surviving author.[49]

Crown Copyright

A number of provisions of the Act apply to copyright of the state or commonwealth crown. In the case of literary, dramatic and musical works, copyright subsists until fifty years after the year of first publication.[50] Copyright exists in perpetuity in an unpublished work. For artistic works, the copyright period is fifty years after the year in which they are made.[51] With engravings and photographs, copyright exists for fifty years after they are published,[52] with the exception of photographs made before the beginning of the Act. In that case, the fifty years runs from the end of the year in which the photograph was made.[53] The duration of crown copyright in films and recordings is the same as for films and recordings generally.[54]

Publication

Obviously, critical to the calculation of the duration of copyright protection is the date on which a work can be said to be published. Section 29 of the Act defines 'publication' as it relates to the different classes of subject matter in which copyright can subsist under the Act. The definitions adopted by the Act essentially provide that a work is published when supplied to the public by sale or otherwise.

Excluded from the definition are unauthorized publications and 'colourable' publications. The latter involve publication of a nominal number of copies of a work in order to secure copyright protection, but without the intention of meeting any expected demand for the work.[55]

OWNERSHIP OF COPYRIGHT

The ownership of copyright means the ownership either wholly or partially of the exclusive rights comprised in the copyright of a work. Ownership arises either under the Act or as the result of a transfer from the copyright owner.

Authors

The general rule is that the author of a literary, dramatic, musical or artistic work is the owner of the copyright in it.[56] The Act does not define the term 'author', but essentially it is the person who creates a work in which copyright can subsist. Thus a person who turns mere ideas into a tangible expression is the author of the work even where the ideas are supplied by another. Thus in *Donoghue* v. *Allied Newspapers Ltd*[57] the ghost writer of the life of a person who supplied the writer with all the relevant information was held to own the copyright in that life. Similarly, in *Springfield* v. *Thame*,[58] the sub-editor of a newspaper was considered to be the author of a news item submitted by a journalist and substantially rewritten by the sub-editor. On the other hand, where a journalist takes down a speech dictated by another, word for word, the copyright owner is the person who gave the speech and not the 'mere amanuensis'.[59] The question is obviously one of degree. Where a speech is edited by the journalist, the journalist may become the copyright owner because of the application of labour, skill and judgment.[60] For the same reason, the translator of a work from one language to another becomes the author of the translated work.[61]

Compilers

A compilation, such as an encyclopaedia, dictionary, year book, newspaper, magazine or periodical, usually involves the aggregation of the work of a number of authors. The coordination and arrangement of those works may be considered to have created an original work separate from and independent of the works of the contributors. In most cases, the relationship between the compiler and the contributors will be spelt out in a contract, which will be a contract of employment in the case of journalists. In compilations, such as *Who's Who*, the contributions for each entry will be so insubstantial that the copyright of them will be owned by the compiler.[62]

Journalists and Media Proprietors

Section 35(4) of the Act says that where a literary, dramatic or artistic work is made by an employed journalist, the proprietor of the newspaper or magazine is the owner of the copyright in the work. That ownership is limited, however, to the right to publish the work, to broadcast it or to reproduce it for the purpose of being published or broadcast.

Section 213 of the Act provides that s. 35(4) does not apply to works made before the beginning of the Act, in which case the author is entitled, subject to contract, to restrain publication of the work otherwise than in a newspaper, magazine or similar periodical.[63]

Employees and Freelance Contractors

A diverse group of people have their work disseminated by the media. Copyright in the work of employees of the media will become that of the employer if it is made 'in pursuance of the terms of his employment ... under a contract of service or apprenticeship'.[64] The relationship of employer and employee may not be easy to determine. In *Sun Newspapers* v. *Whippie*,[65] for example, a cartoonist agreed to supply a weekly comic strip to the *Sun* at a weekly remuneration. In the agreement between the parties, the cartoonist agreed to obey all directions given by the newspaper and he was prohibited from being engaged in any other undertaking or carrying on the business of an artist in competition with the newspaper. The court held that the degree of control exercised by the newspaper was such that the relationship between the parties was one of employment and thus, that the newspaper owned the copyright in the cartoonist's work. On the other hand, in *Re Beeton & Co.*,[66] a person employed by a magazine on a fixed annual salary to provide weekly cookery articles and a correspondence column was held to be a contributor rather than an employee because she had no obligation to provide her exclusive services to the magazine.

The problem with applying this 'control' test to media activities is that the creativity demanded by the activities is not amenable to rigid controls. As the High Court pointed out in *Zuijs* v. *Wirth Brothers Pty Ltd*,[67] however, 'the fact that the performance of a task depends on a natural gift or on some laboriously acquired accomplishment does not necessarily mean that the performer cannot be a servant'.[68] The test in such cases is the possibility or likelihood of direction. In *Beloff* v. *Pressdram Co. Ltd*,[69] Ungoed Thomas J suggested that, in work involving the application of a high degree of skill, control may be replaced by other factors such as the test of whether an employment relationship exists. That case concerned the parody by *Private Eye* of a memorandum written for the London *Observer* by Nora Beloff, who was a well-known journalist on that paper. In an action for breach of copyright, the defendant printers and publishers at the *Eye* successfully established that Beloff had no standing to bring the action because copyright in the memorandum belonged to her employer, the *Observer*. The employment relationship was established by the fact that Beloff was employed full time by the paper on a substantial salary, with pension rights and regular holidays. She was a member of the general editorial staff and her equipment, office and secretary were supplied by the paper. On the other hand, the fact that Beloff undertook radio and television work and wrote articles for other journals did not affect this finding.

The Crown

As was recently illustrated by the suppression of Walsh and Munster's book, *Documents on Australian Defence and Foreign Policy*

1968-1975,[70] the crown owns the copyright in documents and correspondence emanating from government departments. It is irrelevant whether the author of the work is an employee of the crown or an independent contractor. The test in s. 176(2) of the Act is whether the work was made 'under the direction or control of the Commonwealth or the State'.

In addition to the rights conferred by the Act, the crown owns copyright in certain items as part of the royal prerogative. These include the rights to print the authorized version of the Bible, the Book of Common Prayer and the Acts of parliament,[71] but this prerogative does not extend to cover the right to print or authorize others to print any material which would breach someone else's copyright.[72]

Makers of Sound Recordings

The maker of a sound recording is the owner of the copyright in that recording, subject to the rights of the crown or to the terms of any agreement to the contrary.[73] The owner is the person who owns the matrix or master tape at the time the recording is made and not the sound engineer.

Makers of Cinematograph Films

The maker of a film owns the copyright in that film.[74] The owner will be the producer who arranges the first negative copy. The directors, actors and technical staff will not be copyright owners unless they are also producers.

Broadcasters

The owner of copyright in a radio or television broadcast is, subject to crown copyright, the ABC, SBS or radio or television licensee.

Assignees of Copyright

Section 196(1) of the Act provides that a copyright owner may assign all or part of the rights constituting copyright to one or more persons. An author, for example, may assign the right to perform a work to one person and the right to reproduce it to another. Such assignments may be limited in geographic scope and duration. An author may also assign future copyright, in works not yet in existence.[75]

RIGHTS OF COPYRIGHT OWNERS

Copyright, it will be recalled, is a constellation of exclusive rights in original works. In other words, it is the existence of these rights which is the copyright. The rights possessed will depend on the subject matter of the original creation. The owners of copyright in literary, dramatic, musical and artistic works have the exclusive rights to reproduce the work in a material form, to publish and to broadcast the work and to cause it to be transmitted to pay or cable television subscribers. The owners of literary, dramatic and musical works have the right to have the works performed in public or adapted.[76]

The owner of copyright in a sound recording has the exclusive right to make a record embodying the recording, to cause the recording to be heard in public, and to broadcast the recording. Similarly, the owner of a cinematograph film has the exclusive right to make a copy of the film, to cause it to be viewed or heard in public, and to be broadcast or transmitted to pay or cable television subscribers.

The owner of copyright in a television or a sound broadcast has the exclusive right, in the case of a television broadcast, to make a film of the broadcast or a copy of the film, and similar reproduction rights in the case of a sound broadcast. Finally, the owner of copyright in a television or a sound broadcast has the right to rebroadcast it. 'Rebroadcast' is not defined in the Act, but probably means 'rebroadcast by wireless telegraphy'.[77]

The owner of copyright in a published edition has the exclusive right to make a reproduction of that edition.

THE EXERCISE OF COPYRIGHT

The copyright owner may exercise his exclusive rights personally or may assign those rights partially or fully, or may license others to exercise all or some of those rights. In the event of an assignment or exclusive licence of copyright, the recipient of the copyright will be able to bring action for breach of the copyright by others, including the original owner. The Act in s. 196(3) requires an assignment or exclusive licence to be in writing.

An assignment of copyright may be held to be void if on terms that are harsh or unconscionable and there is an inequality of bargaining power between the parties. Most contracts are in a standard form and offered on a take-it-or-leave-it basis to copyright owners, but in two recent cases standard form printed contracts were set aside. In *A. Schroeder Music Publishing Co. Ltd* v. *Macaulay*,[78] a young song writer, who had not previously published, entered into a standard form of contract with a large American musical publishing company. The contract provided that the writer assigned to the company 'the full copyright for the whole world' in every musical composition 'composed, created or conceived' by him alone or in collaboration for the next five years, with a possible extension for the next ten years. The writer was to receive no payment unless his work was published, but the company was under no obligation to publish. The company, but not the writer, could terminate the agreement or assign the agreement. These terms were all standard for the company's agreements but the House of Lords ruled that the terms were unenforceable because there was unconscionable abuse of the superior bargaining power of the company. Similar standard form agreements were set aside by the English Court of Appeal in *Clifford Davis Management Ltd* v. *WEA Records Ltd*.[79] They were described by Lord Denning as giving to the publisher 'a complete stranglehold over each of the composers'.[80]

The difference between an assignment of copyright and a licence has generated much difficult law. The critical distinction appears to be that on the termination of a licence the copyright reverts to the copyright owner, whereas an assignment may be irrevocable.

COMPULSORY LICENCES

The technicalities of copyright theory do not necessarily harmonize with the realities of the modern media. For example, the granting by an author of a literary, dramatic or musical work to a media proprietor of a licence to broadcast that work does not involve the granting of the right to reproduce that work. With broadcasting through national networks and in different time zones, it is necessary for a broadcaster to make recordings of programmes to be transmitted at a later date. To enable this to be done the Act establishes a system of compulsory statutory licences. Accordingly, a broadcaster with the authority to broadcast a work is conferred the right to make an ephemeral record sound recording or cinematograph film of the work, solely for the purpose of the broadcast.[81]

A Copyright Tribunal established by s. 138 of the Act determines the equitable remuneration of copyright owners for the copies of their work made under statutory licence. A complex system of compulsory licences also regulates the manufacture of records of musical works, but discussion of this system is largely beyond the scope of this book.[82] The only matter of immediate relevance is that s. 109 of the Act provides that it is not an infringement of copyright in a published sound recording for a record to be broadcast provided the prescribed royalties are paid to the copyright owner. The Copyright Tribunal has jurisdiction to fix this royalty.

INFRINGEMENT OF COPYRIGHT

In addition to the exclusive rights of the copyright owner, mentioned above, the owner may bring an action in court to restrain and obtain compensation for infringements of copyright. Infringement is defined in the Act to include the doing of things exclusively within the preserve of the copyright owner; the impermissible authorization of such things; the importation of infringing articles for trade purposes; the sale of infringing articles; and permitting a place of public entertainment to be used for a public performance of a literary, dramatic or musical work protected by copyright. The Act provides a number of defences to infringement actions and prescribes a range of remedies for copyright owners.

Direct Infringement

A direct infringement is the doing in Australia of an act which only the copyright owner can do. As we have seen, these include unauthorized reproduction, publication, performance in public, broadcasting and adaptation of an original work. The doing of each of these acts is a separate infringement. If a work is produced as the result of independent creation, it will not breach the copyright of another original creation. It will be recalled that copyright protects the skill and labour which transmutes raw information or ideas into a 'work'. Where a sub-stratum of information is common to two works, similarity is inevitable. In *Ravenscroft* v. *Herbert*,[83] however, the author of a novel based on information supplied by a spiritual medium was able to sustain an infringement action against a person who also employed that information in a similar publication because the author's novel was the only source of that information. Had the information been readily available or ascertainable from a standard reference work, it would not have been protected.[84]

Authorization

The authorization of acts of infringement is prohibited by s. 36. Authorization was recently considered by the High Court in *University of New South Wales* v. *Moorhouse and Angus & Robertson (Publishers) Pty Ltd*.[85] The court held that photocopying in breach of copyright on machines installed in the university library was authorized by the university because of the likelihood of breaches and the failure to take adequate steps to prevent them. The case suggested that the failure to exercise control over users of the photocopiers beyond an incorrectly worded notice was an important determinant against the university.

Copying

The typical breach of copyright is a simple copying of a protected work. For a contravention to occur, it is not necessary that the whole of a work be copied, but merely a 'substantial part'. The Act does not define substantiality and the decisions reiterate that each case must be decided on its own facts. In the leading case of *Hawkes & Son (London)* v. *Paramount Film Service Ltd*,[86] fifty seconds of the musical work 'Colonel Bogey's March' was reproduced in a newsreel showing the opening of a new school. Although the entire work takes some 270 seconds, the English Court of Appeal held that this was a substantial part of the musical work as it contained the principal air of the march, which everyone would recognize. The test of recognition does not seem to have been adopted in later cases. Petersen J suggested 'a rough practical test that what is worth copying is *prima facie* worth protecting'.[87]

A proportion test is impossible on the contradictory facts of the cases, but a rule of thumb may be implied from the 1980 amendments to the Act concerned with fair dealing with copyrighted works for the purposes of research and study. The Act now permits copying of no more than a 'reasonable portion' of a work for those purposes. Section 10 of the Act defines a reasonable portion of a literary, dramatic or musical work with not less than ten pages as being not more than 10 per cent of the pages of the edition or, where the work is divided into chapters, in excess of 10 per cent provided only the whole or part of a single chapter of that work is copied.

Proof of copying will invariably be the degree of similarity between works combined with the likelihood of access to the plaintiff's work. Without proof of access, even complete identity between works may not be conclusive evidence of copying. In *Francis Day & Hunter Ltd* v. *Bron*,[88] the owners of the musical work 'In a Little Spanish Town', first published in 1926, were unable to establish an infringing use in a 1959 musical work 'Why'. Although the judge conceded a high degree of similarity between the works, he accepted the evidence of the composer of the latter that he had neither consciously nor unconsciously copied the former. The Court of Appeal agreed that a causal connection between the infringing work and the original work had to be demonstrated.

An infringing copy may be made even where it is made from a copy of the original work. In *King Features Syndicates Inc.* v. *O. & M. Kleeman Ltd*,[89] the marketing of dolls in the image of the cartoon character 'Popeye' was held to be an infringement of the copyright of the cartoonist.

Related to the question of whether a 'substantial part' has been copied is the determination of whether the result is a 'copy'. The general test applied is that of Kekewich J in *Hanfstaengl* v. *W. H. Smith & Sons*:[90] 'a copy is that which comes so near to the original as to suggest that original to the mind of every person seeing it'.[91]

Non-infringing Copies

In addition to the defence of 'fair dealing', which is discussed below, the courts recognize that the use of another's original work invariably involves a degree of copying, which they consider legitimate, provided the copyist does more than reproduce the original work. It has been held permissible to compile guide books, dictionaries and similar books, for example, from earlier compilations, provided that the latter publications betray independent effort.[92] Difficulties arise in the area of parodies and burlesques since the success of these literary forms depends upon some evocation of an original work. In the United States, two cases with opposite results illustrate the problems in this area. In *Benny* v. *Loew's Inc.*,[93] CBS produced a burlesque of the film 'Gas Light', the rights to which were owned by MGM. The copying was verbatim, but 'enhanced' with comic devices supplied by Jack Benny. These distortions did not prevent the show from breaching the owner's copyright. In *Columbia Picture Corp.* v. *National Broadcasting Co.*,[94] however, a burlesque of 'From Here to Eternity' entitled 'From Here to Obscurity', presented on TV by Sid Caesar and Imogene Coca, was held not to be a breach of copyright. The distinguishing feature between the two cases was that the latter programme did not borrow the actual words of the original drama.

ACTS NOT CONSTITUTING INFRINGEMENT

A large number of acts, otherwise a breach of copyright, are rendered permissible by defences contained in the *Copyright Act 1968*. The compulsory statutory licence for the making of ephemeral recordings for the purposes of broadcasts has already been mentioned. The most important defence as far as the media are concerned is that of 'fair dealing', which is discussed below. A defence noted but not sustained in *Commonwealth of Australia* v. *John Fairfax & Sons Ltd*[95] was that acts 'in the public interest' may override copyright. The publication of a document revealing details of an espionage operation in Australia, for example, may be permitted. Mason J explained that this defence was limited in scope:

> It makes legitimate the publication of ... material in which copyright subsists so as to protect the community from destruction, damage or harm. It has been acknowledged that the defence applies to disclosure of things done in breach of national security, in breach of the law (including fraud) and to disclosure of matters which involve danger to the public. So far there is no recorded instance of the defence being raised in a case such as this where the suggestion is that advice given by Australia's public servants, particularly its diplomats, should be ventilated, with a view to exposing what is alleged to have been the cynical pursuit of expedient goals, especially in relation to East Timor.[96]

Fair Dealing

The copying of a literary, dramatic or musical work protected by copyright is permissible provided the copying can be said to be a fair dealing. The situations in which the Act envisages that a fair dealing may occur are copying for the purposes of research or study; criticism or review; reporting news in a newspaper or periodical or by broadcasting; and giving professional advice by a legal practitioner or patent attorney. The Act does not define 'fair dealing'. Indeed, Lord Denning has declared it to be impossible to define. 'It must be a question of degree', he declared, or 'a matter of impression'.[97]

Research or study

Following the report of the Copyright Law Committee on Reprographic Reproduction (the Franki Committee Report), the Act was substantially amended in 1980 to provide a code to deal with the copying of works for research and study and general educational purposes as well as for library and archival purposes.[98] A number of provisions deal with photocopying by educational institutions. Their meaning is somewhat opaque. An injunction was granted to a group of publishers varying a memorandum by the Director-General of Education for New South Wales which sought to explain the fair dealing provisions.[99] An appeal against this decision was dismissed, and the Federal Court ordered the memorandum to be withdrawn from circulation and destroyed.[100] This litigation merits careful reading as it contains the best recent discussion of fair dealing in an educational context.

Criticism or review

In s. 41 of the Act, fair dealing with a literary, dramatic, musical or artistic work or with an adaptation of the same is permitted if it is for the purpose of criticism or review provided 'a sufficient acknowledgement of the work is made'. A 'sufficient acknowledgement' is defined in s. 10 of the Act as an acknowledgement identifying the work by its title or other description and identifying the author. In *Commonwealth of Australia* v. *John Fairfax & Sons Ltd*,[101] which was concerned with a newspaper review of a book reproducing and criticizing government documents dealing with the East Timor crisis in 1975, a defence of fair dealing for the purposes of criticism and review was rejected by Mason J, who held that the publication of 'leaked' documents could not be a fair dealing. His Honour observed that the defence implied the consent of an author at least to the circulation of a work, as it was unfair that an unpublished work should, without the consent of the author, be the subject of public criticism or review.[102] Finally, Mason J observed that both the newspaper and the book did not represent that they were reviewing the documents but that they were publishing them. Thus, the attraction of the publications was not that they had been undertaken for criticism or review, but that a person 'was able to read for the first time documents which were so important that the government had maintained a secrecy blackout on them'.[103]

Reporting news

A fair dealing with a literary, dramatic, musical or artistic work, or with an adaptation of such a work, other than an artistic work, is not an infringement of copyright under s. 42 of the Act if it is done for the purpose of, or is associated with, the reporting of news. The section requires that the reporting of news be: in a newspaper, magazine or similar periodical, with a sufficient acknowledgement made; or by means of broadcasting, transmission to subscribers to cable television or in a cinematographic film, provided that, in the case of a musical work, the playing of the work forms part of the news being reported.

Although Mason J, in the *Timor Documents* case, allowed that news was not restricted to current events, he was not prepared, for the reasons already discussed, to hold that there had been a fair dealing in the first place.[104]

Reports of Judicial Proceedings

Completely separate from the fair dealing defence is the provision in s. 43 of the Act that copyright is not infringed by anything done for the purposes of a judicial proceeding or by way of a report of a judicial proceeding. It should be remembered, of course, that this defence will not prevent an improper report being either contemptuous or defamatory.

INTERNATIONAL PROTECTION OF COPYRIGHT

Australia is a member of a number of international conventions for the protection of copyright and industrial property.[105] The effect of the Berne Convention is to give nationals of signatories to that convention the same protection against copyright infringement in this country as Australians. The property protected by this convention includes literary, dramatic, musical or artistic works. The published works of foreigners are protected by Australia's ratification of the Universal Copyright Convention. Published works are protected under this convention provided they display the international copyright notice © in a prominent place, together with the name of the copyright owner and the first date of publication. Sound recordings are protected if the Phonograms Convention notice Ⓟ is placed upon authorized duplicates.

COPYRIGHT PROTECTION AND THE TRADE PRACTICES ACT 1974

Copyright infringement may also be misleading or deceptive conduct which is prohibited by the *Trade Practices Act* 1974. The High Court indicated in *Phillip Morris Inc.* v. *Adam P. Brown Male Fashions Pty Ltd*[106] that a copyright action and a trade practices action may be brought simultaneously in the Federal Court of Australia, provided that the relevant facts are common to each action. An illustration is *Coonan & Denlay Pty Ltd* v. *Superstar Australia Pty Ltd*,[107] in which the manufacturer of a cricket helmet alleged both breach of copyright and deceptive conduct on the part of a competitor who imitated the design of its helmet. Copyright breaches have also been alleged in relation to deceptive package designs or advertising campaigns which suggest an affiliation between the copyright owner and the imitator.[108]

REMEDIES AND PENALTIES

The remedies available to a copyright owner for infringement of copyright include injunctions to restrain future infringements, damages or an account of profits from the infringer. In the case of deliberate infringement, certain criminal penalties may be imposed, and the copyright owner or licencee may be able to obtain the infringing copies.

Injunctions

An expeditious remedy available to those seeking to prevent a breach of copyright is the injunction, which may be obtained on an interim basis to preserve the situation, or on a more perpetual basis. In order to obtain interim relief, the applicant merely has to establish a *prima facie* case that 'the inconvenience or injury which the plaintiff would be likely to suffer if the injunction were refused outweighs or is outweighed by the injury which the defendant would suffer if an injunction were granted'.[109] In *Hubbard* v. *Vosper*,[110] for example, the founder of the Church of Scientology sought to restrain the publication of a book critical of the church which contained some writings of the founder. Conceding that copyright might be breached, Lord Denning was unwilling to grant an injunction to prevent the publication of material exposing what he regarded as quack scientific beliefs, since he considered this exposure to be in the public interest.

In cases where evidence of copyright infringement might be destroyed, the English courts have granted injunctions to allow a person bringing an action to enter the premises of a defendant.[111] In Australia, these orders are usually sought in connection with record 'piracy'.[112]

Compensation

Section 115(2) of the Act says that in an action for breach of copyright a person may either seek damages or an account of profits. In assessing the measure of damages, the court has regard primarily to 'the depreciation caused by the infringement to the value of the copyright'.[113] This amount will usually represent the loss of sales to the copyright owner attributable to the infringement. Section 115(4) of the Act envisages the award of damages additional to compensation in the case of flagrant infringements. Additional damages are usually awarded where a person is 'aware or had reasonable grounds for suspecting' that he was in breach of copyright.[114]

Instead of compensation for the loss suffered by infringement, a copyright owner may seek an account of profits, by which means the infringer is obliged to disgorge the gains made from a breach of copyright.[115] An account of profits is ordered only to cover the period after the infringer became aware of the breach. Where a protected work has been incorporated into a larger work, the copyright owner will be able to recover the proportion of profits attributable to his contribution.

Delivery Up of Infringing Plates or Copies

A copyright owner is entitled by s. 116 to obtain the plates from which infringing copies are made, as well as the infringing copies. Damages are recoverable also for copies already sold, which are deemed by the Act to have been the property of the copyright owner.[116]

False Attribution of Authorship

Where authorship is falsely attributed to a work, the copyright owner may obtain damages from or an injunction restraining people who make the false attribution or who knowingly offer for sale, or for hire or public exhibition a work carrying a false attribution of authorship.[117] The same remedies are obtainable in relation to reproductions of artistic works carrying false authorship attribution.[118] Finally, a copyright owner may bring actions under the Act for injunctions or damages in relation to the publication, hire or sale of copyrighted works that have been altered.[119]

Criminal Actions

Those who make, sell, let for hire, exhibit for trade purposes or import articles knowing them to be infringing copies are liable to penalties under s. 133 of the Act. In relation to articles other than films, the penalty is not to exceed $150 for each offending item, not exceeding $10 000 in aggregate for articles comprised in the same operation or transaction, where action is brought in the Federal Court. For films, the fine is $1500 per item. The Commonwealth Crimes Act also imposes a penalty of three years' imprisonment on persons conspiring to commit offences against a law of the commonwealth such as the Copyright Act.[120]

Seizure by Customs

The owner of copyright in a published literary, dramatic or musical work may under s. 135 of the Copyright Act give a notice in writing to the Comptroller-General of Customs objecting to the importation of infringing works. These may be seized by the commonwealth.

Unjustifiable Threat of Action

In the Act, s. 202 provides that a person shall not by 'circulars, advertisements or otherwise', threaten a person with an action for infringement of copyright which is unjustifiable. Such threats may also constitute the torts of injurious falsehood or interference with business relations.[121] This remedy is, of course, necessary because of the considerable potential for using the threat of infringement actions in the manner of 'stop writs' for defamation actions.

6
SUB JUDICE PUBLICATIONS

Mark Armstrong

There are many ways in which the media may break the law by publishing material relating to cases which are *sub judice*.[1] The most common way is to publish something which may prejudice or bias a jury. Examples are mentioning the criminal record or confession of an accused person, and publicly deciding on the particular issues awaiting judgment in a case. Other kinds of prejudicial contempt include intimidating a party to a case or a witness by public vilification or by threats of bad publicity, and virtually any publication made with the actual intent of prejudicing the outcome of a case. Similar principles, although usually more lenient ones, apply to publications affecting a number of tribunals and commissions which are not courts.

The best way to appreciate the danger which the media face is to consider some recent contempts for which the courts imposed fines. Two of these cases arose from the trials of Murphy J in 1985 and 1986. Murphy J was accused of attempting to influence magistrates in relation to charges laid against Morgan Ryan. About three months before Murphy's first trial commenced, ABC television broadcast a current affairs item which would have been taken by the audience to mean that there was material in the '*Age* tapes', obtained by unauthorized phone tapping, which 'revealed' that Murphy J had made improper overtures on behalf of Morgan Ryan in connection with Ryan's trial. In other words, the item would have brought viewers to conclude that Murphy J was guilty of the charges pending against him. The ABC was fined $100 000 and the producer/director of the item was fined $2000.[2]

Whether because of such publicity or not, Murphy was convicted at his trial. But that conviction was quashed by the NSW Court of Appeal, which ordered a retrial of Murphy. Shortly after Neville Wran, Premier of NSW and a close friend of Murphy, heard the news of the retrial, he agreed to an impromptu press conference, at which he said how highly he regarded Murphy J. Asked whether he was convinced that Murphy would be found innocent at the retrial, he replied that he had 'a very deep conviction that Murphy J is innocent of any wrongdoing'. The *Daily Telegraph* published a front-page report of the interview, under the heading 'MURPHY INNOCENT: WRAN. COURT ORDERS RETRIAL'. On the same page was a photograph of Murphy with the caption 'Murphy ... admired and loved'. Wran and the *Telegraph* were found guilty of contempt because of the likelihood that Wran's remarks would make a strong impression on the mind of a juror. Wran was fined $25 000, and the *Telegraph* was fined $200 000.[3]

In 1986 the Melbourne radio broadcaster Derryn Hinch called for the removal of the manager of a children's youth organization. The manager was Michael Glennon, a former Catholic priest. Hinch said in his broadcasts on 3AW that Glennon, who was awaiting trail for indecent assault and other offences relating to children, should be removed because he had previously been convicted and gaoled for indecently assaulting children. The court said that the broadcast was a serious contempt because it was likely to prejudice the jury at Glennon's trial. It fined Hinch $15 000 and sentenced him to 28 days in gaol. It fined 3AW $40 000 for its responsibility for the same broadcasts.[4]

The control of the courts over publications which prejudice *sub judice* proceedings is a part of the law of contempt of court. *Sub judice* means literally 'under a judge'. It is only another way of referring to a proceeding which has started on a course which will ultimately lead to some decision by a court. Contempt law also covers things which are no special concern of the media such as misconduct in the courtroom, disobedience to a court injunction, and bribing of jurors. Contempt by vilification of the courts themselves is considered in the following chapter. The word 'contempt' sometimes misleads laypeople: it should not be taken too literally. Many acts punishable as contempts involve only a notional kind of contempt, not an actual attitude of disrespect. Despite recent recommendations for a uniform Contempt of Court Act, there are almost no statutes of the commonwealth or the states dealing with contempt by the media in Australia. This absence of legislation has some advantages. It has left the judges free to relax much of the old severity of the law through a number of recent decisions. It also means that there is, for practical purposes, one uniform law of contempt throughout the country; a pleasant contrast with the eight separate defamation laws in Australia.

As this chapter shows, some material which looks innocent to a reporter may be contemptuous, and a reporter, editor, programme executive or media company may be guilty of contempt, without having any intention of interfering with the course of justice. The law of contempt does recognize the public interest in freedom of speech. A principle discussed later in this chapter allows some discussion of matters of public interest to continue, even though there may be incidental prejudice to a pending trial. The freedom of discussion, however, is limited and defined. It can be safely exercised only by someone well aware of the strict limits which the courts have set. Commenting on a matter awaiting decision by a court has variously been described by the judges as playing with fire, skating on thin ice or walking a tightrope.[5] This does not mean that the journalist or media executive should despair. Contempt law does not depend on a knowledge of technicalities. In the various recent cases, the courts have looked to the actual substance of what went wrong. They have not taken a legalistic attitude. In practice, what a person responsible for news or current affairs must do is:

1. Know enough about the way litigation works and about contempt principles to be aware of the main ways in which a trial can be prejudiced by publications;
2. Be prepared to consult a lawyer when one of the sensitive areas is approached in an item which is being prepared for publication; and
3. Avoid publishing any material which can affect the central issues in a trial, such as whether the accused person is guilty, or has been convicted before, whether the defendant in a negligence action was negligent or careful, or whether a witness in the trial is a liar.

As earlier chapters have shown, liability for defamation is in all but rare and extreme cases a civil matter, with the usual remedy being an award of damages. For historical reasons, contempt is a criminal matter, with the usual punishment being a fine, although the courts sometimes imprison an offender. The courts will not confine the punishment to the media company which published the contemptuous material. They may fine or even imprison the individual editor, reporter, producer or executive responsible for publication.

WHAT IS 'PREJUDICIAL'

The High Court has said that it is a punishable contempt to publish anything which will raise 'a real risk, as opposed to a remote possibility' that justice will be interfered with[6] and that the essence of contempt by prejudicial publication is 'a real and definite tendency to prejudice or embarrass pending proceedings'.[7] For obvious reasons, these very general formulations do not indicate what may be said in particular borderline situations. They do serve as a reminder that any kind of publication which falls within those broad formulae can be punishable, even if it is not similar to a publication held contemptuous in an earlier case. That is important for people preparing material for the electronic media, since most of the cases have been concerned with the potential of the written word, not with the impact of a medium like television. The fundamental principles of contempt are the same, however, for all media, print or electronic. The concept of 'a real risk' of prejudice is illuminated by the cases in the law reports. Four major cases, namely *Packer* v. *Peacock*, the *Sunday Times* case, the *BLF* case and the *Rigby* case, may serve as points of reference for charting the rest of the law.

Packer v. *Peacock*,[8] decided by the High Court in 1912, arose from a suspected murder. Dr Peacock had been charged with the murder of Mrs Davies but had not yet been committed for trial. The body of the alleged victim had not been found. The *Age* published a somewhat rhetorical set of articles about the murder allegations, which would have left many readers with no doubt that Mrs Davies had indeed been murdered, that her body had been disposed of, and that Peacock was the culprit. The court considered this a very serious contempt. An article in the *Argus* summarized alleged facts, including a statement by another person that Peacock had done the acts of which he was accused, and disposed of the body; it included what were said to be expert views about the time which would be taken to disintegrate a body with chemicals so that it could be cast into a sewer without trace. The *Argus* was in contempt because, on balance, it had created an impression that Peacock had committed the murder, and had implied that the only major question unanswered was what he had done with the body. The *Herald* published an interview with a person which set out in narrative form a series of alleged facts showing a clear case of murder against Peacock. That was also contemptuous.

The case demonstrates obvious categories of contempt. It certainly does not establish that nothing may be published about pending litigation. Indeed, the judgment of the court states that the media may report the 'bare facts' of a crime:

In our opinion the public are entitled to entertain a legitimate curiosity as to such matters as the violent or sudden death or disappearance of a citizen, the breaking into a house, the theft of property, or any other crime, and it is, in our opinion, lawful for any person to publish information as to the bare facts relating to such a matter. By 'bare facts' we mean (but not as an exclusive definition) *extrinsic ascertained facts to which any eyewitness could bear testimony*, such as the finding of a body and its condition, the place in which it is found, the persons by whom it was found, the arrest of a person accused, and so on. But as to alleged facts depending upon the testimony of some particular person which may or may not be true, and may or may not be admissible in a Court of Justice, other considerations arise. The lawfulness of the publication in such cases is conditional, and depends, for present purposes, upon whether the publication is likely to interfere with a fair trial of the charge against the accused person [emphasis added].[9]

Naturally enough, the recently publicized major crimes which attract headlines in the media are often crimes in relation to which an accused person has been arrested or charged, so that there are journalistic pressures to inform the public contending against legal pressures to protect the fairness of the eventual trial. It is the 'extrinsic ascertained facts' principle which allows some reporting of them, as illustrated by *Davis* v. *Baillie*,[10] a case which arose from press coverage of the pursuit of a man charged with housebreaking who had absconded from bail. The judge said that the media were entitled to report the pursuit of the absconder and his arrest, and the circumstances leading up to them, as prominently and in as much detail as editors chose. But because he had already been charged with housebreaking, they were not allowed to set out his record of previous convictions or speculate that he was 'back to his old habits'. They were allowed to warn the public of housebreakings by him in the course of his flight. It appears from this case that the law will tolerate some incidental prejudice created in the course of warning the public about the presence or activities of a fugitive from justice.

Packer v. *Peacock* was concerned with a criminal case, but there are no fundamental differences in the principles which apply to civil cases, as demonstrated in *Attorney-General* v. *Times Newspapers Ltd*,[11] decided in 1973 and commonly known as the *Sunday Times* case. In it, the House of Lords approved an injunction preventing publication of an article in the London *Sunday Times* about tragedies caused by the drug thalidomide and attempts to obtain compensation for the children deformed by it from Distillers Co. (Biochemicals) Ltd ('Distillers'), who marketed and manufactured the drug. A number of actions against Distillers were pending, and negotiations for a settlement of those actions were in train, albeit slowly. The degree of Distillers' culpability and responsibility to the thalidomide victims was a matter of public controversy, which had been canvassed in the media and in parliament. The *Sunday Times* had already published an article criticizing what it regarded as a mean offer of settlement by Distillers. It proposed to publish an article consisting of detailed evidence and argument apparently intended to show that Distillers did not exercise 'due care' to see that thalidomide was safe before putting it on the market.

The House of Lords considered that the proposed article would be contemptuous because it prejudged an issue in the pending litigation, namely whether Distillers had been negligent, and the article could lead to public prejudgment of that issue. Prejudging of *sub judice* issues was condemned by the House of Lords not only because of its potential for influence on jurors and witnesses at a trial, but also because public prejudgment of an issue awaiting decision by a court was 'intrinsically objectionable'.[12]

The *Sunday Times* case is an obstacle to 'investigative' reporting, the essence of which is careful and detailed analysis of an issue. The problem is that investigative reporting of a matter which is *sub judice* almost inevitably produces a contemptuous prejudging of an issue which a court will be asked to decide. It is not insignificant that the editor of the *Sunday Times* seeking to push the law of prejudicial contempt to its limits was Harold Evans, a pioneer of investigative journalism. Publication of the results of 'media sleuthing', of the kind often portrayed in TV dramas, is contemptuous if it could affect the outcome of a pending case.[13]

Eight years after the *Sunday Times* case, the High Court of Australia delivered its decision in the *BLF* case.[14] It is an authority, on contempt of court by the media, even though the actual decision was about an attempt to restrain a royal commission rather than directly to restrain the print or electronic media. In 1981, a royal commission was established to inquire into allegations of illegal, improper or corrupt conduct of the Builders' Labourers Federation (BLF) and its officers, including Mr Norm Gallagher. The commission opened in a blaze of publicity, with allegations of corruption being made against Gallagher by counsel assisting the commission. The allegations were very widely reported. Two weeks after the opening, Victoria and the commonwealth began deregistration proceedings against the BLF in the Federal Court of Australia. The BLF claimed, among other things, that the royal commission would be in contempt of the Federal Court by publicly investigating matters relevant to the court deregistration proceedings.

The High Court rejected that argument by a majority of four to two justices. The court held that there was not sufficient overlap between the matters being investigated by the royal commission and the matters to be investigated by the Federal Court to put the commission in contempt: the deregistration proceedings were primarily about questions such as whether the conduct of the union or its members had prevented the objects of industrial laws from being achieved and whether the rules of the union had been observed. There was an overlap between the inquiries of the commission and the court, but it was not such that the royal commission would prejudice the deregistration case. That decision of the High Court, quite consistent with many earlier ones, is a reminder that it is rare for a whole topic to become *sub judice* and 'untouchable', let alone a whole person. The scope of potential contempt is sometimes exaggerated in the minds of media practitioners, to become broad and absolute to an extent which the law does not require. Only publications which raise a real risk of prejudice are in contempt; publications which refer to or even discuss some matter awaiting decision by a court in a non-prejudicial manner are not contemptuous.

The judgments of the High Court justices in the *BLF* case were more sensitive to the claims of freedom of speech than the judgments in the *Sunday Times* case. Mason J spoke of 'the overriding importance of freedom of discussion and speech to which should be added the equal importance of the public having access to information which it has a legitimate interest in knowing'.[15] That was so even though 'in a given case it is not easy to point to specific and tangible benefits that flow from preserving that freedom.'[16]

APPLYING THE TEST

In his words quoted earlier, Mason J was not suggesting that a general principle of freedom of speech is to supplant or vary the certainty of the existing law of contempt. He was drawing attention to differences in the permissible degree of comment which arise from the different kinds of people likely to be influenced by publications. The situation in the *BLF* case was clearly at the permissive end of the spectrum. First of all, it was the unusual situation where an injunction was sought *before publication* to prevent potentially prejudicial statements being made. As in the law of defamation, the courts are much more reluctant to impose restraint *beforehand* than to punish a publication which has already been printed or broadcast.[17] Secondly, the person being restrained was an experienced barrister sitting as a Royal Commissioner, not a media company. Thirdly, and of greater practical importance, the pending proceeding was not a criminal trial by jury but a deregistration proceeding to be determined by judges of the Federal Court.

At the other end of the spectrum from the *BLF* situation would be a media report about an issue to be determined in a pending criminal trial by jury.[18] Sometimes the courts are more lenient towards comment about a pending civil case than about a pending criminal case. Most criminal cases involve hazards to the accused greater than any faced by parties in civil cases. But one cannot generalize much more than that. There are a number of kinds of publications which will always be very dangerous for the media before a criminal trial. The media should never suggest, for example, that an accused person has confessed to a crime, refer to any previous offences by the accused, or publish a photograph or other material which would identify the accused, without obtaining careful legal advice.

Variations in Time, History and Medium

The courts have been anxious in the last few years to look at the likely effect of a publication which is said to be in contempt, with a view to confining punishment to situations where the right to a fair trial appears to allow no alternative. The main factors which have been recognized so far as alleviating the prejudice which would otherwise occur are: the lapse of time expected to fall between the time of publication and the trial in question; the fact that the material published was nothing new to the public; and the coverage and impact of the medium used to publish.

Unless a contemptuous publication is very striking and memorable, the courts will allow for the fact that members of a jury may be expected as the months pass to forget it, or forget its sting, before they come to consider the evidence at the trial. For example, the *Bacon* case[19] arose from an article in the *National Times* which was strongly critical of Detective Sergeant Rogerson, who was charged with bribery. It included suggestions that he was suspected of murder, attempted murder, supplying drugs, suborning witnesses and perverting the course of justice. The court decided that the article was not likely to prejudice the trial of Rogerson, because it would not be remembered for seven months, the shortest period which would have been foreseen to occur between the date of the article and Rogerson's trial. There were two other factors present in the *Bacon* case to lessen the impact of the article. The first was that most of the material in the article was not new. There had been a whole series of similar articles published before charges were laid. The second factor was that the article appeared in the *National Times*, a paper with a fairly small circulation.

The way in which the courts attempt to allow for the human factors in the minds of potential jurors is captured in the following statement of Glass JA about the ABC 'Four Corners' items which associated William and Robert Waterhouse with the Fine Cotton scandal and other wrongdoing.

> The circumstances of the publication to be considered included the following. It would be published to an estimated audience of 210,000 on the first presentation and to an unstated number of viewers on the second and third presentations. Any trial of [Robert Waterhouse] would not take place for at least twelve months following the three presentations. In the intervening period a daily succession of scandals, real and imaginary, would be revealed in the print and electronic media. Any forecast as to the capacity of the potential juror to retain impressions over a twelve months period must allow for the ephemeral character of television images and sounds as well as the viewer's scepticism and memory loss during that period. Another circumstance properly to be taken into account ... is a tendency of jurors heeding the warning of the trial judge and responding to the dynamic of the trial to banish from mind any prior impressions and concentrate on the material before them.[20]

If there is a striking or particularly graphic publication, such as a reference to the prior criminal record of an accused person, or something unusual which would stay in the public mind, time may be unable to erase the recollection. The concern of the courts to deal with the realities of effects on the media audience can also work against the media if, for example, a reading of the newspaper context shows that a television programme had a meaning which was not literally there in the words spoken.

Jury Trials

The differences between pending jury trials and non-jury trials are sometimes overlooked. Where a jury trial is pending, the greatest caution is needed. It is fairly clear, for example, that if a jury were to sit in the deregistration proceedings in the *BLF* case, a majority of the justices of the High Court would have held that the royal commission should be restrained from publicizing the alleged misdeeds of Gallagher and his union. As the main question was whether judges would be influenced by the publicity, it was necessary to show a real risk of serious prejudice. It was not to be assumed that the generalized 'atmospheric or environmental' effect of ventilating the alleged failings of the union and its officers through the royal commission would involve contempt of court.[21]

Where there will be no jury, it is not contemptuous to publish material which may lead the public to form an opinion adverse to one of the parties to litigation. The effect of a publication on the public at large in that situation is probably not relevant to prejudice.[22] The court in the *BLF* case was allowing much greater freedom to report matters relating to non-jury trials than those involving juries. In a country with so many state and federal jurisdictions as Australia, it is difficult to say in general terms which cases are tried by juries. If proceedings are pending and it is not clear whether a jury will be empanelled, there is no alternative to checking with a lawyer. As a broad generalization, serious criminal charges are tried by jury throughout Australia. The right to a jury trial for less serious offences varies from jurisdiction to jurisdiction. Jury trials of civil matters are not common, except in Victoria and New South Wales.

Cases Heard by Judges Alone

I am and have always been satisfied that no judge would be influenced in his judgment by what may be said by the media. If he were, he would not be fit to be a judge.

That statement of Lord Salmon was adopted by Gibbs CJ and Mason J in the *BLF* case.[23] One of the major points of law clarified by the court in that case was that judges may be expected not to be influenced by media comment. Older cases contained suggestions that it was contempt to 'embarrass' a judge by a publication which required him to put some prejudicial material out of his mind, or that it was contempt to create the possibility of even subconscious pressure. But those suggestions were clearly rejected by a majority of the court in the *BLF* case.[24] Gibbs J pointed out that it is an everyday task of a judge to put out of his mind evidence of the most prejudicial kind that he has heard in court and rejected as inadmissible, and that it is not uncommon for a judge to try a case which was the subject of emotional public discussion before proceedings started.[25] On the facts of the *BLF* case, it was not necessary for the court to say whether *any* public comment may be so prejudicial as to raise a real risk of prejudicing a judge.

In a 1980 decision, the New South Wales Court of Appeal fined the publisher of the Sydney *Sun* $10 000 for an allegation which was possibly 'one of those unusual cases where a magistrate or judge might find it hard to excise the allegation from his mind'.[26] On its front and second pages, the *Sun* had published the tragic story of a father who was said to have strangled his infant son in hospital after learning that he would be retarded and deformed for life. The headline, 'Father Accused, Sick Baby Murder', took up about half the front page. In a prominent block of text, the father was quoted as saying, 'I couldn't bear to see him suffer in future'. The article said that the father had confessed to police. It did not name him, but gave his age and said that he was 'from a South Coast town'. The *Sun* gained no protection by omitting the name, as what matters is whether the jury and others involved in any trial will connect the article with the accused. The main prejudicial elements in the article were the allegations that the father had confessed, and the attribution of guilt in the *Sun*'s emotional account of the child's death. As the court said:

> It would be a rare person indeed who would not have some emotional reaction, either against the man charged or in his favour, on reading the account published in the *Sun*.[27]

Magistrates and Justices of the Peace

Even if the *Sun* did raise the unusual risk of prejudicing the mind of a judge, it is clear that judges can be assumed to be capable of dismissing much prejudicial matter from their minds. The principle probably extends to all the courts of which the members are judges, such as the Family Court of Australia, and the various District, County and Industrial courts. But what of Magistrates' courts, Petty Sessions and inferior courts presided over by magistrates and justices of the peace with varying degrees of qualification? The law would be unlikely to disregard the capacity of such persons to exclude prejudicial material from their minds, but they are not to be regarded universally and automatically as having the same capacity for excluding prejudice as judges. Where a magistrate is not required to have been qualified to practise law to be eligible for appointment, he or she should be treated by the media with some of the same caution required with potential jurors.[28]

Inferior courts do not themselves punish for the kinds of contempt considered here, but they are protected by the Supreme Courts, which have jurisdiction to punish contempts of courts below them.

Appeals

It must follow from what the High Court said in the *BLF* case that the media have considerable freedom to comment on the issues in a case even when an appeal is pending, or when the time for parties to lodge appeals has not yet run out. That is illustrated by a 1960 English decision, *R* v. *Duffy; Ex parte Nash*.[29] The day after Nash was found guilty of causing grievous bodily harm and sentenced to five years' imprisonment, a newspaper published a hostile article about him, describing him as violent and vicious-looking. It said he was 'a small-time hooligan with big ideas' who had believed the police could not touch him; a man who had been destined to end up in the dock and 'an obscure thug'. Nash claimed that immediately after sentence, the press had been informed that he would appeal, and that some statements in the article were untrue as well as prejudicial. The court held that there was no risk of the appeal judges being influenced by such an article, and therefore no prejudicial contempt. An Australian court would be likely to reach the same conclusion today.

Pressuring Parties

It is a contempt to pressure a litigant by holding him or her up to 'public obloquy' for exercising his constitutional right to have his rights and obligations determined in court.[30] It was contempt, for example, for an English newspaper to quote the secretary of a company as saying that appointment of a receiver by certain plaintiffs 'smashed the goodwill and organisation of the business in a day' and that nobody could understand such conduct.[31] This kind of contempt does not require a risk that the disputed issues in a case should be prejudiced. It is concerned with intimidation of plaintiffs, defendants, accused persons, prosecutors, appellants, respondents and other parties. For example, there can be a situation where the trial will be heard by a judge alone, who is not likely to be influenced by advance publicity about the issues. However, a publication which strongly suggests that one side of the pending case is wrong, and so creates a public atmosphere of hatred or contempt against that side, will nevertheless be contemptuous.[32]

Pressuring of parties was an issue in the *Sunday Times* case. The Law Lords made remarks about another *Sunday Times* article which had already been published. It said, among other things, that 'the thalidomide children shame Distillers', compared the amount of compensation offered by Distillers with the amount of profits made by the company in the preceding year, and urged Distillers to reconsider the amount of compensation offered in settlement. Three Law Lords thought that was permissible, but Lords Diplock and Simon thought it overstepped the mark, because of the amount of 'obloquy' or abuse it heaped on Distillers. The more liberal majority view is the one which prevails, and states the law for the future.

It is quite permissible to seek by fair public comment to dissuade a litigant from proceeding with his or her case. It is impermissible to express the comment so strongly or intemperately as to undermine public confidence in the courts by intimidating the litigant. Australian courts are unlikely to be more sensitive about the feelings of litigants than were the majority of the House of Lords in the *Sunday Times* case. The *Sunday Times* case was applied in a New South Wales decision, *Commercial Bank of Australia* v. *Preston*.[33]

Litigation was pending between the bank and Preston, who outside the bank's premises distributed a pamphlet attacking it. Preston's pamphlet said that the bank was paying thousands of dollars to take him to court and intimidate him, and that one of the bank's managers (who was likely to be its principal witness in the litigation) had been found by a court to be a deliberate liar. Hunt J held that the article was contemptuous because it was intemperate and because it vilified the witness.

Witnesses

The decided cases contain a number of statements that it is contemptuous to publish material which may affect the minds of witnesses called to give evidence in trials.[34] If this principle were taken to the extreme, it would mean that reporting about matters pending even in non-jury trials would be as restricted as in jury trials. As most trials involve the giving of evidence by witnesses, reporting would be severely limited in practice. However, the modern law of contempt is much more liberal. It does not assume that witnesses will be influenced at all by the publication of material affecting the issues in a trial. Gibbs CJ said in the *BLF* case:

If the allegations made ... are true, an honest witness, called to give evidence in ... court, and aware of the facts, will give evidence in support of those allegations; if they are false, an honest witness, if aware of the falsity, will say so.[35]

Mason J said that the risk of a witness in the *BLF* case being influenced by media reports of evidence in the earlier royal commission inquiry was 'a mere matter of speculation, not a matter of genuine inference'.[36] Wilson J said that although material tending to influence witnesses will be in contempt, the tendency must be established, not based on speculation.[37] The High Court also rejected the view that it is contemptuous merely to create an 'atmosphere of prejudice' where no jury is involved.

Photographs, Film and Identification

It is clear from the *BLF* case that a court may not automatically assume that the testimony of witnesses will be influenced by publications concerning the matters about which they will testify. Before a publication can be in contempt through prejudice, a real likelihood of influence is necessary. Identification by eyewitnesses, however, is one situation where that likelihood is universally recognized. Witnesses must sometimes strain memory to the limit in criminal cases. Identification may also relate to a vehicle, a weapon, a document or some other object. It may arise as an issue in a civil case as well as in a criminal one. Understandably, the courts are hostile to any publication which may confuse the process of recollection.

The *Bradley* case[38] illustrates this. A schoolboy named Graeme Thorne was kidnapped and murdered by a person seeking a ransom payment shortly after his parents won the New South Wales lottery. The police search for the murderer lasted three months and was accompanied by almost unprecedented media publicity. Bradley was arrested and charged with the murder. The *Daily Mirror* published a large picture of Bradley on its front page under bold headlines which read 'Man held. First photo.' The subheading was:

These are the first pictures published of Stephen Leslie Bradley (right) and his wife, Mrs Magda Bradley (below). Bradley was arrested yesterday on the liner Himalaya at Colombo on a warrant charging him with the murder of eight-years-old Graeme Thorne. More stories, pictures on pages 3, 4 and 5.

In finding the publisher and editor of the *Mirror* guilty of contempt, the court pointed to the obvious dangers to a fair trial where identification will be an issue if photographs of the accused are published, and to the unanimity with which the courts have condemned such publications. It was no defence for the editor to say that in the course of the police search for the murderer, the *Mirror* had at the request of the police published an artist's impression of the wanted man; or to say that he was sure that photographs of Bradley had already been shown to witnesses capable of identifying him as the kidnapper.

The same principle applies to television coverage of trials. Film of an accused person entering or leaving the court building is fairly commonplace. News film has at least as much potential for prejudice as hard copy. It is not contempt to film an accused whose identity is in issue, but it is contempt to broadcast such a film. The onus of concealing identity does not lie on the accused, or on the police, as some producers and editors appear to believe.

CONTINUING A PUBLIC CONTROVERSY

The law of contempt does make a concession to freedom of speech in allowing public controversy to touch a *sub judice* matter. That important concession is the principle first spelled out by Jordan CJ in the *Bread Manufacturers* case.[39] His words quoted below have been repeatedly endorsed by Australian and English courts. They have almost the character of an Act of parliament. He said:

> It is of extreme public interest that no conduct should be permitted which is likely to prevent a litigant in a Court of justice from having his case tried free from all matter of prejudice. But the administration of justice, important though it undoubtedly is, is not the only matter in which the public is vitally interested; and if in the course of the ventilation of *a question of public concern* matter is published which may prejudice a party in the conduct of a law suit, it does not follow that a contempt has been committed. The case may be one in which as between competing matters of public interest the possibility of prejudice to a litigant may be required by yield to other and superior considerations. The discussion of public affairs and the denunciation of public abuses, actual or supposed, cannot be required to be suspended merely because the discussion or the denunciation may, *as an incidental but not intended by-product*, cause some likelihood of prejudice to a person who happens at the time to be a litigant.
>
> It is well settled that a person cannot be prevented by process of contempt from continuing to discuss publicly *a matter which may fairly be regarded as one of public interest*, by reason merely of the fact that the matter in question has become the subject of litigation ... [emphasis added].[40]

As with most classic formulations of the law, the important practical question is how the words have been applied in the cases. The *Bread Manufacturers* case itself is a simple illustration of the principle. In a style of journalism now almost extinct, the Sydney *Truth* had been campaigning against price-fixing and other activities of bakeries which, it alleged, were inflating the price of bread. After that campaign had started, a bread carter began an action for defamation and conspiracy against Bread

Manufacturers Ltd, the bread trade protection association which he claimed had 'blacklisted' him. While this action was awaiting trial by jury, *Truth* continued to allege boycotting and blacklisting of vendors selling bread cheaply by the 'avaricious food ring' controlling the bread industry. It did not refer to the bread carter's case, being unaware of it. The court found no contempt in the articles published while the case was pending, as any tendency to influence the case was 'fortuitous'. It appears from his judgment, however, that Jordan CJ may have found *Truth* guilty of contempt if the staff had known, or had reason to know, that the case was pending.[41]

The *Rigby*[42] decision of the High Court takes the law much further. In particular, it extends the freedom to publish to cases where the media do know that litigation is pending. The main items in the *Sydney Morning Herald* under attack in that case were the text of a statutory declaration made by Rigby, which alleged in some detail police violence against him; and a letter from Rigby's solicitors to the Premier of New South Wales calling for an investigation of his allegations. These items were alleged to be contemptuous because when they were published Rigby had been charged with offensive behaviour, unlawfully assaulting a police officer, and resisting arrest in connection with the events about which his complaints were published. The charges would normally be tried by a magistrate, although it was not impossible that some of them would ultimately be tried by a jury. The High Court held there was no contempt. The court's reasons may be summarized under two aspects of the dictum of Jordan CJ. The most important words are italicized in the preceding quotation.

1. *Is there a 'question of public concern' or a 'continuing matter of public interest'?*
In the *Rigby* case, the court took note of the background to publication of Rigby's allegations. The *Herald* and other papers had been publishing articles and allegations about police misconduct, including brutality, for some time. The Rigby allegations were part of a continuing controversy. The *Herald* had recently published articles demanding an open inquiry into the administration of the police force. On the day before it published Rigby's statutory declaration, the Premier of New South Wales had announced the appointment of a judge to inquire into another incident of alleged police violence. It is notable that in both the *Rigby* and the *Bread Manufacturers* cases the

public controversy had been running long before the challenged articles were published.

2. *Is any prejudice 'an incidental and unintended by-product'?*
The letter from Rigby's solicitors spoke of their client's high integrity and good reputation in the commercial world. It said also: 'That he could be without any reason assaulted by police officers and falsely charged is a matter of the utmost gravity'. Taken on its own such a statement in a newspaper would involve so much prejudgment of his innocence as to be contemptuous, regardless of whether a jury would hear the case or not. The court, however, was prepared to read that dangerous statement in the context of the several columns of text about calls for a public inquiry published in the *Herald* on that day. The court read all that material as a whole. The context was one of calling for the terms of reference of the announced inquiry to be extended to cover Rigby's allegations, not of passing judgment on the charges against him.

The *Herald* was able to publish material about Rigby's allegations and even refer to the charges against him because the articles were not about the subject matter of the pending trial. Although the statutory declaration did incidentally imply his innocence of the police charges, Rigby's main allegations were about police violence *after* his arrest. The trial would be concerned with what happened at the time of arrest and before it. The publication of his statutory declaration would have been contemptuous if the police had obtained a confession from Rigby. Then, evidence of police violence after arrest could have been relevant to whether the confession was made voluntarily or not.[43] Of course, the statutory declaration, the solicitors' letter, and the other material published in the *Herald* tended to create a *general* prejudice against the police. But in this case as in the *BLF* case, a mere 'atmosphere' of prejudice was not specific enough to the pending case to raise a real risk of prejudice.[44]

REVIEW OF THE CASES

The second *Willesee* case[45] demonstrates how far the courts can go in treating prejudice as 'an incidental and unintended by-product'. The Willesee television programme broadcast an item which continued the public controversy about allegations of corruption made by James Anderson. In that item, it implied that Anderson had a criminal background and had little credibility. Anderson's jury trial on a charge of stealing a necklace was at that time nearing its end. The trial was aborted by the judge because of the obvious danger of prejudice caused by the TV item. Nevertheless, Willesee and the others responsible were not found guilty of contempt, because it was not proved that they knew of Anderson's trial. Unless it was shown that they knew of the trial, the prejudice to it had to be 'unintended'. However, the court was critical of the station management because it did not have a system for checking whether cases were pending. A major media outlet which cannot point to such a system risks at least criticism by the courts and responsibility for costs, and also a conviction where it was a matter of widespread public knowledge that a trial was taking place.

At the beginning of this chapter, it was said that what a journalist or media executive must do is know what aspects of trials are sensitive, be prepared to consult a lawyer in doubtful situations, and avoid publishing material affecting the central issues in a trial. Now that a number of judgments of the courts about actual situations have been discussed, it is possible to make a practical list of cases mentioned in this chapter to illustrate just how important is the distinction between prejudice to *the issues to be decided* in a trial, and other situations where the issues in a trial are *touched upon* but not prejudiced.

Cases where publications were contemptuous, because of likely prejudice
In *Packer* v. *Peacock*, the newspaper articles suggested that Dr Peacock was guilty of the murder with which he was charged.

The *Sunday Times* suggested in its investigative article that Distillers had indeed been negligent in the manufacture of thalidomide. Whether Distillers had been negligent was one of the questions the court was going to decide.

Neville *Wran* said that Murphy was innocent of the crime with which he was charged, and the ABC suggested that the *Age* tapes showed Murphy to be guilty through the improper associations which the tapes were said to reveal.

Derryn *Hinch* drew the previous indecent assault convictions of Glennon to public attention whilst Glennon was facing charges for similar offences. Similarly, the first *Willesee* case[46] involved disclosure of the similar criminal record of a person facing charges.

Publication of the photograph of *Bradley* raised the prospect that witnesses at his trial would not know whether they recognized him from the newspaper or from a scene relevant to the kidnapping.

The articles in the *Gordon* case[47] suggested that Gordon had been executed to prevent him from giving evidence against the people accused of drug offences, with obvious potential for prejudice to their fair trial.

Cases of some likelihood of prejudice, but no contempt conviction because the Bread Manufacturers principle saved the publication
The articles in the *Rigby* case could have had some slight impact on Rigby's offensive behaviour trial, but were principally about a wider issue of police behaviour generally.

The *Brych*[48] articles merely reported recent developments in the Brych cancer-cure controversy, and did not have a direct bearing on Brych's defamation action.

The current affairs item in the second *Willesee* case reflected on Anderson's character, but was not concerned with the larceny charge which he was facing. It was about the different issue of the allegations of corruption which Anderson had made.

Cases where there was no contempt
In the *BLF* case, the royal commission was inquiring into questions different from those which would be answered by the Federal Court, even though there was some overlap in the areas of investigation, and both were concerned with the affairs of the same union.

The article by Wendy *Bacon* certainly disparaged Rogerson, who had been charged with bribery, and even mentioned the bribery accusation against him, but allowing for the time which would elapse before trial, it was not likely to influence a jury against Rogerson.

Similarly, the ABC programme in the *Waterhouse* case was very critical of Robert Waterhouse, but it did not say that he was guilty of offences through the Fine Cotton affair, nor was it likely to influence a jury to convict him by the time his trial would come about.

STOP WRITS

As an English judge has said, 'it is a widely held fallacy that the issue of a writ automatically stifles public comment.[49] The use of 'stop writs' or 'gagging writs' inevitably arises when media coverage of public controversies is discussed. It is still believed in some quarters that a person who fears exposure by the media can prevent that exposure continuing by starting a defamation action. That will mean that a defamation action will be pending and, so the fallacious theory goes, that any further exposure will be in contempt of court. It is true that as a matter of defamation law a person who repeats defamatory material may aggravate the amount of damages ultimately awarded, or undermine a defence of qualified privilege or fair comment by providing evidence of malice, as discussed earlier in this book. But the issue of a defamation writ should very rarely prevent a well-advised media writer from continuing to publish news. The problem lies not in contempt law but in misunderstandings about the law, or in the tactical brinkmanship which distinguishes so many defamation actions.[50]

The courts have repeatedly dismissed the idea that the law of contempt enables a defamation writ to stifle discussion. In the second paragraph of his *Bread Manufacturers* statement quoted above, Jordan CJ clearly indicated that the beginning of litigation does not mean the end of public discussion. In the *Rigby case*, the High Court said:

> There have been occasions where summary proceedings for contempt have been commenced, or threatened, not with the real object of ensuring the impartial administration of justice, but solely for the purpose of stopping public comment on, or even public inquiry into, a matter of public importance. A court possessing the summary jurisdiction [over contempt] will not allow itself to the made the instrument for effecting such a purpose.[51]

Lord Reid said bluntly in the *Sunday Times* case that 'a gagging writ ought to have no effect'.[52]

The *Brych* case[53] illustrates these principles. There had been protracted, intense and bitter controversy over Brych, who conducted a cancer clinic in the Cook Islands. His clinical methods, qualifications, and capacity to cure cancer had been publicly and vigorously debated in Australia. Brych sued the Melbourne *Herald*, alleging that it had defamed him in an article about his clinic. A fortnight later, the *Herald* published two further articles about adverse developments in Brych's affairs, which nevertheless did not attack him. One article, headed 'PM Orders Brych Ban', was about current and threatened restrictions on his practising in the Cook Islands. The other article, headed 'Brych Won't Get in Here: Hunt', reported the attitude of the Australian Minister for Health towards Brych's prospects of obtaining medical admission in Australia. Brych claimed that these articles were prejudicial to his defamation action, and in contempt of court. Anderson J held that there was no contempt. The articles would not prejudice Brych's defamation action. They did not relate to the pending proceedings: they appeared 'to report factually current events and some background information'. The defamation action was not to be heard for several months, and the public had already heard a great deal about the Brych controversy. Any element of influence on a potential juror would therefore be so remote as not to be worth considering. Anderson J took into account the fact that the subject under discussion was 'a question of public concern' within the meaning of the *Bread Manufacturers* dictum.

A case in which a defamation plaintiff did succeed in stopping discussion of an issue for a time is *Watts* v. *Hawke*.[54] It involved a dispute over the Australian Journalists' Association (AJA) Code of Ethics. Robert Hawke, a public figure (later Prime Minister of Australia), complained to the AJA and to the Press Council that Barry Watts, a journalist with the *Australian*, had written and published a telex which attributed to Hawke statements he had never made, and statements he had made off the record. Hawke claimed that Watts had thereby contravened the AJA Code of Ethics. Hawke published the substance of his complaints about Watts in a telex. Watts then started a defamation action against Hawke; and obtained an order from the Supreme Court of Victoria restraining the Judiciary Committee of the AJA from hearing Hawke's complaint because the results of the Judiciary Committee investigation could prejudice his defamation trial.

Kaye J was prepared to grant the order as the AJA committee would be adjudicating on questions central to the defamation action, and the committee had no power to ensure that its findings would remain confidential. As a result, there was a danger that the jury in the defamation case would learn that the AJA would have investigated and reached a conclusion on matters which they were to decide. It may be seen that this situation was far removed from the usual 'stop writ' situation where all the media seek to do is to continue reporting some matter. In *Watts* v. *Hawke*, the danger was thought to be that the public would learn of an investigation and determination of matters awaiting decision, something more prejudicial even than the thalidomide article restrained in the *Sunday Times* case. The AJA committee would formally adjudicate on the propriety of Watts's conduct. Furthermore, it is doubtful whether the conduct of Watts was a 'question of public concern' so as to attract the right to continue a public controversy.

WHEN ARE PROCEEDINGS PENDING?

The Beginning of Criminal Proceedings

The time when criminal proceedings are pending, and the reason why it is so important to identify that time, are best illustrated by the decision of the High Court in *James* v. *Robinson*.[55] The Perth *Sunday Times* published sensational articles about two murders, which they indicated Robinson had committed, and about the ensuing 'manhunt' for him. Robinson was being pursued by a large number of police at the time of publication, but he had not yet been arrested or charged. The articles included photographs of Robinson and his alleged victims; a verbal description of him; eyewitness accounts of the crime; a statement that he had said 'I'll get two more'; and a statement by a taxi driver that Robinson 'knew what he was doing'. In short, the articles would have been paradigms of prejudice. But the High Court held that there was no contempt of court, whatever might be said about the good or bad taste of the articles.

There was no contempt because no court was legally destined to consider Robinson's alleged crimes. He was simply a person being pursued by police. It was not enough that criminal proceedings against him were imminent. They had to be actually 'pending'. The court said that criminal proceedings are not pending when a person has not been arrested or charged.[56] Anyone preparing material for the media should assume that proceedings are pending if a person has been arrested *or* charged, if a warrant has been issued for his or her arrest, or if any other act, such as the issue of a summons, or information has occurred to set the criminal process in train.[57] If no legal process of that kind has occurred, and if, for example, a suspect is only being sought or questioned by police, there can be no danger of prejudicial contempt. If a newsworthy crime occurs, it is important for the media to watch out for the happening of any of the legal events mentioned, and where necessary to check before publishing. It is particularly important for radio, the medium with the shortest editorial 'lead time'. There is no interim period for contempt in these situations. The *sub judice* period begins immediately a person is charged, for example.

Before criminal proceedings are pending, it cannot be said that 'anything goes' in crime reporting. There is no danger of prejudicial contempt, but there is still the danger that a person whose reputation is damaged may sue for defamation. The Perth *Sunday Times* must have been confident that it could successfully defend any defamation action brought by Robinson. Furthermore, if a report was published with a *deliberate* intention to pervert the course of justice, then the publisher with that intention would risk prosecution for attempting to pervert the course of justice.[58] An example might be a publication designed to ensure that a particular person likely to be charged was convicted. It is unlikely, however, that a newspaper or broadcasting station with no ulterior purpose would find itself prosecuted for that crime. Of course, the beginning of the *sub judice* period does not mean an end of publication about a crime. It means that publications must be made subject to the law of contempt already outlined.

The Beginning of Civil Proceedings

The principles which determine the beginning of civil proceedings are the same as the criminal ones already mentioned. It is generally accepted that the time at which proceedings begin is more sharply defined, as it is the issue of the writ, statement of claim, summons or similar document.[59]

Termination of Criminal and Civil Proceedings

The exact time when proceedings end is much harder to identify. The broad rule appears to be that civil proceedings have ended as soon as a judgment has been delivered, regardless of any appeals to higher courts against the judgment.[60] On the other hand, a criminal case may remain pending until judgment has been delivered in any appeal against the original judgment, or until the time for appealing has run out.[61] Most kinds of appeal are heard by judges alone, so the media usually have more freedom once the original judgment has been delivered, even in criminal cases. Appeals from some convictions by magistrates, however, are reheard by a judge and jury.

As outlined earlier, the law of contempt is more generous to the media when no juries or witnesses will be involved.

It is possible that courts may in future allow otherwise prejudicial comment on the subject matter of a case which has become inactive or dormant through the inaction of the parties. The English Court of Appeal thought that the *Sunday Times* case was such a case, as about four years had elapsed since the thalidomide action started but no trial had yet begun. But the House of Lords overruled the Court of Appeal, considering that negotiations for settlement with Distillers had continued throughout that time. The proceedings were not therefore dormant. It would be necessary to point to a very long period of inactivity in a case before it could be treated as dormant. The courts appear not to have so treated any current proceedings in a reported contempt case.

RESPONSIBILITY AND PUNISHMENT

Intention

Before a person can be convicted of most criminal offences, an intention to commit the offence must be demonstrated to a court. Provided that there is an intention to publish, however, a person can be found guilty of contempt without having any actual intention to prejudice proceedings. The court itself judges contempt on the basis of the *inherent tendency* of what was published, not on the basis of what a reporter, editor or producer intended it to mean.[62] 'Inherent tendency' refers to the nature of the publication, not to its actual, ultimate effect. So it is almost irrelevant to inquire whether the course of a trial has actually been influenced one way or another.[63]

Intention is rarely decisive, but it is always relevant. If a publisher does not know that proceedings are pending, for example, or does know but has no intention to prejudice them, a court will be more likely to allow that publisher to continue discussion of a public controversy.[64] Conversely, if there is an actual intention to prejudice, a person may be convicted even if the publication does not of itself have any inherent prejudicial tendency. So a media campaign to have a conviction quashed would almost certainly be a contempt, despite the unlikelihood that it would influence the appeal judges. When contempt has been found, and the court comes to decide in its discretion how severe the punishment should be, intention is a very important factor.

Responsibility

In deciding who was actually responsible for publishing a contempt, the courts often 'look over the editor's shoulder' in a media organization to investigate every step on the way from initial gathering of material to final publication. They often investigate the extent to which legal advice was obtained in advance, and whether the legal advice was acted upon. The essence of the contempt is *publication* of material rather than *preparation* of material. So the person or company primarily responsible is the publisher, typically a newspaper company or broadcasting company. Editors are virtually always held responsible by the courts, even when they have no actual knowledge of the offending material.[65]

Reporters, sub-editors, executives and others can be punished for contempt, but their responsibility tends to be based on actual, immediate responsibility for offending material, unlike the stricter responsibility of editors and publishers, which arises from the very nature of their position. It is contempt of court to distribute or print prejudicial material, regardless of any actual knowledge of what is printed.[66] The tendency in the modern cases is to impose little if any penalty on distributors and printers who had no reason to know that they were disseminating contemptuous print material; but the company or corporation responsible for a radio or TV station cannot claim to be an 'innocent distributor' of the material which it transmits.

Two modern Australian cases will illustrate how responsibility for contempt is apportioned.

The *Gordon* case[67] arose from the trial of the Zampaglione brothers for drug dealing offences. The crown was to call a former drug dealer named Gordon to give evidence against the Zampagliones, but he was murdered. The crown agreed at the beginning of the trial not to tell the jury of this murder, because it could easily prejudice their minds against the accused. While the trial was underway, however, the *Age* published a series of articles by its 'Insight' team about the drug trade. These included a headline saying 'Killings Show the Trade is Booming' with a captioned photograph of Gordon's body and text which unmistakably linked his murder to the Zampaglione drug ring, among others. It was no help to the *Age* that the Zampagliones were not actually named. Marks J found that the jury could, in the context of the trial, have taken the articles to mean that the Zampagliones were guilty of the drug offences charged, and that Gordon had been murdered to stop him giving evidence against them. Such a prejudicial publication was obviously contemptuous. He fined Davie, the editor of the *Age*, $4000, rejecting Davie's contention that the editor of a large newspaper should not be held personally accountable for the mistakes of his subordinates. The judge said that although one man cannot know everything happening in a large newspaper office, there must be a system designed to ensure compliance with the law of contempt, including special treatment of dangerous copy to ensure that it cannot be published unless certain checks are made. For similar reasons, David Syme & Co, the publisher, was fined $75 000.

The allocation of responsibility for contempt by electronic media was unclear until the first *Willesee* case,[68] decided in 1980. As a result of the murder of a warder at Long Bay gaol in Sydney, the warders went on strike, leaving prisoners locked in their cells. The *Willesee at Seven* programme broadcast by ATN Channel 7 included film of an unidentified prisoner speaking through a cell window and recorded by a long-range camera and microphone. Among other things, the prisoner said: 'The inmate who allegedly killed [the dead warder] had previously assaulted two other officers with weapons'. The New South Wales Court of Appeal found that broadcast contemptuous, even though the context of the segment was the strike at the gaol, because of the grave risk of prejudice caused by publicizing previous offences of an accused person, particularly in such an arresting and dramatic way through the television medium. The court expressed concern that in recent contempt cases large corporations, such as television station licensees and newspaper proprietors, had not ensured that obviously sensitive material was viewed or read and approved by a lawyer before being disseminated.[69]

Willesee at Seven had been produced for the licensee company of ATN Channel 7 under a contract with Trans Media Productions, which was an independent production company, and with Willesee. Willesee was the managing director of Trans Media and also compere and co-ordinator of the programme. The court fined the licensee, the production company and Willesee, finding little distinction between the responsibility of any of them. The licensee was guilty because it was responsible for everything which it transmitted. That was so although it had no actual knowledge of the contemptuous film. The production company was responsible because its employees had made the film. Willesee was responsible, although he had not personally previewed the film, because he was the person 'with direct and immediate control of the programme and its contents'. The aggregate of the fines imposed on all three was only $5000, because such a case of television contempt was novel. But the court warned that similar cases would incur more serious penalties in future.

Reliance on Police

As already mentioned, the court in the *Willesee* case expressed concern about the failure of media companies to obtain legal advice on the exact content of sensitive publications. Assurances or hints from the police are no substitute for this independent legal advice, as illustrated by *R* v. *Pacini*.[70] In that case, Melbourne newspapers and a radio production executive were found guilty of contempt because of prejudicial publications about an attempted murder. The papers published a photograph of the accused (partly blanked out in one case) and stories conveying the impression that the crime had been *successfully solved* by the arrest of the accused. The station broadcast an interview with a police officer conveying the same impression. The papers and the radio executive had relied on information supplied by police officers responsible for investigation of the crime. The officers had assured them that identity would not be an issue in the case, and that the accused had already confessed. The judge pointed out that the accused might at his trial wish to repudiate any confession, set up an alibi, or take some other course which would be prejudiced by the publications. More important, the police had no power to dispense anybody from the law of contempt: 'By no collaboration of police and reporters can an editor be permitted to determine what is or is not a contemptuous publication.'[71] He referred to another case,[72] in which Jordan CJ had indicated that it would not be safe to publish a photograph of an accused because the police predicted that identity would not be an issue at his trial. Jordan CJ there rejected the suggestion that:

a junta of police officers and journalists can hold a sort of preliminary settling of the issues likely to be tried at the hearing, and that this Court ought not lightly to interfere in their rulings as to the probability of identity being raised.

TRIBUNALS

The courts are outnumbered by the hundreds of statutory tribunals, both state and federal, which conduct hearings and make decisions in many areas of human activity, including employment, town and country planning, licensing, discrimination, mining, and social security. Although generically described as tribunals, they may actually have names such as 'board', 'commission', or 'committee'. The same principles of contempt discussed in this and the next chapter apply to some of them although they are not courts. That is because the Act of parliament setting up a tribunal sometimes expressly gives it the protection of the law of contempt. Unless an Act does that, a non-court is not protected against contemptuous publications made outside its hearing room. This means that the Act establishing a tribunal must be read and interpreted by a lawyer before the media can know whether the proceedings of the tribunal are to be treated with the circumspection necessary for courts.

Tribunals which can affect the media are examples of how an Act may adopt principles of contempt law. Section 25AB of the Broadcasting Act makes it an offence punishable by a court to insult a member of the Broadcasting Tribunal in relation to an inquiry, or to 'do any other act or thing that would, if the Tribunal were a court of record, constitute a contempt of that court'. The Administrative Appeals Tribunal has the same protection,[73] as does the Trade Practices Tribunal.[74] Contempt law does not protect any tribunal in the Media Council of Australia scheme for self-regulation of advertising, as that scheme is a private one, not based on any law of a parliament. Among the better known tribunals, the Taxation Boards of Review have no contempt protection, but s. 182(1)(d) of the commonwealth Conciliation and Arbitration Act makes it an offence by writing or speech improperly to influence an arbitration commissioner or witness appearing before the commission. It is an offence to use words false and defamatory of a federal royal commission, or to be 'in any manner guilty of any *wilful* contempt' of it,[75] but royal commissions established under the corresponding Victorian and New South Wales laws do not have the same protection.

There are few cases to explain the exact effect of a section of an Act which, like those mentioned in the preceding paragraph, says that contempt law will apply to a tribunal. The main case, *R* v. *Arrowsmith*,[76] concerned a 1949 Victorian royal commission into the Communist Party. The Act establishing the commission deemed it to be a proceeding of the Victorian Supreme Court. The *Guardian* published vehement attacks on the royal commissioner and on one of the leading anti-communist witnesses. Lowe J pointed out that the law of prejudicial contempt of court simply could not be applied without modification to something which was not actually a trial, and that freedom of speech had to be given more weight than when a trial was pending. He did fine those responsible for contemptuous items, such as depiction of the witness in words and a cartoon as a 'rat' who betrayed his associates and whose evidence contradicted his previous writings. Lowe J did apply a more lenient standard, however, for determining prejudice than would have applied to proceedings in court, and did exonerate from contempt some material, including abuse of the witness, which was not related directly to the proceedings of the royal commission. A modern court would probably be at least as liberal towards contempt of a tribunal protected by a contempt clause in its Act, while still attempting to protect tribunal witnesses and parties from intimidatory publications.

Even if an Act does not expressly say that a tribunal is protected, it may analytically be a court, despite its name, so as to share the protection of the courts themselves. But the decided cases do not provide any simple test for saying what is a court. In one case, the New South Wales Court of Appeal decided that a New South Wales Coroners Court was a court for the purposes of prejudicial contempt.[77] That conclusion was not reached by applying any one simple rule, but by a detailed consideration of the Coroners Act and the functions of the coroner. It was held that even though there was not the usual adversarial contest between parties, proceedings at the coroner's inquest were still a part of the administration of justice, which could profoundly affect the interests of citizens. In *Attorney-General* v. *British Broadcasting Corporation*,[78] the House of Lords held that a local valuation court was not a court for contempt purposes. The valuation 'court' was empowered to hear evidence on oath, and required to sit in public in order to determine questions obviously involving the rights of citizens. But the Law Lords considered that its function was to deal with administrative issues rather than to administer justice. Their judgments indicated a reluctance to extend the law of contempt beyond the traditional courts. It is not lightly to be assumed that the contempt law considered in this chapter applies to bodies other than the traditional courts, unless an Act of parliament says so.

In 1983, responding to the sentencing of the trade union leader Norm Gallagher to gaol for contempt, the commonwealth Attorney-General referred to the Law Reform Commission a wide-ranging inquiry into contempt law, of which the kinds of contempt discussed in this chapter and the next were a major part. The report of the commission was published in mid-1987, to a generally favourable reception.[79] The report has 730 pages, including draft bills to enact the reforms. Judging by the rate of adoption of earlier law reform reports, such as the *Unfair Publication* report on defamation and privacy mentioned in Chapter 2, it may be a number of years before the recommendations of the commission become law. Even if the recommendations are implemented at the federal level, that will not necessarily produce changes at the state level. The most effective reform would be a uniform national one supported by all states, enacting the new Bills drafted by the commission.

A summary of such a long report can mention only some highlights. Generally, the report proposed moderate changes through a restatement and clarification of existing law. It recognized the importance of freedom of speech and the role the media play in informing the community about proceedings in court. If the report were implemented, the situations of possible contempt would be organized into a planned spectrum. At the most sensitive end would be current jury hearing of a criminal case. At the least sensitive would be an appeal waiting to be heard by a higher court. The law would become more tolerant of comment as it moved away from the current jury trial end of the spectrum. The only publications capable of creating prejudice in relation to a criminal trial be jury would be those saying or implying that: the accused is innocent or guilty; the jury should acquit or convict; the accused has a prior conviction or has committed another offence, or is suspected of doing so; the accused was or was not involved in an act relating to the offence, or similar conduct; the accused has confessed, or behaved in a guilty manner or has a good or bad character; the accused or any likely witness is credible or not; a document likely to be in evidence is reliable or not; or the prosecution has been undertaken for a improper motive. Among defences to contempt charges would be the need to facilitate an arrest or protect the public (typically by publication of a photograph of a wanted person) and a broad public interest defence similar to the current *Bread Manufacturers* doctrine. The only publications which could be contemptuous in relation to civil trials by jury would be those saying or implying that: a likely witness or evidence is credible or not; a party has good or bad character; or a certain outcome of the case is likely or proper.

7

COURTS AND PARLIAMENTS:
Criticizing and Reporting

Mark Armstrong

CRITICIZING AND 'SCANDALIZING' THE COURTS

'Justice is not a cloistered virtue: she must be allowed to suffer the scrutiny and respectful, even though outspoken, comments of ordinary men.'[1] Those famous words of Lord Atkin reflect the tolerance which the courts have generally shown towards criticism. Most of the cases where the media have been punished for contempt by 'scandalizing' have involved specific accusations of bias or corruption which go beyond mere criticism of the work of the courts. A writer or broadcaster who is aware of these very limited danger zones has no other need to treat the reputations of courts or judges with special care. Before turning to the cases, it should be pointed out that whereas the prejudicial contempts considered in the preceding chapter can be committed only when legal proceedings are pending, 'scandalizing' contempt can be committed at any time by a publication which brings the courts into disrepute or deters the community from resorting to them. There is no 'safe period'.

Criticism

The main decision of the High Court on scandalizing contempt is *R* v. *Dunbabin; Ex parte Williams*.[2] Dunbabin was editor of the Sydney *Sun*. The court found him and his publisher guilty of contempt for producing a sarcastic article headed 'Courts and Cabinets' which in a confused manner attacked the High Court for allegedly frustrating the federal government. It said: 'Well may the Caseys and the Kellys cry like the historic British monarch for some gallant champion to rid them of this pestilent Court.' Casey was a federal cabinet minister. The article spoke of the court putting into 'suspended animation ... the law which was relied upon to keep Australia white' by the exercise of 'keen legal intelligences', this 'to the horror of everybody except the Little Brothers of the Soviet and kindred intelligentsia'. That was a reference to a High Court decision which had temporarily stopped government moves to deport Egon Kisch, the Czechoslovakian communist writer. The article also suggested that as an alternative to getting rid of the High Court, it should be given some 'real work to do' so that it would not have 'time to argue for days and days on the exact length of the split in the hair'. The court held that the *Sun* had overstepped the mark of honest, reasoned criticism. Rich J said:

> Any matter is a contempt which has a tendency to deflect the Court from a strict and unhesitating application of the letter of the law or, in questions of fact, from determining them exclusively by reference to the evidence. But such interferences may also arise from publications which tend *to detract from the authority and influence of judicial determinations*, publications calculated *to impair the confidence of the people in the Court's judgments* because the matter published aims at lowering the authority of the Court as a whole or that of its Judges and *excites misgivings as to the integrity, propriety and impartiality brought to the exercise of the judicial office*. The jurisdiction is not given for the purpose of protecting the Judges personally from imputations to which they may be exposed as individuals [emphasis added].[3]

If taken out of context, the words quoted may suggest a stricter rule than actually applies. The inflammatory nature of the article, the topic and the year of the decision should be borne in mind. Furthermore, the article was brought before the court by a person whose case was awaiting decision by it. She claimed that the article would *prejudice* her appeal, which involved the validity of broadcasting legislation; and that the publisher of the *Sun* had an interest in that case, because of a shareholding in the radio station 2UE.[4] The courts will, for obvious reasons, be more ready to punish a scandalizing contempt which has in it some element of prejudice to a particular case.

Later cases positively indicate what the courts will tolerate as 'honest criticism based on rational grounds of the manner in which the Court performs its functions'.[5] In *Ambard* v. *A-G for Trinidad & Tobago*,[6] decided the year after the *Dunbabin* case, the Privy Council upheld the right of the media to criticize the work of the courts. A newspaper had criticized what it saw as 'the human element' in sentencing by judges, claiming in particular that there were inconsistencies between the sentences imposed in two recent cases. Unlike the *Dunbabin* article, the

Ambard article did not include vituperation or ridicule. The Privy Council made it clear that Ambard's paper had a right to criticize the courts even if the actual criticism was ill founded. Lord Atkin said:

> The path of criticism is a public way: the wrong headed are permitted to err therein: provided that members of the public abstain from imputing improper motives to those taking part in the administration of justice, they are immune ... If criticism of decisions could only safely be made by persons who accurately knew the relevant law, who would be protected?[7]

R v. *Brett*[8] arose from an article in the Melbourne *Guardian* headed 'Mr Justice Sholl: Die-Hard Tory', denouncing the appointment of Sholl J to the bench. It said, among other things, that 'he has earned the gratitude of the notorious Holloway Government', that his main mission had been 'defending the positions of power and privilege of the wealthy', and that the judiciary was an integral part of 'the repressive machinery of the State'.

O'Bryan J said that it would have been contempt to state that the poor and uninfluential had no hope of justice from the Supreme Court because of some bias, but it was not contempt to criticize the range of persons from whom appointments were made to the bench, or to say that a judge would be influenced by his character and general outlook in his approach to a problem. Similarly, in *R* v. *Commissioner of Police*; *Ex parte Blackburn*,[9] the English Court of Appeal upheld the right of *Punch* to publish an inconsistent and even incorrect criticism of the court. *Punch* had spoken of judicial 'blindness' and said that the gambling laws had been rendered unworkable 'by the unrealistic, contradictory and, in the leading case, erroneous, decisions of the courts, including the Court of Appeal'. The court said that it would not use contempt law merely to uphold its own dignity, as freedom of speech was at stake.

A-G v. *Mundey*[10] arose from an impromptu criticism of a trial just concluded. Mundey said that the trial judge had wrongly excluded from evidence certain United Nations documents and political material which he should have considered, that there had been a miscarriage of justice, that the judge had shown himself a racist, and that there was racism throughout Australian society. He went on to speak about immigration policies and maltreatment of Aboriginals. Hope J dismissed the contempt charges brought against Mundey because of this statement. He said that Mundey's remarks about the judge being a racist should be taken in the context of his allegation of racism in most areas of Australian society: it *would* have been contempt to suggest that the particular trial judge had been actuated by a racist bias against the accused.[11] This case appears to allow stronger criticism than does *R* v. *Brett*, in which it was regarded as contemptuous to characterize the courts as biased capitalist institutions.

Allegations of Bias or Misconduct

Hope J found that Mundey was guilty of contempt because of another remark he made in the same interview. Mundey had said, in effect, that the trial judge would have sentenced the accused to gaol, but had instead only fined him because the workers had walked off their jobs to attend the trial, and because a national strike was threatened. Such a claim would wrongly suggest that the judge had been overawed, and that an accused person had not received 'ordered and fearless' justice. Hope J imposed no penalty, however, partly because the interview by television reporters who had approached Mundey as he left the courthouse was unsolicited, because Mundey had no contemptuous intention, and because those at the TV station who edited and transmitted the interview had not been charged. He pointed out that the news media transmitting an interview in that kind of situation have at least as much responsibility for contempt as the person interviewed.[12]

A decade after the *Mundey* case, Mr Norm Gallagher was sentenced to three months' gaol for remarks very similar to Mundey's. He told television reporters that the action of his union members in demonstrating and walking off jobs was the main reason that the Federal Court had 'changed its mind' so as to decide an appeal in his favour. The severity of the punishment caused much public criticism of this area of contempt law. The Federal Court pointed in its judgment to a number of factors which made the *Gallagher* case an exceptional one.[13] These included Gallagher's failure to apologize, as Mundey had done, the greater premeditation in his statement, and his public indications that any fines imposed for contempt would ultimately be paid for by employers in the building industry. The court was most concerned that an unfounded suggestion that it had been deflected from its duty by union pressure had received widespread media publicity. The High Court refused Gallagher leave to appeal against that decision. In refusing leave, the court mentioned the importance of freedom of speech, including the right of everyone to make even 'outspoken, mistaken or wrong-headed' comments about the administration of justice. But it mentioned the competing need to prevent 'baseless attacks on the integrity or impartiality of courts or judges'.[14] Applying the same approach, the Federal Court fined two people dissatisfied with a decision of the Family Court who had published a strongly-worded and illustrated brochure which portrayed the court as having bowed to wealth and influence in a custody case.[15]

Parties, Witnesses and Juries

The law of contempt protects courts, not judges. It is not contempt even to allege that a judge is corrupt or vicious if that allegation does not relate to his judicial office. Of course, anyone making such an allegation must be prepared to defend it in a defamation action.

Publications which may intimidate a litigant out of pursuing his or her legal rights are contemptuous, as well as publications intended to prejudice pending proceedings. There is no sharp dividing line between prejudicial contempt, discussed in Chapter 6, and scandalizing contempt when parties, witnesses and juries are concerned. A court may find that a publication so undermines the confidence of the public in the administration of justice that it is punishable as scandalizing contempt, quite apart from any prejudicial effect. The best example of the principle is *A-G* v. *Butterworth*,[16] a case which did not actually involve the media. An honorary union official gave evidence unfavourable to a case being put by his union to an industrial court. After the proceedings, some other members of the union condemned his conduct and attempted to remove him from office. The English Court of Appeal punished those who had attempted to remove him, saying that it was just as much contempt to intimidate or victimize a witness *after* proceedings had terminated as during them. The court made it clear that the same principle applies to jurors.

Clearly, a publication which calls for a boycott of a witness because of the testimony he or she has given, or otherwise tries to intimidate the witness through the media, is contemptuous. Juries must in principle enjoy the same protection as judges. A campaign to influence potential jurors entering court precincts against certain kinds of prosecution evidence is contempt.[17] An allegorical report of a Canadian murder trial at which the accused was convicted and sentenced to death spoke of 'the twelve people who planned the murder, and the judge who chose the time and place and caused the victim to suffer the exquisite torture of anticipation'.[18] The judge held that the court must protect jurors from such insults and ensure that juries in future trials would not be apprehensive of finding guilt where the facts required it. In another Canadian case, the court condemned a report which said that a man had been tried by a 'poisoned' jury and a 'poisoned' judge, because of the suggestion of bias on the part of the jury.[19]

Fair Comment

There are no formalized defences to charges of contempt, as there are in defamation cases. But Australian courts have repeatedly adopted a statement of Griffith CJ in *R* v. *Nicholls*.[20] He said:

> I am not prepared to accede to the proposition that an imputation of want of impartiality to a Judge is necessarily a contempt of Court. On the contrary, I think that, if any Judge of this Court or of any other Court were to make a public utterance of such character as to be likely to impair the confidence of the public, or of suitors or any class of suitors in the impartiality of the Court in any matter likely to be brought before it, any public comment on such an utterance, if it were a fair comment, would, so far from being a contempt of Court, be for the public benefit, and would be entitled to similar protection to that which comment upon matters of public interest is entitled under the law of libel.[21]

There appears to have been no Australian case in which a court has actually said that a comment would have been punished as contempt, except that the conduct of the judge was such as to merit the comment, and the *Nicholls* case itself was decided on another point. But the freedom to criticize misconduct on the bench is not in doubt.

ACCESS TO COURTS

A reporter, as a reporter, has no particular rights or privileges. He or she is not normally entitled to information, save what is open to any member of the public.[22] It is desirable for a court to provide special accommodation for the media, but they have no right to that accommodation.[23] Some space must be provided for the public, including the media, but once that space is filled, they are not entitled to more.[24]

The courts recognize a clear general principle of open justice, burdened by exceptions which vary from state to state and jurisdiction to jurisdiction. The basic principle was stated as follows in 1829 by Bayley J:

> It is one of the essential qualities of a Court of Justice that its proceedings should be public, and that all parties who may be desirous of hearing what is going on, if there be room in the place for that purpose—provided they do not interrupt the proceedings, and provided there is no specific reason why they should be removed—have a right to be present for the purpose of hearing what is going on.[25]

The need for open justice has been repeatedly emphasized, as in the famous words of Lord Atkin which begin this chapter, and in the equally famous statement of Lord Hewart that justice should not only be done but should 'manifestly and undoubtedly be seen to be done'.[26] Lord Diplock expressed the publicity principle as follows in *A-G* v. *Leveller Magazine*:

> If the way judges behave cannot be hidden from the public ear and eye this provides a safeguard against judicial arbitrariness or idiosyncrasy and maintains the public confidence in the administration of justice. The application of this principle of open justice has two aspects: as respects proceedings in the court itself it requires that they should be held in open court to which the Press and public are admitted and that, in criminal cases at any rate, all evidence communicated to the court is communicated publicly. As respects the publication to a wider public of fair and accurate reports of proceedings that have taken place in court the principle requires that nothing should be done to discourage this.[27]

In *Scott* v. *Scott*,[28] the House of Lords held that the public can be excluded only if it can be shown that by nothing short of their exclusion can justice be done. The recognized examples which meet this strict test are cases concerned with trade secrets, the very subject matter of which would be destroyed by an open hearing, and cases where there is such a justified fear of tumult or disorder that justice cannot be done without exclusion of the public. *Scott* v. *Scott* clearly establishes that a court cannot be closed just to save witnesses or parties from embarrassment or ridicule.[29] That is important on the frequent occasions when prominent people involved in litigation seek to avoid publicity. The other common law exceptions to the open justice principle are cases involving the affairs of wards of court and lunatics. The fact that a case has legitimately been heard in private does not mean that nothing may ever be known of it. A court is required to make public the judgment and orders arising from such a case so far as that can be done without disclosing confidential material.[30] The open justice principle does not apply to matters heard in chambers, usually administrative matters or procedural or non-contentious aspects of a case. The final hearing of a civil action or suit or criminal prosecution is very rarely heard in chambers. The public, including the media, are not entitled to observe proceedings in chambers. The law about reporting what happens there is unclear.[31] It is not necessarily contempt to publish what happens there, but it is certainly dangerous; not least because a media report will necessarily be second-hand.

The most important exceptions to the open justice principle have been those imposed by Acts of parliament in courts dispensing family law and in children's courts. Both deal with universal human problems of interest to the media. At one time, these courts were generally closed. However, the current trend is towards opening them to some extent but preventing the media from identifying parties and witnesses in the cases. The Family Court is an open court now, but s. 121 of the *Family Law Act* 1975 prevents the media from identifying parties, their families, or witnesses whether by name, address, description, photograph, film, sound broadcast or in any other way. Children's courts are still usually closed throughout Australia.[32] In South Australia, however, representatives of the news media may be present at a trial in the Children's Court. They may, unless the court otherwise orders, publish a brief summary of the circumstances of an offence for which a child is sentenced, without identifying the child in any way; and in Victoria a children's court is open, subject to a power to restrict publicity. The Australian Law Reform Commission has recommended that the media should have a right of access to proceedings in the ACT Children's Court, and a right to report proceedings provided the child is not identified.[33] This new approach seems likely to be accepted throughout Australia before long.

RESTRICTIONS ON PUBLICATION

Even if a court is sitting in public, the judge or magistrate may sometimes prohibit reporting of the proceedings, or of part of them. That is sometimes a lesser evil than closing a court altogether. But there is doubt about whether courts have inherent power, not conferred by Act of parliament, to prohibit publication of the names of parties or witnesses, especially in the absence of some compelling reason for secrecy.[34] The prospect of harm or distress to personal or business reputation will rarely, if ever, provide a sufficient cause for a court to suppress the name of a person involved in a case.[35] It is otherwise where there is some more specific reason, connected with the administration of justice, for concealing identity. For example, a court has inherent power to prevent publication of the name of a blackmail victim in proceedings against the blackmailer.[36] Otherwise, the proceedings would fulfil the blackmailer's threat of public exposure of the victim. Similarly, a ward of court can be protected from identification in the media.[37]

Three states and the ACT confer a power on their courts to prohibit publication of evidence or of material which may identify those involved in their proceedings. In South Australia, the power can be exercised only in the interests of justice or to prevent undue prejudice or hardship and its exercise must be reported to the Attorney-General.[38] A Tasmanian court may prohibit publication of material in a case before it only to avoid prejudice to that case.[39] A Victorian court may pronounce it improper to publish any part of its proceedings until they have concluded.[40] If the court does so, it is an offence to publish. An ACT court may restrict publication of its proceedings 'in the interests of justice'.[41]

For an order suppressing identity to bind the media, it must normally be clearly expressed to do so. *A-G* v. *Leveller Magazine*[42] arose from acceptance by magistrates of a request that a witness in an official secrets case be referred to as Colonel 'B'. They gave no direction to the press not to publish his real name. From evidence which the colonel gave under cross-examination, without any objection by the crown or the magistrates, it was possible to deduce what his real name was. The House of Lords overturned the contempt convictions of magazines which had published it. The basis for that decision appears to have been that the magistrates had appeared to accept revelation of the colonel's identity during the case. Had they not done so, it could have been contempt to publish the name.

One of the situations in which courts have inherent power to ban disclosure of identity is where a witness such as a police informer will be in danger of retaliation or violence.[43] However, courts are most unlikely to suppress media publication in a situation where the danger is not clearly demonstrated, or where disclosure in an open hearing will have already created the danger. This is illustrated by *Fairfax* v. *Police Tribunal of NSW*, a case in which the NSW Court of Appeal invalidated orders of the police tribunal restricting media publication of the name of a witness.[44] The court pointed out that anyone attending the tribunal hearing would have been able to learn that the witness was alleged to be an informer, so that there was little protection to be conferred by preventing the media from republishing the allegation. Furthermore, the order of the tribunal had prevented *any* publication of the name of the witness. Assuming that the power to suppress the name existed, it could have extended only so far as a publication in a context which would link the witness with the tribunal inquiry or the informer allegation. This was one of the recent cases in which the role which the media can play in reporting the proceedings of courts to the public has been recognized. Fairfax was a newspaper publisher, with no interest in the police tribunal inquiry other than the wish to publish what occurred there. It was not in any sense a party to the inquiry. Nevertheless, the court recognized the right of Fairfax to take the restrictive order to court and have it invalidated.

Sometimes, it is so clear from circumstances that part of the proceedings is not to be reported that it is contempt to publish, even in the absence of any statement from the presiding judge or magistrate. If the judge or magistrate is obviously maintaining confidentiality inside the courtroom, it is contempt to destroy that confidentiality by some publication outside.[45] Often, the jury are sent out of the courtroom while there is a 'trial within a trial' about the admissibility of evidence, or some other matter which could prejudice their minds. Although the court remains open at such a time, it is contempt to publish that matter until the jury have completed their task.[46] It is contempt to publicize a payment into court by a defendant, since the jury may take that to be an admission of liability, which it is not.[47]

On a number of occasions in the 1980s, accounts of what had been discussed and decided in the jury room were published by the media after a celebrated trial. Examples were the trials of Lindy Chamberlain for murder, of Murphy J for conspiracy, and of Norm Gallagher for fraud. On occasions, there was virtually a radio debate between one school of thought and another among the former jurors. There has been a reaction against that kind of disclosure, because of the perceived damage to the jury system, particularly having regard to protection of jurors who wish to remain anonymous and do not wish to be forced to defend their decisions in public.[48] That reaction has led to some new laws being passed to protect the secrets of the jury room,[49] with the likelihood of more such laws to come. For example, a new Victorian law makes it an offence to publish, solicit or obtain statements about jury deliberations.[50] Unless or until such a law is enacted in the state or territory where a trial is held, it appears that it is not unlawful to publish jury room secrets, provided that the publication is not one which would intimidate or ridicule the jurors.[51]

Most permissible reports of cases will consist of summaries of what was actually said in the course of the proceedings. Apart from the exceptions already mentioned, everything which occurs in the court while it is hearing a case may be reported, including disruptions and incidents, 'so long as the incident arises out of, and is substantially connected with, the matter which the court is investigating, whether it is technically part of it or not'.[52] In the case from which those words are quoted, for example, the court held headlines like '"Dirty Mongrel" Is Father's Cry' and '"Hope He Burns" Cries Father of Dead Child' were permissible, as were reports of a demonstration against the suspected murderer in the precincts of a Coroner's Court. Defamation law may be less tolerant of reports about statements and events which are only incidental to a case.[53] No privilege attaches to writs, statements of claim or defence, answers to interrogatories, or other documents which are not actually read out in the course of the proceedings.[54] Even when all or part of a document has been read out, it is not always safe to report from a copy supplied by one of the parties, as opposed to notes taken in court by the reporter in person, or the official transcript of proceedings.[55]

Principles similar to those discussed above can apply to statutory tribunals. They will do so to the extent that an Act of parliament adopts the 'open justice' principle which applies to the courts or empowers a tribunal to restrict reporting. For example, s. 106 of the Trade Practices Act says that the Trade Practices Tribunal shall hold inquiries in public, although it does have power to exclude the public, and may restrict the publication of evidence or documents. The Administrative Appeals Tribunal and Broadcasting Tribunal are also required to sit in public, unless satisfied that there are reasons for doing otherwise, or for restricting publication of evidence or documents.[56]

FAIR AND ACCURATE REPORTS

One application of the open justice principle is to allow 'fair and accurate' reporting of what takes place in an open court, as explained by Jordan CJ in *Ex parte Terrill; Re Consolidated Press Ltd*:

Not all the public can obtain admission to the public sittings of the Courts, and therefore those who do are at liberty to communicate to the public generally an account of the proceedings which they have witnessed. So long as any account so published is fair and accurate and is published in good faith and without malice no one can complain that its publication is defamatory of him notwithstanding that it may in fact have injured his reputation, and no one can in general be heard to say that it is a contempt of Court notwithstanding that it may in fact be likely to create prejudice against a party to civil or criminal litigation. This applies to preliminary inquiries by a magistrate where such inquiries are held in open Court ... In these respects there is an analogy between the law of contempt and the law of libel ...[57]

The danger of liability for defamation arising from an inaccurate or distorted account of proceedings in a court has already been mentioned in Chapter 3. Although defamation and contempt law make essentially the same demand, the contempt law is judge-made and uniform throughout Australia. The right to report proceedings is a major exception to the strict prohibition which the law otherwise imposes on material which may affect the mind of a jury. The freedom to report preliminary or committal proceedings at which a magistrate determines whether a person should stand trial before a jury means that a good deal of prejudicial material, including prosecution evidence which the crown would not be allowed to place before a jury, is published in the media; although magistrates at committal hearings usually do have statutory power to exclude the public so as to avoid severe prejudice.

A person facing prosecution for different offences in two or more trials faces the prospect of having evidence at the first trial published before or during the second or subsequent trials.[58] When a person is facing trial, however, the media may not dig up reports of old proceedings which could prejudice the pending trial. To be protected, a report must be *contemporaneous*.[59] Thus, the Melbourne *Truth* was fined for contempt when it published a lurid and prejudicial article (which it claimed to be a report of a man's committal proceedings) about a year after those proceedings had concluded, but only about two weeks before his trial.[60]

Some journalists wrongly believe that anything said in open court is thereafter in some kind of 'public domain', quotable in any context. That is a dangerous belief. Jordan CJ explained in *Ex parte Terrill* that 'fairness and accuracy' mean freedom from bias.[61] A fair summary of proceedings is protected as much as a *verbatim* account. That is important for radio and television, which may have to summarize proceedings in less than sixty seconds. It is not necessary to apply the technical knowledge or skills of a lawyer in compiling the summary; something representing the work of 'a person of ordinary intelligence using reasonable care' is sufficient.[62] The report loses protection if it is partial, if it represents that something occurred when it did not, or if it withholds facts which put a different complexion on facts which are truly reported.[63] If these requirements are met, it is permissible to report proceedings as a prominent news item instead of as a dry law report, and to feature some aspect of a case which was not given prominence before the judge or magistrate.[64]

The principles are illustrated by a report found to be contemptuous in *Minister for Justice* v. *West Australian Newspapers Ltd*.[65] A youth was charged with murder, and also with several breaking and entering offences and offences involving cars. While the murder trial was pending, the *Daily News* published a substantially accurate account of proceedings related to the other offences headed: 'Youth on Murder Charge Gaoled on Car Counts'. It focused attention on the charge of stealing a rifle and ammunition. A footnote on the same page said that the murder victim had been shot through the heart. The court held that it was permissible to report the proceedings, but that the report was unfair and contemptuous, because the headline referred to the pending murder charges, the text selectively reported the evidence which pointed to a connection with the murder charge, and the footnote drew a similar connection.

PARLIAMENTS

Freedom of speech in the federal and state parliaments is absolute, controlled only by the parliaments and not by courts. This freedom of speech is particularly important in a country such as Australia, the defamation laws of which often make it dangerous to expose corruption in any other forum. As mentioned in Chapter 3, defamation law allows the media the 'privilege' of publishing fair and accurate reports of parliamentary proceedings. The privilege is almost identical with the privilege of reporting the courts. That was made clear by Cockburn CJ in *Wason* v. *Walter*, the case which established the privilege, when he said:

> It is to be observed that the analogy between the case of reports of proceedings in courts of justice and those of proceedings in Parliament being complete, all the limitations placed on the one to prevent injustice to individuals will necessarily attach to the other. A garbled or partial report, or of detached

parts of proceedings, published with intent to injure individuals, will equally be disentitled to protection.[66]

A brief impression of the highlights of a parliamentary debate is permissible, but the privilege will be lost if, for example, it reports accusations made against a person without mentioning what was said in reply to them.[67]

The ABC has the special duty of reporting proceedings of the federal parliament under the *Parliamentary Proceedings Broadcasting Act* 1946. Parliament itself determines the days and periods of the broadcasts, and the allocation of time between the House and the Senate, through its Parliamentary Joint Committee on the Broadcasting of Parliamentary Proceedings. Section 14 of the Act relieves broadcasts under it from any legal liability, for defamation or otherwise.

In the Colonel 'B' affair mentioned earlier in this chapter, some members of parliament disclosed the colonel's real name in the House of Commons. *The Times* reported their speeches, including the name.[68] That raised the interesting question of whether a fair and accurate report of proceedings in parliament could ever be in contempt of court; but the question did not come before a court. It remains unresolved. In Australian parliaments, the Speakers sometimes prevent members from making statements which could prejudice *sub judice* proceedings in a court, but at other times they appear to let political importance take priority over the risk of prejudice.[69]

Defamation by an unfair or inaccurate report is not the only danger associated with reporting parliaments. There is also the danger of contempt of parliament,[70] which is similar to the contempt of court law discussed above. In practice, the publications which pose the greatest danger of contempt of parliament are those which may be regarded as exerting improper pressure on members of parliament, as bringing the institution itself into disrespect, or as disclosing the secret proceedings of parliamentary committees.

Four examples involving the federal parliament illustrate these categories. The 1955 *Fitzpatrick and Browne* case arose from articles in the *Bankstown Observer* which alleged that Morgan, a member of the House of Representatives, was engaged in an immigration racket. Fitzpatrick, the publisher, and Browne, the journalist who wrote the article, were called before the Privileges Committee of the House, to which they admitted that the article had been published to dissuade Morgan from raising certain matters in the House. This might be compared with an article which intimidates a party or witness in a court case. On the recommendation of the Privileges Committee, the House committed Fitzpatrick and Browne to three months' imprisonment in Goulburn gaol. They challenged the power of the House to do so in the High Court, but the court held that where the House or the Senate framed its writ against a person in sufficiently broad terms, no court could interfere with the exercise of such a power.[71]

The 1981 *Oakes and Wylie* case was about lowering respect for the institution of parliament. The rather exaggerated headings and 'pointer' on an issue of the *Daily Mirror* said:

MPs BLUDGERS, DRUNKS! It's not all hard work and stress for Australia's federal members of Parliament. Many have little or nothing to do other than to sit around the members' bar, boozing and whingeing. Today, on page 9, Australia's top political commentator Laurie Oakes reveals the truth about the drunks and bludgers on Canberra's back benches.

The article itself said, among other things, that 'the Parliamentarians with reputations as drunks and those regarded as workers are two quite separate groups'. The committee found that the headings and article were both in contempt, but that the matter was not worthy of occupying the time of the House any further.[72] Its report also repeated earlier calls for urgent reform of this area of law.

An example of reporting confidential material was the *Walsh and Rothwell* case of 1971. Both the *Sunday Review* and the *Sunday Australian* published some of the contents of a Senate committee report on drugs before it had been presented to the Senate. The Senate Privileges Committee noted that publication of any such leak was contemptuous, as was publication of the proceedings or evidence of a committee meeting behind closed doors.[73] Walsh and Rothwell, the editors of the respective papers, both apologized. They were called before the bar of the Senate and formally reprimanded.[74] In 1984, the *National Times* published evidence and proceedings of confidential sessions of a Senate committee which was inquiring into allegations of misbehaviour made against Murphy J. The Senate committee produced a report which found that this was a serious contempt of parliament.[75]

The scope of the offence of contempt of parliament by the media varies between jurisdictions. The federal, Victorian and South Australian constitutions confer on their parliaments the same powers in this area as were enjoyed by the House of Commons in England at the time when the respective constitutions were passed.[76] These somewhat ancient powers include the power to imprison offenders. It appears that the three parliaments do not have power to impose fines for these offences. Queensland, Western Australia and Tasmania also give their parliaments statutory power to punish for contempts committed outside their walls; but they limit that power to specified offences. Most of the offences specified are not relevant to the media, although it is an offence to endeavour to compel a member by insult or menace to declare himself in favour of or against any proposition or matter expected to be brought before the House.[77] The New South Wales parliament has not conferred on itself the power to punish for contemptuous publications made outside its walls, although it does, like all the other Australian parliaments, have an inherent power to exclude representatives of offending media from its precincts.

For many years there has been concern and discussion about the need to clarify and confine the operation of contempt of parliament principles in the federal sphere. In 1984, a joint committee chaired by Mr J Spender produced a comprehensive report on this area, with specific proposals for reform.[78] The recommendations in the report were not radical, but they would have prevented the media from facing jeopardy for publications which did no more than defame the institution of parliament. The Bill proposed by the committee would also have confirmed the power of the parliament to punish unauthorized disclosures of evidence taken in private or premature publication of reports. The power to impose fines was to be confirmed, in addition to the power to imprison offenders. The parliament was to retain the power to punish offences against itself, but there were to be improved procedures with greater opportunity for those accused to defend themselves, and some limited opportunity for review of contempt findings by the High Court. A Bill introduced but not passed in 1986 would have implemented some of these recommendations, as well as reaffirming the traditional exclusion of the courts from questioning what was said or done in parliament.[79]

8

OBSCENITY, BLASPHEMY AND SEDITION

Michael Blakeney

For hundreds of years, laws have prohibited blasphemy, obscenity and sedition.[1] The promulgation and enforcement of these laws was originally in the hands of the church. Not surprisingly, given their origins, they presuppose the inherent moral weakness of the human vessel. The use of the church courts by Archbishop Laud to attack the political opponents of Charles I resulted in their abolition by the victorious Puritans. Despite the secularization of the laws, an ecclesiastical flavour permeates their administration. Ultimately, as was perceived by Archbishop Laud, it is probably true to say that blasphemy, obscenity and sedition are all political offences in that they are considered to be destructive of society.

No evidence, beyond vague references to the excesses of Rome in its decline, has ever proved the damage caused by these offences. The courts are placed in the difficult position of having to predict whether other people might be harmed by the material before them. The assumption of human frailty would seem to be indispensable before an accused person can be found guilty. Changing moral attitudes make prediction of future results difficult. A general decline in religious observance, sexual modesty and, it is hoped, jingoism, means that most people found guilty of these offences in earlier times would probably be acquitted today. Prosecutions, however, still sometimes occur.

BLASPHEMY

The crime of blasphemous libel is committed when a publication vilifies the Christian religion, the Bible, the Book of Common Prayer, or God. Originally, the crime included the denial of the existence of God or divine providence, but the House of

Lords in 1917 declared that irreligious utterances were not in themselves punishable unless they had a tendency 'to endanger the peace then and there, to deprave public morality generally, to shake the fabric of society, and to be a cause of civil strife'.[2]

Reflecting a similar tolerance, s. 574 of the New South Wales Crimes Act says that no person is guilty of blasphemy if the publication complained of 'is by way of argument or statement and not for the purpose of scoffing or reviling, nor of violating public decency, nor in any manner tending to be a breach of the peace'. Section 119(3) of the Tasmanian Criminal Code declares that it is not blasphemy for a person 'to express in good faith and in decent language, or to attempt to establish by argument used in good faith and conveyed in decent language, any opinion whatsoever upon any religious subject'.

Although blasphemy is a crime in Australia, and is extended to the electronic media by s. 118 of the Broadcasting and Television Act, there have apparently been no prosecutions. In England, there were only four prosecutions in the 120 years before 1976. In 1922, a man was prosecuted for a statement in a pamphlet comparing Christ's entry into Jerusalem with 'a circus clown on the back of two donkeys',[3] and in Jersey, in 1940, a man was sentenced to gaol for two months for doodling on his passport photograph so as to turn it into a representation of the crucifixion.[4] Following the European Cup Winners' victory of Tottenham Hotspur in 1963, the UK Home Secretary declined to prosecute for blasphemy three men who accompanied the team in their triumph through North London regaled in the robes of priests and carrying placards saying 'They Shall Reign for Ever', 'Hallowed be Their Names' and 'Adore Them for They are Glorious'. Although fourteen Tottenham clergymen petitioned for a prosecution, the Home Secretary declined to act because he did not believe that a prosecution would succeed in court.[5]

Until 1976, official reluctance to bring blasphemy prosecutions made the offence almost irrelevant for the media. But in that year Mrs Mary Whitehouse successfully obtained permission to prosecute *Gay News* and its editor for publishing a poem and cartoon suggesting that Christ was a promiscuous, practising homosexual. *Gay News* was fined £1000 and the editor was sentenced to nine months' imprisonment, suspended for two years, and fined £500. The House of Lords dismissed the editor's appeal that he had not intended to publish a blasphemous libel, explaining that the offence was demonstrated 'by proof only of intention to publish material which in the opinion of the jury is likely to shock and arouse resentment among believing Christians'.[6] In an era when privately appointed watchdogs of community morals have become vociferous, the *Gay News* prosecution may have significant implications.

OBSCENITY

The classic definition of obscenity is that of Cockburn CJ in *R v. Hicklin*:

> I think the test of obscenity is this, whether the tendency of the matter charged as obscene is to deprave and corrupt those whose minds are open to such immoral influences, and into whose hands a publication of this sort may fall.[7]

This Hicklin test has been incorporated into numerous statutory definitions of obscenity in Australia, but it has caused more problems than it has solved. Material has been found to be obscene even though having no influence on the relevant vice squad or jury who have given it the closest scrutiny.[8]

In *R v. Close*, Fullagar J in the Supreme Court of Victoria suggested that 'obscene in its ordinary sense denotes something which is indecent or disgusting ... which offends against good taste or decency'.[9] This approach was endorsed by the High Court in *Crowe v. Graham*, in which Windeyer J observed:

> Courts have not in fact asked first whether the tendency of a publication is to deprave or corrupt. They have asked simply whether it transgresses the bounds of decency and is properly called obscene. If so, its evil tendency and intent is taken to be apparent.[10]

As *Crowe v. Graham* recognized, the obscenity of a publication or broadcast depends on its 'setting and circumstances'. Mass media will be judged by the modesty of the average member of the public. In considering, for example, whether language in the play 'Norm and Ahmed' was obscene when performed in a Brisbane playhouse, Stable J said: 'We are concerned with the contemporary standards which ordinary decent-minded people accept'.[11] The use of community standards as the touchstone of obscenity has been reiterated in decisions of the Supreme Courts of South Australia[12] and Western Australia.[13] Probably the best summary of the position established by the High Court in *Crowe v. Graham* is that of Bray CJ in the South Australian decision, *Romeyko v. Samuels*.[14] He took the High Court to have established that indecency and obscenity were synonymous and that the test of indecency was whether the matter complained of was offensive, to a substantial degree, to the contemporary standards of the Australian community; and whether it had that character in the context of the publication as a whole.[15]

When a medium is addressed to a limited section of the community, the propensity to be obscene is determined by the standard of that limited section. In some Australian cases, for example, courts have accepted that university students are less likely to be offended by material published in university newspapers than the general public would be.[16] On the other side of the coin are sections of the community considered to be particularly sensitive to obscene material. A 'School Kids Issue' of *Oz* magazine was successfully prosecuted. Its explicit and allegedly grotesque depiction and discussion of sex was considered offensive to the audience of school children for which it was intended.[17]

These decisions seem to suggest that a pornographic subscription TV service would not be obscene because the subscribers would not easily be offended. The House of Lords has ruled, however, that already depraved people can be further corrupted, and it upheld the conviction of people who sold 'hard core' pornography to selected customers.[18] In two cases involving the publication of advertisements for female[19] and male[20] prostitutes, the House of Lords held not only that the publications were obscene, but that the publishers were guilty of conspiracy with the prostitutes:

> to induce readers to resort to the said advertisers for the purpose of fornication and of taking part in or witnessing other disgusting and immoral acts and exhibitions, with intent thereby to debauch the morals as well of youth and divers other liege subjects of Our Lady the Queen and to raise and create in their minds inordinate and lustful desires.[21]

Print Media Legislation

In addition to the common law of obscenity, laws in each state and territory prohibit the publication or circulation of indecent or obscene matter.[22] The laws generally define indecent and obscene publications as those which tend to deprave and corrupt people whose minds are open to immoral influences, and those which 'unduly emphasise matters of sex, crimes of violence, gross cruelty or horror'. In some states, literary, artistic or bona fide medical or scientific works are exempt;[23] in others, such works may be exonerated if they display literary or other merit.[24]

Superimposed on these prohibitions of obscene or indecent

publications is a system of classification which allows the limited display and sale to adults of certain marginally obscene publications.[25] The relevant Acts generally require that those publications be kept out of view of the public, or that they be available only on a request made by an adult.

Imported printed works are subject to a system of censorship established under the federal Customs Act.[26] Regulation 4A(2) of the *Customs (Prohibited Imports) Regulations* prohibits the importation of goods which are 'blasphemous, indecent or obscene' or which 'unduly emphasise matters of sex, horror, violence or crime, or are likely to encourage depravity'. It also prohibits advertising matter related to such goods. The *Customs (National Literature Board of Review) Regulations* establish the National Literature Board of Review which may, when called upon, advise the Minister for Customs whether a publication falls within the prohibited category. A work may be refused importation, or allowed into Australia subject to conditions restricting distribution. The minister is not obliged to refer a publication to the board, or to follow its advice. Among books prohibited in the past, following review by the board, were *Fanny Hill*, *Myra Breckenridge* and *Portnoy's Complaint*, but many such books have been allowed into Australia following reviews by the board. After negotiations, the states agreed with the federal government some years ago not to prosecute for obscenity books allowed into the country under the customs regulations, which do not have any legal application to locally printed books.

Radio and TV Legislation

Under s. 118 of the *Broadcasting and Television Act* 1942, it is an offence to broadcast or prepare for broadcasting 'blasphemous, indecent or obscene matter', thus adopting the common law definitions of those offences. The considerable and various powers of the Broadcasting Tribunal to censor radio and television are discussed in Chapter 9. The tribunal is particularly concerned with blasphemy and obscenity through s. 119, which allows it to suspend from broadcasting the people responsible for broadcasts which may have given offence to a section of the public.

The tribunal has the power to cancel or restrict the grant of a radio or television station licence where there has been a contravention of s. 118. It has taken the view that it should use that power to punish obscenity. In 1982 it renewed the licence of the radio station 4ZZZ-FM (Brisbane) for two years instead of the usual three because the station had broadcast a number of items which the tribunal considered obscene.

In giving its reasons for shortening the renewal period, the tribunal laid down for future reference the principles which it would apply in interpreting s. 118 and in using its other powers:

(a) In a consideration of s. 118 the test of obscenity is the same as the test of indecency.
(b) The test of indecency (obscenity), pursuant to s. 118 of the Act, is whether the matter in question offends to a substantial degree the sexual modesty of the average man or woman in the Australian community or offends to a substantial degree the contemporary standards of decency currently accepted by the Australian community.
(c) It is the standards applicable in the Australian community at the time of the broadcast or telecast that must be applied and not the standards of some past age or era.
(d) It is the standards for the whole community that must be applied and not the standards of groups or classes within the community to whom broadcast or telecast of the matter is intended or likely. However, the standards do not include special susceptibilities over and above those of the average member of the community.
(e) All the circumstances and the setting of the broadcast or telecast must be considered. The fact that a matter had a restricted publication, and the classes of persons and the ages of those persons to whom (the) broadcast or telecast is made or likely, are relevant circumstances.
(f) The words complained of must be looked at in the context of the broadcast or telecast as a whole. For example, was their use accidental or deliberate? Was it a gratuitous use or a deliberate use as part of a serious presentation of a matter of artistic or literary merit, or a social or moral issue?
(g) The influence and pervasiveness of the broadcast medium concerned must be taken into account as a relevant factor. As the material discussed previously illustrates, this will vary in degree depending on the medium. In the Tribunal's view, in the context of the broadcast media, commercial television has the greatest degree of influence and pervasiveness and public broadcasting (i.e. public radio) the least. Consequently contemporary community standards are likely to be more liberal as they apply to public broadcasting than as they apply to commercial television but less liberal for commercial broadcasting than public broadcasting.
(h) There is no absolute ban on the broadcast or telecast of particular language. However, for practical purposes, without setting out an exhaustive list, the following factors are likely to be relevant in a consideration of whether the broadcast or telecast of language substantially offends contemporary community standards of decency and is indecent or obscene pursuant to s. 118:
   (i) The broadcast medium involved—television (commercial or ABC), radio (commercial, ABC or public) and the nature of the broadcast market in which the station is located.
   (ii) The nature of the language broadcast or telecast.
   (iii) The nature of the broadcast or telecast as a whole. Was the use of

the language in context? Was it gratuitous? Was it deliberate? What was the overall purpose of the broadcast or telecast? Did it involve a serious matter of artistic or literary merit? Did it involve a serious discussion or presentation of some moral or social issue?
(iv) The time at which the broadcast or telecast was made.
(v) The probable demographic composition and size of the audience of the broadcast or telecast. Will a significant number of children or young people be included in that audience?
(vi) Were warnings and other precautions taken regarding the broadcast or telecast and if so the nature and likely effectiveness of those measures.
(i) The Tribunal does not believe that the use of words such as 'fuck' and 'cunt' on commercial television would be acceptable to current contemporary community standards of decency unless very exceptional circumstances were applicable ...[27]

Apart from the legal requirements of the tribunal, the Federation of Australian Radio Broadcasters (FARB) and the Federation of Australian Commercial TV Stations (FACTS) operate private schemes of censorship for commercial radio and TV advertisements, as outlined in Chapter 12. The schemes are designed to avoid contravention of the legal requirements, and also to ensure that 'taste and decency' are observed, especially in references to sex.

Other Media

The Film Censorship Board, established under the *Customs (Cinematograph Films) Regulations*, controls obscenity in films. Imported films will not be cleared by Customs until approved by the board. If the board considers that a film is 'blasphemous, indecent or obscene' or 'likely to be injurious to morality', or if it depicts 'any matter, the exhibition of which is undesirable in the public interest', it will not be approved by the board.[28]

Under arrangements with the states, the board also classifies all films for exhibition, whether they are made locally or imported, into the familiar categories of (G), (NRC), (M) and (R). In performing its role, the board particularly restricts violent material, as well as sexual material. The Cinematograph Films Board of Review hears appeals from decisions of the board. Apart from imported films, the Film Censorship Board classifies films intended for television in accordance with the Programme Standards made by the Broadcasting Tribunal, namely: 'Unrestricted for TV' (G); 'Parental Guidance Recommended' (PGR); 'Suitable only for Adults' (AO); or 'Not Suitable for TV'. The federal *Postal Service Regulations* prohibit a person from knowingly sending by post or courier an article containing indecent, obscene or offensive matter, or advertisements for it; and the federal *Telecommunications Regulations* prohibit transmission of similar matter by telephone, telex or other telecommunications services.

SEDITION

In political turmoils dating back to the seventeenth century in England, prosecutions for sedition have been used to intimidate critics of the government. In *R* v. *Tutchin*,[29] a critic of corruption in the ministry of Queen Anne and of its management of the navy was sentenced to seven years' imprisonment, with a whipping every fortnight for the duration of that sentence. Lord Chief Justice Holt explained:

> If people should not be called to account for possessing the people with an ill opinion of the government, no government can subsist. For it is very necessary for all governments that the people should have a good opinion of it. And nothing can be worse to any government, than to endeavour to procure animosities as to the management of it; this has been always looked upon as a crime and no government can be safe without it be punished.[30]

Since *Tutchin*'s case was decided, prosecutions for sedition in England have become rare. There have been no successful prosecutions in that country for over a hundred years. The last case involved the unsuccessful prosecution in 1947 of the editor of the *Morecambe and Heysham Visitor* for publishing an article attacking British Jews for tacit support of outrages against British troops in Palestine.[31] The article said of the Jews that violence may be the only way to bring them to the sense of their responsibility to the country in which they live. Birkett J in his direction to the jury said:

> You will recollect how valuable a blessing the liberty of the Press is to all of us, and I am sure that that liberty will meet no injury—suffer no diminution at your hands.

The editor was acquitted.

There has been less tolerance in Australia. The targets have been more the people whose statements the media report than the media themselves. The High Court has upheld three convictions for sedition in the last thirty-five years.[32] Under s. 24D of the federal *Crimes Act* 1914, a maximum penalty of three years' imprisonment may be imposed on 'any person who writes, prints, utters or publishes any seditious words'. 'Seditious words' are those which express an intent, among other things, 'to bring the Sovereign into hatred or contempt', 'to excite disaffection against Government or Constitution of the Commonwealth or against either House of the Parliament of the Commonwealth', and 'to promote feelings of ill-will and hostility between different classes of Her Majesty's subjects so as to endanger the peace, order or good government of the Commonwealth'. Exemptions from those prohibitions are listed in s. 24F, including endeavouring in good faith to show that an Australian or foreign government is mistaken in any of its policies, counsels or actions; pointing out defects in legislation or the administration of justice, with a view to reform; and doing anything in good faith in connection with an industrial dispute. In New South Wales, Victoria and South Australia, the common law of sedition applies; but Queensland, Western Australia and Tasmania are like the commonwealth in having made sedition a specific statutory offence.[33]

In *Burns* v. *Ransley*,[34] decided in 1949, the High Court convicted a member of the Communist Party who, in answer to a question at a public meeting, said that in event of a war between the Soviet Union and the Western powers, the party would 'fight on the side of Soviet Russia'. Six months after this case, Lawrence Sharkey, the secretary of the Communist Party, was telephoned by a *Daily Telegraph* reporter for a statement about what policy the party would adopt if Australia were invaded by 'communist forces'. Sharkey was convicted for saying to the reporter that in the hypothetical event of an invasion by communist forces, Australian communists would welcome the invaders if they were 'resisting aggression'.

In these cases, the High Court declined to adopt a distinction which had been drawn by the United States Supreme Court between 'agitation and exhortation calling for present violent action which creates a clear and present danger of public disorder' on the one hand, and on the other hand permissible 'doctrinal justification or prediction of the use of force under hypothetical conditions at some indefinite future'.[35] In *Cooper* v. *The Queen*,[36] decided in 1961, the High Court sustained the conviction of a man whose exhortations were more immediate and violent. He had exhorted some New Guineans to gain self-government by tying up the local police officer, breaking into the stores for rifles and other goods, expelling white people, blockading the airstrip and looking to 'the Russians' for help.

It is probable that the 1949 prosecutions were inspired by the post-war anti-communist fears of United States origin, but the point has been made that 'other fears could lead to similar decisions'.[37] Certainly, the law of sedition is always available to unscrupulous political leaders who wish to create or deepen divisions in the community for their own partisan advantage.

9
RADIO AND TELEVISION
Mark Armstrong

Radio and television law involves a complex structure of intersecting legal rules and institutions. There are two main reasons for this complexity. The first reason is that radio and television, like other users of the radio spectrum, depend on government planning for their existence. Without regulation of natural resources like the airwaves, newspapers and magazines could still be printed, goods could still be manufactured, and transport systems could still run. But the potential for technical interference in use of the airwaves is so great that planning is the necessary basis for radio and television. The second reason for complexity is the more important one, however. That is the extreme political sensitivity of rules limiting the control of major media, especially television. The laws reflect many attempts over the years to balance competing commercial and political forces, whilst at the same time attempting to provide at least some protection for the public interest. Given the nature of this process, it is little wonder that the result is complicated and sometimes inconsistent. This chapter outlines the laws which have the most direct impact on programmes and the services provided to the public. The more complex laws relating to licensing and ownership of stations are discussed in more specialized books.[1] They are only summarized here. To understand even the basic laws it is necessary to remember that there are four different sectors of the broadcasting system:

the *commercial broadcasting services*;
the *public broadcasting services*;
the *national broadcasting service* of the ABC; and
the *special [multicultural] broadcasting service*.

As the law is made by the federal parliament rather than by state parliaments, only one Act, the *Broadcasting Act* 1942, needs to be consulted on most points, although a separate *Australian Broadcasting Corporation Act* 1983 governs the ABC. Other federal Acts, considered in earlier chapters, such as the Copyright Act and the Trade Practices Act, apply to all media, including radio and television. In the rest of this chapter, references to sections or to 'the Act' refer to the federal *Broadcasting Act* 1942 unless otherwise stated. The term 'broadcasting' is used to refer generically to both radio and television, although for historical reasons some official sources still use 'broadcasting' to refer to radio only. The Act is not an exclusive code covering all aspects of radio and television programmes. It says nothing, for example, about contempt of court and virtually nothing about defamation. So a defamatory broadcast will be governed by the relevant state law.

Among other things, the Act establishes the Australian Broadcasting Tribunal. Contrary to a common misconception, the tribunal is not responsible for administration of the Act: that responsibility belongs to the Minister for Communications. The Act does give the tribunal a pervasive role in commercial and public broadcasting, but virtually no role in ABC and SBS broadcasting. The tribunal grants licences for commercial and public stations. It also decides on renewal, suspension and revocation of those licences, and on changes in the control and ownership of the licensees (the corporations which hold the licences). It also has a responsibility to assemble and make available information about broadcasting,[2] and to inquire into matters referred to it by the minister. It also determines standards for programmes and advertisements. Of more everyday concern to broadcasters, the tribunal now holds a somewhat miscellaneous collection of powers over programmes and advertisements. The tribunal is based in Sydney, with a large office in Melbourne and small offices in other state capitals. Its members are a chairman, a vice-chairman and several other members. Virtually all decisions of the tribunal are made at meetings of the members (which are not open to the public) or by single members to whom the tribunal has delegated some powers. Decisions of the tribunal are implemented by its staff, headed by the general manager.

Until World War II, postal services, telecommunications and broadcasting were all controlled directly by the Postmaster-General, a minister in the federal government. In 1949, the Australian Broadcasting Control Board took over some of the Postmaster-General's powers to control programmes, and had an advisory or quasi-departmental position in other areas such as licensing of stations and approving changes in their ownership and control. The Broadcasting Tribunal replaced the Broadcasting Control Board in 1977. Unlike the board, however, it was given independent power in licensing, ownership and control decisions. As an independent statutory corporation, the tribunal has a duty to act independently of the government in the exercise of its powers. Of course, it examines government policy and takes it into account, but as a matter of law it must not be dictated to by that policy, or blindly follow it. As a matter of principle, it appears to be almost universally acknowledged that governments and ministers of all persuasions have an obvious conflict of interest in control of the mass media. Whereas the community may expect the media to be fearless and impartial, governments and ministers naturally seek the opposite, whatever their good intentions. Governments and ministers around the world seek favourable media publicity, and wish to be well regarded by those who control the media. By removing the more immediate decisions about radio and television from the control of ministers, the Act tries to insulate those media from government sway. It should be mentioned in passing that there are a number of senior bureaucrats who acknowledge no such principle. They seek to impose uniformly on radio and television the same kind of control as is appropriate to other federal areas, such as primary industry and transport, which involve no freedom of speech issues. That provides a tense environment for the Broadcasting Tribunal, as it does for the ABC and SBS.

Most of the powers still held by the minister involve planning and technical aspects of the broadcasting system. These aspects are regarded as requiring government control, as opposed to independent control, because they involve national resources such as the radio frequency spectrum, and because they often affect the national economy. The minister also has some residual powers over programmes. A phrase such as 'planning and technical' connotes something abstruse, but in reality some of the most vital practical issues in broadcasting come into this category, such as the effective radiated power of a station and its service area. The minister plans and finally decides on all major aspects of the ABC and SBS networks. It is the minister who initiates the licensing of each new commercial or public station. The tribunal's role starts only after the minister has formally invited people to submit applications for a licence. It is also the minister who specifies the nature, purpose and engineering characteristics of a station. Whereas the operations of the tribunal have a court-like form, in which most decisions are based on submissions and evidence presented at public hearings or in documents submitted by parties, the minister's decisions are reached through the internalized, departmental form. The two environments are different. The Sydney-based tribunal is mainly a lawyers' forum, but the department is dominated by Canberra public servants and to some extent by Melbourne engineers. Each group brings its own set of values and ambience, with results which are sometimes Byzantine. The minister reponsible for administering the Act is currently designated the Minister for Communications.

Until recently, Australia had a dual broadcasting system, consisting of the national broadcasting service provided by the ABC and the commercial broadcasting service provided by separately licensed stations. The ABC sector of the system was roughly modelled on the British Broadcasting Corporation and the licensed, commercial sector was roughly modelled on the US system. The 1970s saw each of these two sectors unwillingly spawn another sector. The result is the system of four sectors mentioned at the beginning of this chapter. From a lawyer's viewpoint, the SBS is modelled on the national service of the ABC and the public broadcasting service is modelled on the commercial broadcasting service. That produces the following overall structure of the Act.

The Australian Broadcasting Tribunal
Part II (ss. 7–29) constitution, powers and functions of tribunal

Sectors operating under statutory authority
Part III (ss. 30–79A): Australian Broadcasting Corporation [now largely removed to the *Australian Broadcasting Corporation Act 1983*]
Part IIIA (ss. 79B–79ZJ): Special Broadcasting Service (SBS)

Sectors operating under licence from Broadcasting Tribunal
Part IIIB (ss. 80–94) Licences and Licence Warrants

Provisions common to all sectors
Part I (ss. 1–6) Preliminary
Part IV (ss. 95–119AB) Broadcasting Requirements
Part V (ss. 119A–134) General

Even this relatively simple list requires some historical explanation. There was an important change to the Broadcasting Act in 1986, when the whole Act was rearranged and given its present name. Until 1986, it was called the Broadcasting and Television Act. At the time of the renaming, an important change to the licensing system was introduced. The legal machinery was introduced to define the area served by each commercial and public station, after which they would no longer need a separate licence for each transmission facility within the area. This was intended to simplify the licensing system, which had previously required a number of separate licences for the one area. However, the new licensing system was designed in such a way that each existing station needs to be converted to the new approach separately. Some radio stations are likely to remain for a time under the old system, to which the old requirements of the Broadcasting and Television Act will continue to apply. If this appears complicated, then appearance reflects the reality of the conversion process. Another change to the rearrangement of the Act had occurred earlier, in 1983. As noted in the above list, in 1983 most of the laws relating to the ABC were removed to a separate Australian Broadcasting Corporation Act. However, a few requirements affecting the ABC are still to be found in Parts III and IV of the Broadcasting Act.

As for the character of the services provided by the four sectors outlined above, the predominant character of the ABC is national and non-commercial. By s. 65 of the Act, the ABC is prohibited from broadcasting most forms of advertisement. The ABC is national in the sense that it has always been expected as a matter of policy to provide an integrated service of interest to the whole Australian community, although many concessions have been made to state and regional demands. Individual ABC stations do not have great legal significance, as they are largely outlets for the one national service provided by the one corporation, for all of which the corporation is responsible.

The SBS is modelled on the ABC, and is said to result from the unwillingness of ABC executives to depart, in the 1970s, from their BBC model by providing multicultural programmes and programmes in languages other than English. By s. 79D of the Act, the transmission of multilingual broadcasts is made the primary object of the SBS, while the government is also allowed to make regulations conferring other special functions on it. Both the ABC and SBS are legally independent of the government in providing programmes; although the members of both bodies are government appointees. On the executive side, the managing director of the ABC is appointed by the board; whereas the government appoints the executive director of the SBS.

The commercial broadcasting service is not one unified service so much as a number of separately licensed commercial broadcasting stations. There are about 140 radio stations and about 50 television stations in Australia. Virtually all of them were licensed on the basis that they would be controlled by local business interests and would serve local communities. Rational allocation of markets between stations is supposed to be effected by the service areas which the minister specifies for each licence, and through the licensing policies applied by the Broadcasting Tribunal. As the commercial stations are allowed to advertise, the majority of their programmes consist of entertainment for a mass audience.

The newer public broadcasting sector was said to arise from the failure of the commercial stations and the ABC to provide community oriented programmes which were not directed to a mass audience. There are about 60 stations operating in this sector in Australia. The term 'public' is intended to indicate a degree of involvement by the public in the running of the stations and the making of the programmes. It sometimes creates confusion with the ABC and SBS services, which are not properly described as 'public' although they are provided by public authorities. Public broadcasting stations are licensed in the same way as commercial stations, the main difference being that under s. 119AB of the Act, they are allowed to broadcast only a limited range of sponsorship announcements, other advertisements being prohibited.

PROGRAMME LAWS AFFECTING ALL STATIONS

As explained earlier, it is only the individual stations in the commercial and public services (as opposed to the ABC and SBS) which are licensed. The word 'licensee' is a convenient way of referring to one of these stations which gains its right to broadcast from a Broadcasting Tribunal licence. There is more external regulation of the licensed, commercial and public stations than there is of the ABC and SBS, all of whose programmes are internally controlled by the government appointed members of their respective governing bodies. The main historical reason behind the different treatment has been that legislators in the past sought to remedy certain programme deficiencies in the commercial stations which they did not see or apprehend in the ABC stations. There are some sections of the Act, however, which affect all sectors of radio and television.

Australian Content

The SBS has no specific legal obligation to produce Australian programmes, although it does in practice generate a lot of Australian production, mostly with an ethnic character. The other three broadcasting sectors are all required by s. 114 of the Act to use the services of Australians 'as far as possible' in the production and presentation of programmes. A prosecution for breach of such a general obligation could be imagined only in an extreme case, and there has not been one. However, it would be wrong to assume that the exhortation is ineffective. It serves as a statutory guideline which the ABC and Broadcasting Tribunal are not likely to disregard: the ABC in planning its service and the Broadcasting Tribunal at its licensing inquiries. By s. 114(2), an Australian composers' quota for radio stations is imposed. Not less than 5 per cent of the programme time of ABC, commercial and public radio stations must be devoted to the work of Australian composers. The Act does not indicate the period of time over which the percentage is to be calculated, but a licensee would clearly be in breach if it had not met the quota on the aggregate of programmes throughout its licence period. Other obligations of licensees are mentioned later.

Current Affairs and Political Broadcasts

In s. 116, the main restrictions on political broadcasts are set out. Sub-section 116(1) introduces an important safeguard for the ABC, by saying that *subject only to s. 116* the ABC may determine the extent and manner in which it will broadcast 'political or controversial matter'. That sub-section is designed to prevent outsiders, including government ministers and commonwealth bureaucrats, from interfering with ABC news and current affairs programmes.[3] Until recently there were other restrictions on political broadcasts in s. 116 which applied to the ABC, SBS and licensees as well. There was formerly a ban on dramatization of political matter, and a restriction on political programmes during a three-day 'blackout' before elections. With the removal of those laws, s. 116 has become a section which gives freedom to the ABC, and does not restrict it. The SBS has no such safeguard. As for licensees, the section imposes on them an obligation to afford reasonable electoral broadcasting opportunities to political parties, and it prohibits them from broadcasting election advertisements in the three days before the election. Those two requirements are discussed later.

Section 117 of the Act is concerned not with restricting the content of controversial broadcasts, but with ensuring that the identity of those behind them is disclosed to the community. In outline, it requires a station to announce the name of every speaker who 'delivers an address or makes a statement relating to a political subject or current affairs'. Where the speaker is not the author, the speaker's name must be announced. The announcement must be made after an address or statement of less than a hundred words and before *and* after a longer one. The station must keep records of names, addresses and occupations of the authors of such statements and addresses, and provide them to the Broadcasting Tribunal if required. These obligations apply all year long. They apply not just to electoral matter, or even political matter, but to all current affairs broadcasts. Many talk-back radio programmes, for example, should comply, although s. 117 appears not to be enforced against those programmes.

Similar obligations are imposed in respect of elections to the commonwealth parliament and commonwealth referendums. Section 333 of the *Commonwealth Electoral Act* 1918 requires that the name and address of the author must be included in any 'announcement, statement or other matter commenting upon any candidate, political party or the issues being presented to the electors'. In 1985, the government accepted recommendations of a Senate committee that the requirements of ss. 333 and 117 should be simplified, and that s. 117 should not apply to talk-back programmes and 'man in the street' interviews—but there was a delay in introducing the necessary changes to the two Acts.[4] Section 350 of the same Act forbids the making or publication of a false or defamatory statement about a candidate for election, and allows him or her to obtain an injunction to restrain repetition of such a statement. Section 351 makes it an offence to link a candidate with an organization, such as a political party, without written permission of the candidate. Section 329 of the Electoral Act prohibits a wide range of misleading or untrue statements about how to cast a vote or matters relating to an election. These Electoral Act provisions apply to all media, not just to radio and television.

Section 117A of the Broadcasting Act affects current affairs broadcasts in yet another way, by requiring written transcripts or sound recordings of them to be kept. It affects all 'matter relating to a political subject or current affairs, being matter that is in the form of news, an address, a statement, a commentary or a discussion'. Current affairs producers will note with understandable exasperation that this is only one of several overlapping but different definitions which operate in the same area. The main purpose behind s. 117A is to ensure that people who consider themselves to have been defamed in current affairs broadcasts should be able to obtain an accurate record of the words used against them, but it is not limited to defamation. It embodies a scheme in which the station must retain the transcript or recording for six weeks, unless a person serves a notice requiring the record to be preserved until some imminent or pending litigation is completed. However, if the litigation is not started within three months of service of the notice, the ABC, SBS or licensee affected may then destroy the record.

The section does not provide any way for a person to get access to the record. To do that, it is necessary to rely on the ordinary rights of discovery, production and inspection available from the court in which the case is brought. The minister has a power to require that the initial period for keeping the records be longer than six weeks in special cases, and to require that records of historic importance be handed over for safe keeping. Commercial and public licensees are required to provide any records kept under s. 117A to the Broadcasting Tribunal on request. Furthermore, s. 99(4) of the Act requires them to provide to the tribunal on request 'any writing, record, film or other device' used in connection with a programme. These powers can obviously be used when complaints are made about programmes. A person seeking redress or even simply complaining about a current affairs programme can be sure that if action is taken within six weeks, an accurate record will still be in existence. As outlined in the preceding chapter, s. 118 of the Act expressly prohibits blasphemous, indecent and obscene broadcasts.

The powers of the government (through the usual statutory persona of 'the Minister') to intervene directly in the broadcasting of programmes are almost the same for the ABC and SBS as they are for licensed stations, although the powers are conferred by different sections of the Broadcasting Act and the ABC Act. They have rarely been used, but some broadcasters believe that their very existence gives the government more persuasive power than it should have; for example, in requests for prime ministerial addresses to the nation. Until recently the minister had power to prohibit a station from broadcasting virtually any kind of programme. Those powers have been repealed, but there are still powers to require that specified programmes be broadcast. The ABC and SBS must transmit free of charge any matter the broadcasting of which the minister considers to be 'in the national interest'.[5] Licensees have a similar obligation to transmit free of charge 'such items of national interest as the minister specifies' up to a maximum of thirty minutes in any 24-hour period.[6] The Governor-General is able, under s. 131, to authorize the minister to take complete control over any station in an emergency. The minister must report his or her reasons for using these powers to parliament within seven sitting days.[7]

Sporting Broadcasts and Entertainments

Despite suggestions which have been made from time to time, the Act does not regulate the acquisition of exclusive rights to broadcast sporting events. The only section directly concerned with sport is s. 115, which applies only to television. It prohibits television stations from broadcasting coverage of 'a sporting event or other entertainment' held in a place for which an admission charge is made 'if the images of the sporting event or other entertainment originate from the use of equipment outside that place'. It is therefore unlawful to broadcast transmissions from cameras on a tower erected outside a sporting ground or a helicopter flying around it, even when the body responsible for the ground has no objection.

By this clumsy prohibition, s. 115 attempts to prevent unauthorized television coverage of sport. But for the section, television stations would be free to broadcast virtually anything their cameras could scan. The common law does not prevent a person from broadcasting coverage of events taking place on the land of another, and radio stations are still free to do so.[8]

ABC AND SBS PROGRAMME LAWS

The main limits on ABC and SBS programmes are not laws applying from the outside, but the internal chains of command which extend down from the governing bodies of these two services, consisting of government appointees. The two services could almost be regarded as having their own inbuilt broadcasting tribunals. The brief 'charter' of the SBS to provide multilingual services, and other services which the government prescribes, has been outlined earlier. The ABC has a more formal and detailed charter set out in s. 6 of its Act. The charter is not legally enforceable in a court, but is nevertheless the basic reference point of the whole service. The main functions set out in the charter are:

(a) to provide within Australia innovative and comprehensive broadcasting and television services of a high standard as part of the Australian broadcasting system consisting of national, commercial and public sectors and, without limiting the generality of the foregoing, to provide:
   (i) broadcasting programs that contribute to a sense of national identity and inform and entertain, and reflect the cultural diversity of, the Australian community; and
   (ii) broadcasting programs and television programs of an educational nature;
(b) [to transmit overseas programs through Radio Australia]; and
(c) to encourage and promote the musical, dramatic and other performing arts in Australia.

The charter says that in providing its broadcasting services, the ABC is to take account of: the services provided by the other sectors of the system; the Standards set by the Broadcasting Tribunal; the responsibilities of the states for education; and the the need for balance between programmes of wide appeal and specialized programmes.

Corresponding to the Programme Standards which apply to commercial and public broadcasters are the internal programme guidelines of the ABC and SBS. Among other things, the internal guidelines of the ABC lay down standards of fair play for interviews; divide up the time for electoral broadcasts between the political parties; and restrain commercially motivated 'plugs' (without restricting legitimate publicity for forthcoming events or recommendations for good products, by brand name or otherwise). The SBS guidelines have been criticized by many ethnic leaders for the restrictions which they impose on political discussion. These guidelines are entirely the product of the ABC and SBS themselves, which are free to remove or change them at any time. They do not have the force of law, but the ABC and SBS naturally have the same kind of power to discipline employees who disobey instructions as other public authorities.

In the programme area, the board of the corporation receives advice from the national ABC Consultative Council, which is required to be representative of the Australian community. The national advisory council is in turn advised by state and territory advisory councils.[9] On the recommendation of the councils, the managing director of the corporation appoints community affairs officers, who are to investigate programme complaints about matters like errors of fact and invasions of privacy. Where an officer decides that a complaint is justified, there must be a prompt on-air retraction or apology (s. 82(5)). Some particular responsibilities, as well as the general programme obligations, are laid down by the ABC Act. The corporation is to maintain an independent news service, and broadcast daily from all national stations regular news and current affairs sessions (s. 27). It may maintain and use orchestras, bands and other groups of musicians, and arrange for public concerts and entertainment (s. 28). That is the authority on which major undertakings such as the ABC orchestras rest. The corporation may also prepare and distribute literature (including programme schedules), and make, promote and distribute films and tapes relating to its programmes and concerts (s. 29). It can form subsidiary companies to assist in the marketing operations resulting from these ancillary activities (s. 25A).

COMMERCIAL AND PUBLIC PROGRAMME LAWS

Programme Standards

Unlike the ABC and SBS, licensees of commercial and public stations are obliged by s. 99 of the Broadcasting Act to comply with the Programme Standards made by the Broadcasting Tribunal. ABC spokesmen have sometimes said that the ABC voluntarily complies with those standards, and the ABC is obliged by its Act to 'take account of' the standards, without being obliged actually to follow them. Copies of the standards are issued by the tribunal, which also has power to revise them at any time. This does not mean that changes can be made easily. In 1986 considerable formality was imposed on the standard-making process by new legislation and regulations made by the government. Under these new laws, anyone can apply to have new standards imposed or old standards removed, but the elaboration and formality of the process of change is much greater than it was before. In the few years before 1986, there was rapid revision of some parts of the standards. The greatest changes were in radio, where a booklet of rules was reduced to three pages. This was not a frivolous 'deregulation', but a response to the greater choice now available between radio services, their specialization, and the decrease in community controversy about what should be broadcast on radio.[10] In fact, the restrictions laid down in the Radio Programme Standards are brief enough to quote in full:

2. A licensee may not transmit a program which may:
    (a) incite, encourage or present for their own sake violence or brutality;
    (b) simulate news or events in such a way as to mislead or alarm listeners;

(c) present as desirable the misuse of alcoholic liquor; or
   (d) present as desirable the misuse of drugs or narcotics.
3. A licensee may not transmit a program which is likely to incite or perpetuate hatred against, or gratuitously vilifies, any person or group on the basis of ethnicity, nationality, race, gender, sexual preference, religion or physical or mental disability.
4. A licensee shall ensure that not less than 20 per cent of the time occupied in the broadcasting of music each day by a licensee shall consist of performances by Australians.
5. News programs (including news flashes) transmitted by a licensee must:
   (a) present news accurately;
   (b) not present news in such a way as to create public panic, or unnecessary distress to listeners; and
   (c) distinguish news from comment.
6. Any contest transmitted by a licensee must be conducted fairly.
7. A licensee must not transmit words of an identifiable person unless:
   (a) that person has been informed in advance that the words may be transmitted; or
   (b) in the case of words which have been recorded without the knowledge of the person, that person has subsequently, but prior to the transmission, indicated consent to the transmission of the words.

The situation is different with television. Unlike radio, television is the battleground of many debates over Australian production, materialism, violence, sexual exploitation, sexism, political bias, children's programmes, and community standards generally. The television programme standards have been officially under revision since 1971, but the only significant change has been an interim rearrangement in 1986. The history of the standards, and the more elaborate inquiry regime for changing standards mentioned above, suggest that radical change to the 'interim' 1986 text of the standards is unlikely in the near future. The television standards are more extensive than the radio standards. They contain rules about news programmes, contests, and broadcasting of interviews similar to the radio rules quoted earlier. However, there is no equivalent of Radio Programme Standard 3 which deals with incitement to hatred on ethnic and other grounds. The topic which occupies the greatest number of pages is the system for classification of television programmes (including advertisements) for appropriate time zones of the day and night, which has no radio equivalent. It dates from the beginning of television in 1956, when it was more practicable than it is today to minimize community problems by isolating programmes suitable for adults to times when children would not be expected to be watching. Changing viewing habits and new devices such as videocassette recorders reduce the effectiveness of this system. The table, reproduced from Television Programme Standard 9, sets out the classifications which related to each time zone. The text of the standards attempts to indicate broadly what level of programme content is appropriate to the various classifications, whose symbols must be transmitted at the start of most programmes and from time to time during them. In very brief summary, the classifications are:

G (General)	Programmes suitable for children to watch without adult supervision.
PGR (Parental guidance recommended)	Suitable for children to watch subject to the guidance of an adult.
AO (Adults only)	Unsuitable for viewers under 18 years.
C (Children)	Classified in advance by the tribunal on advice of its children's programme committee as having special value to children.
Not suitable for television	Unsuitable for television at all, principally because of violence, obscenity or drug content.

A licensee may transmit a programme outside the times prescribed if it is a serious presentation of a moral or social issue and if there is clear on-air warning of its content. These classifications apply to all television programme material, including advertisements. Primary responsibility for administering the standards lies with the individual licensees. In practice, this means that the major network licensees in Sydney or Melbourne classify the programmes before providing them to other stations. Licensees employ FACTS (the Federation of Australian Commercial Television Stations) to classify programmes for them, or to give advice about classification, particularly in relation to advertising. The Programme Standards previously required that films for television be classified by the Commonwealth Film Censor, but that requirement has been removed by legislation. When complaints are made to it about the suitability of a programme or advertisement for its time slot, the Broadcasting Tribunal investigates. Where it is found that a licensee has clearly breached the standards, the licensee is liable to sanctions under the licensing system discussed later in this chapter. Under the system which applied until recently, a licensee did not face any jeopardy once material had been cleared in advance by the Commonwealth Film Censor. The only programmes to which that kind of certainty still applies are those classified 'C' as specially suitable for children.

Restrictions on Programme Makers

It can be argued in principle that there should be no rules about the content of the media. Rightly or not, all societies in

Table: PROGRAMME CLASSIFICATION CHART

TIME	WEEKDAYS				SATURDAY AND SUNDAY		
			(1)	(2)			
	C	G	PGR	AO	AO	G	PGR	AO

Time markers: 12MN, 5AM, 6AM, 8.30AM, 12 NOON, 3PM, 4PM, 5PM, 7.30PM, 8.30PM, 12MN

Weekdays:
- G: 5AM – 7.30PM (with C sub-block 4PM – 5PM)
- PGR: 5AM – 8.30AM; 8.30AM – 3PM; 4PM – 5PM; 7.30PM – 8.30PM
- AO (1) School days: 12MN – 5AM; 3PM blocks; 8.30PM – 12MN, with G or PGR 12 NOON – 3PM
- AO (2) School holidays: 12MN – 5AM; 8.30PM – 12MN

Saturday and Sunday:
- G: 5AM – 7.30PM
- PGR: 5AM – 6AM; 7.30PM – 8.30PM
- AO: 12MN – 5AM; 8.30PM – 12MN

(1) WEEKDAYS WHICH ARE SCHOOL DAYS
(2) WEEKDAYS WHICH ARE SCHOOL HOLIDAYS.

all political systems impose restrictions in one way or another, whether by private or by public sanctions. The usual basis for the restrictions is not to restrict adult viewing, but to protect children. So it is important to consider the fairest way to balance the competing interests of community demands for observance of minimum standards, and the broadcaster's demand for freedom of speech. One approach is directly to prosecute in the courts those who break a general law about programme content. That approach is embodied in s. 118 of the Act, which allows prosecution of a person responsible for a blasphemous, indecent or obscene programme. It involves subjecting a person to a criminal sanction because a progamme may have crossed a line drawn between cultural values. Such a prosecution would not be launched lightly, and in fact none is known to have occurred. It is similarly possible to prosecute a licensee which fails, after an appropriate direction from the tribunal under s. 99(2) of the Act, to take measures to ensure that programmes do comply with the standards. This raises the same kind of problem as an obscenity prosecution in a court, and could involve unfairness because probably no programme standards will ever be able to formulate precise rules in advance about the kind of material which is unsuitable. Even if such standards could be drafted, they would probably be an over-intrusion into programme-making.

Apart from criminal prosecutions, the range of other sanctions provided by the Act is limited. Section 129 incorporates s. 99(2) into each licence, so that the tribunal does not lack power to pursue breaches of the standards through its licensing process. Penalties like short-term renewal of licences, however, or even revocation or non-renewal, are likely to be out of proportion to the fault which has occurred. They pose the risk of punishing all the staff of a station for the fault of one, or in the case of non-renewal of a licence or revocation, the risk of punishing the public by removing a service from them. At the other extreme, the tribunal is empowered by s. 101 of the Act to 'reprimand or admonish' a licensee, and to require it to broadcast the 'reprimand or admonishment'. The tribunal is not known to have contemplated this particular procedure.

Section 119 attempts to compromise between these different approaches by allowing the tribunal to suspend from broadcasting the person who was responsible for a programme which contravened the standards; but it guarantees that the person in jeopardy will have the opportunity to have his or her defence considered by the tribunal before action is taken, as well as the opportunity of appealing against any unfavourable decision. It has often been said that the tribunal has no adequate sanction in the case of breaches of the standards, other than taking away a licence or giving a warning to the licensee. A Senate committee identified that problem decades ago, and s. 119 was inserted in the Act in 1942 precisely to remove it.

Under s. 119, the tribunal may make an order preventing a person from presenting programmes in live broadcasts or from 'passing or selecting' programmes for broadcasting. It may also place restrictions on the extent to which a person engages in those activities. The words 'passing or selecting' make it clear that producers, editors and directors of broadcasts, and not just performers, are included. In the past, when the words of s. 119 were slightly different, restrictions were imposed on performers such as Graham Kennedy, Peter Cook and Dudley Moore who had uttered four-letter words on air. They were confined for a period of time to prerecorded programmes. It appears that there has been no case in which s. 119 has been used against a programme executive rather than a performer. In the words of s. 119(1), a restriction may be imposed where a person has:

(a) presented in a live broadcast the whole or a part of a programme; or
(b) passed or selected for broadcasting the whole or a part of a programme (being a programme that was subsequently broadcast),
in respect of which, or in respect of the broadcasting of which, the programme standards were not complied with or this Act was contravened ...

In practice, the Tribunal has very rarely used s. 119. It has tended to resort to the more drastic penalties, by looking to the management or shareholders of a licensee company to change its operations so that individuals will not contravene the standards again.[11]

Concluding this survey of general programme standards and penalties for breach of them, it should be mentioned that there are a number of protections for licensees built into the Act. First, it is not a criminal offence to contravene a programme standard. An offence only arises if the tribunal gives the licensee a notice under s. 119(2) actually directing it to comply with the standards. Second, a licensee does not contravene a standard by making a 'reasonable mistake' or reasonably relying on another person. Third, various sections of the Act and modern administrative law in general ensure that a licensee (or another person) cannot be penalized by the tribunal without a full opportunity to put its defence in writing and, if necessary, by oral explanation. It is also worth noting that the tribunal does not have power to require that programmes be approved in advance, except for programmes considered for 'C' time.[12] The view was taken when the Act was amended in 1985 that it would be undesirable to authorize the degree of censorship which would be involved in prior tribunal approval of any adult programmes.

Advertisements

The law governing advertisements generally is discussed in Chapter 12. The following outline is concerned with the law governing television and radio advertisements specifically. As has been mentioned already, the ABC is prohibited from broadcasting most forms of advertisements. The SBS is similarly restricted, although it may derive funds from programme sponsorship of a kind approved by the minister under s. 79ZA(d) of the Broadcasting Act. Public broadcasting stations are allowed by s. 119AB of the Act to make sponsorship announcements consisting of the name and address of the sponsor; and a description, made in accordance with Programme Standards of the tribunal, of the business, undertaking or activity (if any) carried on by the sponsor. Public broadcasters may not broadcast advertisements other than the sponsorship announcements. There was much uncertainty about how far the words of the Act enabled public broadcasters to move their sponsorship announcements towards something resembling the advertisements on commercial stations. The government announced in 1986 that it would change the law to confirm the non-profit character of public broadcasting.[13]

In practice, advertising is what distinguishes the character of commercial broadcasting from that of the other three sectors. Section 100 of the Act allows commercial stations to broadcast advertisements subject to the restrictions imposed under the Act. The main restrictions are the Advertising Conditions made by the tribunal. Not all the advertising sections of the Act are negative. Sub-section 100(3) says that 'a licensee shall not, without reasonable cause, discriminate against any person applying for the use of his advertising service'. Like s. 45(a)(ii) of the Trade Practices Act (which prohibits contracts, arrangements and understandings likely to lesson competition), this sub-section has been neglected by advertisers and agencies, who do not appear to have yet asserted these legal rights of fair, non-discriminatory access to advertising time.

Most of the tribunal requirements about advertising are set out in the Radio Advertising Conditions and Television Advertising Conditions, which were, like the Programme Standards, revised in 1986. There are also some Television Advertising Standards which specifically affect the content of advertisements. The reason for having the confusion of rules bearing different names, namely 'standards' and 'conditions', is that the powers to make them arise from different sections of the Act. The Advertising Conditions follow the same scheme, and are authorized by the Act in a similar way to the Programme Standards. The Radio Advertising Conditions are extremely brief. Their operative words are:

2. Advertisements transmitted by a licensee must:
    (a) not be presented as news programs or other programs;
    (b) comply with the Radio Programme Standards so far as they are applicable.
3. All advertisements transmitted by a licensee must be produced in Australia or New Zealand.
4. A licensee of a commercial broadcasting [i.e. radio] station, being the only commercial broadcasting station licensed to serve the whole or a substantial part of the area which it is licensed to serve, must not transmit more than 18 minutes of advertisements in a period of one hour.

As with the Radio Programme Standards, the current simple requirements replace a former much more extensive set of requirements. In particular, all radio stations used to be restricted to 18 minutes of advertising per hour. With the growth in numbers of stations, and increasing competition to provide an attractive sound to listeners and advertisers, it was found that stations in competitive markets were using much less than 18 minutes per hour.

With television, the dominant medium which finds itself at the centre of so many controversies, there is more complexity. The main television restrictions are summarized here, but it is necessary to read the actual words of the Conditions and Standards published by the tribunal to ascertain exactly how they apply in a particular situation. The topic which takes up the largest number of words is the extent to which advertisements interrupt programmes. Advertisements are to be broadcast only in the periods between programmes, or in 'natural breaks' during programmes; although there is much difficulty in determining exactly what a 'natural break' is. 'Non-programme matter' is to be clearly separated from programmes 'in a readily discernible manner'. There are many exceptions to the Conditions limiting the placement of advertisements, but the basic rule is that no more than four advertisements are to occur in any break in a programme. Between 7.00 and 10.00 p.m., up to 11 minutes of advertisements may be broadcast each hour. At other times, the basic maximum is 13 minutes per hour. In 1986, the tribunal started a review of these rules, which was expected to lead to changes late in 1987.

There are also restrictions on television advertising in particular situations. There are a number of restrictions on advertising directed to children.[14] For example, advertisements directed at that audience may not be designed to mislead or deceive children, or take advantage of their credulity. They may not encourage children to ask their parents to purchase products, or imply that an advertised product makes its owner superior to others; and products which would be unsafe if used by children without supervision may not be 'directed to children'. More rules like these, and an overall time limit of 10 minutes of advertisements per hour, apply to the special C hour between 4.00 and 5.00 p.m. on weekdays. Advertisements for films and tapes which are classified for an adult or restricted audience may, in general, be broadcast only during the corresponding television time zones.[15] When scheduling advertisements for products 'of a personal or intimate nature', licensees are to exercise care with regard to the likely composition of the audience at the relevant time. In particular, advertisements for sanitary napkins, condoms, vaginal deodorants and treatments for haemorrhoids may be transmitted only during PGR and AO time.[16] Advertisements for betting or gambling may not be broadcast when the audience is expected to include large numbers of children. Advertisements for alcohol may be transmitted only after 8.30 at night, or between noon and 3.00 p.m. on a school day. However, alcohol advertisements for sponsors of live broadcasts of sporting events on Saturdays and public holidays are permitted.[17]

Apart from the Advertising Conditions and Standards of the tribunal, there are some sections of the Act which apply directly to particular kinds of advertisements. For example, sub-sections 100(6)–(9) require that an advertisement relating to a medicine be approved by the Secretary of the Commonwealth Department of Health or his delegate. The obtaining of approval is co-ordinated through the self-regulation schemes of the Federation of Australian [Commercial] Radio Broadcasters and the Federation of Australian Commercial Television Stations mentioned in Chapter 12. Those federations also apply the Voluntary Code for the Advertising of Goods for Therapeutic Use. Sub-section 100(5A) of the Act prohibits advertisements 'for, or for the smoking of, cigarettes or cigarette tobacco'. It does not prohibit all smoking advertisements and promotions. Cigar and pipe advertisements are still lawful, as are some kinds of 'corporate' advertisements for cigarette companies. An even greater concession to the tobacco companies is in sub-section 100(10), which excludes from the definition of 'advertisement' any incidental advertisement for which the licensee of a station is not rewarded. Obvious examples are the 'perimeter' advertisements and other commercial paraphernalia now inseparable from many sporting broadcasts, but there is some debate about exactly what 'incidental' means.[18]

Australian Content

The protections for Australian content in radio have already been mentioned. They are: the 5 per cent *composers'* quota in s. 114 of the Act; the 20 per cent Australian music *performers'* quota in Radio Programme Standard 4; and the requirement in Radio Advertising Condition 3 that all advertisements be produced in Australia or New Zealand. Those rules are fairly simply stated, but as in other areas, a higher level of complexity (and controversy about what the rules should be) is to be found in television. The main rules are in Television Programme Standard 14. It sets out the 'points system' for encouraging Australian programmes. There is a scale of points in the standard, which give the highest value to intensive productions like local dramas, ranging down through light entertainment and current affairs to cooking, gardening and live sporting programmes which usually require more limited production resources. A licensee must meet a target of points on the table equal to its number of transmission hours over a year. The allocation of points is such that most licensees are well above their target each year. Less easily met, because of the expense of production and the difficulty of finding products which attract good audience ratings, is the requirement that licensees broadcast at least 104 hours of first-release Australian television drama each year. There is also a requirement that each licensee must transmit at least four 'big budget specials', which must be variety spectaculars or one-shot dramas, using higher than normal budgets and employing large numbers of Australian talent. The final requirement is in Television Programme Standard 18, which says that all television advertisements must be produced in Australia or New Zealand. There are a number of exceptions to this rule, but the two main ones are: that 20 per cent of the audio or video in an advertisement may come from outside

Australia if it is associated with people, places or events which cannot be obtained locally; and that more than 20 per cent overseas material may be used if it was filmed overseas by an Australian production crew sent there for the purpose.

Children's Programmes

The sensitive area of children's programmes is, as already mentioned, the only one in which the Act allows prior classification of programmes to make sure that they are suitable. This reflects a long history of controversy between licensees who say that television is a mass medium which can not depart from its normal commercial role to serve a minority group, and community groups and others who say that commercial television, and not just the ABC, has a responsibility to provide material of special value to children. A major role in developing and applying the current rules is played by the Children's Programme Committee of the tribunal, an advisory committee appointed under s. 29 of the Act. The members of the committee are drawn from television, advertising, education and the general public. The committee makes recommendations to the tribunal about matters affecting children's television generally, and in particular about applications for 'C' classification. The only time of day affected by 'C' classification is 4.00 to 5.00 p.m. on weekdays. The 'C' classification is not, like the other time zone classifications, an attempt to exclude unsuitable material. The criteria for classification set out in Children's Television Programme Standard 2 require, among other things, that a 'C' programme be designed specifically for children older than five years and younger than 14 years, and that it be appropriate for Australian children, not assuming too much of the culture, dialect or environment of some other country. The Children's Standards do not apply outside the 4.00 to 5.00 p.m. timeslot, apart from some of the advertising requirements mentioned earlier and a children's drama quota. Children's Television Programme Standard 14 requires that in each statistical year a licensee must transmit eight hours of first-release Australian drama, to be transmitted at any time before 8.30 p.m. This is not an addition to the general 104-hour drama requirement mentioned earlier, but effectively a part of it. The Children's Television Standards deal with a number of other details, such as rules for moving 'C' time when there is a clash with a major sporting event, and details about advertising during 'C' time. There are also brief Preschool Children's Television Programme

Standards which require licensees to broadcast programmes suitable for children younger than six years for 30 minutes at a suitable time each weekday.

Electoral Broadcasts

There is one electoral programme requirement which applies only to the licensed, commercial and public stations, namely s. 116(3). It says that if a licensee broadcasts election matter during an election period, it must 'afford reasonable opportunities for the broadcasting of . . . election matter to all political parties' which are represented in the parliament concerned. That is as close as Australian law comes to any right of reply or 'fairness doctine' in current affairs broadcasting.

The best way to understand the 'reasonable opportunities' requirement is to see what it does *not* do. First of all, the obligation does not apply outside an election period. Secondly, it does not apply to a station which avoids broadcasting any election matter. Thirdly, s. 116(5) says that a station is not obliged to offer any free time. Parties seeking their 'reasonable opportunity' must be prepared to pay for it. Fourthly, the obligation is not to offer an equal opportunity, but only a 'reasonable' opportunity. However, most commercial radio stations abide by the voluntary FARB Fairness Code, under which they attempt to provide fair presentation of all significant points of view on controversial issues of public importance, and to give a right of reply to people exposed to personal attack through use of the facilities of the station.

There was formerly a 'blackout' on the broadcasting of any political material immediately before an election. It was replaced by a ban which now restricts only paid or sponsored political advertisements for the three days before an election. Section 116 of the Act sets out this ban, and a number of related definitions which prescribe the extent of the ban more precisely.[19] Since electoral boundaries do not correspond to the service areas of radio and television licensees, there are many 'overlap' situations where it would not be entirely clear whether a by-election or state election would be affected by broadcasts. The Broadcasting Tribunal is required to determine the areas which are affected. The ban applies only to licensees which have received a notice from the tribunal informing them that they are covered by it in relation to a particular election. Neither the electoral advertising 'blackout' nor the 'reasonable opportunity' rule apply to local government elections. They apply only to elections for the federal and state houses of parliament. Section 310 of the Commonwealth Electoral Act also requires that after a commonwealth election, each licensee which has broadcast electoral advertisements must provide a return to the Electoral Commission setting out particulars of those advertisements, including the amount which the station charged for them.

Press Reports

Reflecting earlier tensions between newspapers and electronic media, s. 102 prohibits a licensee from transmitting 'news or other information of any kind' published or even collected by a newspaper or news agency, except by agreement with it. This is stricter than the obligation imposed by copyright law. Section 102 contrasts with s. 105, which obliges licensees to make particulars of forthcoming programmes available to the print media.

Religious Broadcasts

Section 103 of the Act requires licensees to broadcast 'Divine Worship or other matter of a religious nature' during periods determined by the tribunal, free of charge if the tribunal so requires. The directions published by the tribunal require that commercial and public radio licensees broadcast religious material for at least one hour per week. Television licensees are required to broadcast religious matter to occupy at least 1 per cent of the normal weekly hours of service, with the minimum period being 30 minutes. For both radio and television, the time must be provided free of charge. It may consist of a continuous programme, or a number of short announcements which make up the total weekly time. There is some doubt about the validity of s. 103, in view of s. 116 of the Australian constitution which says that the commonwealth shall make no law '... for imposing any religious observance ...'[20]

PUBLIC INQUIRIES

The Broadcasting Tribunal derives its name from the public hearing process through which it conducts inquiries before exercising its main powers. There are several kinds of inquiries. 'Directed inquiries' are the only ones commenced at the direction of the minister. They can cover almost any matter relating to broadcasting. Topics of directed inquiries have included the introduction of cable and subscription television, the distribution of programmes by satellite, and self-regulation by broadcasters of programmes and advertisements. The only matters which these inquiries may not investigate are those specifically relating to the ABC or the SBS. There are also 'area inquiries' which investigate the adequacy of broadcasting services in the various areas of the country. Lastly, there are 'ordinary inquiries' which relate to the more usual functions of the tribunal. The main matters dealt with in ordinary inquiries are:

Making new Programme Standards or changing existing ones.

Granting, renewing, or suspending licences or imposing conditions on licences.

Considering licence transfers and changes in control of licensee companies.

Any other matter relating to broadcasting (other than the ABC or the SBS) into which the tribunal decides to inquire.

Until 1986, public hearings were, with few exceptions, the main focus of inquiries, except where Programme Standards were concerned. But in that year, inquiry arrangements were formalized into a uniform set of procedures governing all ordinary inquiries. The procedures place much more emphasis on documentation, with the tribunal deciding what matters, if any, should go to a public hearing or to a conference with the parties. Since 1986, it has been possible for anyone to commence the inquiry process by making an application to the tribunal to exercise one of its powers, whether in relation to a licence, a Programme Standard or various other matters. A person who has made such an application, and a person who has made a written submission to an inquiry which has already begun, is automatically a party to that inquiry. The tribunal had previously interpreted the Act as requiring that in order to be a party a person needed a special interest in the subject-matter of the inquiry, but there is no longer any special interest requirement. Basic rules about the conduct of inquiries are set out in Division 3 of Part II of the Act. In addition, a number of details are set out in the *Australian Broadcasting Tribunal (Inquiries) Regulations*. Among other things, the regulations require the tribunal to maintain a public file for each inquiry containing all relevant documents.[21]

An inquiry into the grant of a licence begins with a public notice by the minister calling for applications. Through the minister, the government controls the commencement of new services, and all planning and technical aspects of broadcasting services.[22] The tribunal is concerned only with what happens after the minister has initiated the process for a new service. It makes its decisions about new or continuing services within the planning and technical framework decided by the government. Thus the tribunal does not decide on the transmitting frequencies to be used, or the areas to be served, by a station, or on changes in those matters. It has no role in relation to the ABC and the SBS, which do not require licences at all. After the minister has called for new licence applications, those interested in providing the service lodge their applications with the tribunal. Others may then lodge submissions about the grant of the licence, whether for or against. Anyone may submit that it is not in the public interest that a licence should be granted, and it is not uncommon for existing licensees to make such a submission, arguing that introduction of a new competitor will dilute the advertising revenue available and so degrade the quality of service to be provided. After submissions have been lodged, the tribunal normally requires further information and supporting documents from the parties, and it may hold one or more conferences with the parties to clarify the issues. Unless the inquiry is entirely uncontroversial, a public hearing then occurs, at which the people who submitted each application explain their plans and sum up their case. The inquiry process is often very lucrative for lawyers representing the major parties, particularly in the voluminous documentation stage. However, the tribunal generally prefers to talk directly with the main people involved, and there is no requirement that parties use a lawyer at any stage of the process.

Once the public hearing is completed, the tribunal issues its decision, accompanied by a report on the issues. If it decides to grant a licence, it then waits for the minister to finalize technical specifications for the service, which are embodied in a licence warrant.

The steps in an inquiry into renewal of a licence are similar, although usually less complex. Where Programme Standards are concerned, there is the same basic process, but the sequence of steps is more likely to be adapted to the nature of the particular inquiry. For example, a conference, with the parties may take the place of a public hearing.

Criteria

At most licensing inquiries, the topics to be investigated are pre-determined by exclusive criteria inserted in the Act in 1981. Before then, the tribunal was able to inquire into any aspect of a matter before it relevant to the public interest. In the *2HD* case of 1979,[23] the High Court upheld public interest as the criterion to be applied by the tribunal in inquiring and making decisions. Certain major media interests objected to such a criterion, with the result that it was replaced by the current exclusive criteria. They are exclusive because the tribunal may not normally base its decisions on matters which fall outside them. The one major matter which does fall outside the criteria is concentration of control over commercial radio and television generally. It was not excluded by accident. The exact naure of the statutory criteria differs from one kind of application to another.[24] The following is a summary of the criteria, in the form of questions which use the key words of the Act.

1. *Has the applicant complied with the conditions of the licence*, if an existing licence is being renewed?
2. *Is the granting, renewal or other change affecting the licence contrary to some provision of the Act?*
3. *Has the applicant given (and complied with, in the case of renewals) an undertaking to comply with the licence conditions and provide an adequate and comprehensive service under the licence, having regard to technical and legal obligations and also to:*

    the nature of the community to be served;
    the diversity of the interests of that community; and
    the nature of other broadcasting services in the area?

    This mechanism of an undertaking is the main focus of tribunal attention to the programmes of a station or proposed station.
4. *Has the applicant given (and complied with, in the case of a renewal) an undertaking to encourage Australian-produced programmes and the use of Australian creative resources?* Coupled with the exhortation in s. 114(1) of the Act mentioned above, this criterion makes Australian content the most prominent programme issue mentioned by the Act.
5. *Is the applicant a fit and proper person to hold an interest in the licence?* This involves more than an inquiry into the personal propriety of those behind an application. The criterion envisages a wide-ranging inquiry into all relevant aspects of

the company making the application, including its connections and associations and its performance in the past. One obvious feature of fitness and propriety is the degree of local involvement and association of the applicant.
6. *Does the applicant have the financial, technical and management capabilities to operate the station effectively?*
7. *Will grant of the application serve the need to avoid undue concentration of influence on radio and TV stations in the local area?* The important qualification is that this criterion applies only *outside* the six state capitals. In those major metropolitan markets, there is no such criterion.
8. *Will grant of the application serve the need for commercial viability of stations in the area?* This protectionist criterion is not as strong as it appears. 'Viability' means survival, not prosperity.[25]

The conduct of licensing inquiries is governed by the procedural rules in the Act and the regulations mentioned earlier. These rules must be read in the light of the case law which the courts have developed to ensure that adminstrative tribunals such as the Broadcasting Tribunal comply with the rules of natural justice. The expression 'natural justice' includes a collection of very concrete minimum standards of procedural fairness. The term sometimes misleads non-lawyers into believing that there is some kind of ambulatory moral law concept which transcends the ordinary law. There is not.

A classic instance of natural justice being denied was *Barrier Reef Broadcasting* v. *Minister for Post & Telecommunications*.[26] That case arose from an inquiry conducted by the Broadcasting Control Board, the predecessor of the Broadcasting Tribunal. Two companies were competing for a licence. The Board allowed one applicant to cross-examine the witnesses of the other, but not vice versa. The applicant denied the opportunity to cross-examine wanted to question its rival about possible breaches of the ownership and control sections of the Act. The court held that the resulting grant of the licence was invalid, because such 'differential and adverse' treatment of one applicant showed that the board was biased against it. Oral cross-examination now occurs much less frequently than it did at the time of the *Barrier Reef* case. The usual approach is to give parties very full opportunities to challenge and question each others' cases in writing. Where oral questioning is still required, the tribunal itself often asks the questions, leaving parties to question only within very limited areas of controversy which have not been covered by the earlier processes.

One feature of the tribunal which lawyers find hard to accept is that it is not a court. Courts nearly always act and inquire at the instance of parties who bring cases before them. They are very reluctant to initiate. The Broadcasting Tribunal, like many administrative tribunals, is in a quite different position, although there is always a tendency to copy the trappings, procedure and approach of the courts. The tribunal has a duty under s. 25(1) of the Act to make 'a thorough investigation into all matters relevant' to the matter before it. In *R* v. *Australian Broadcasting Tribunal; Ex parte Hardiman*,[27] the Broadcasting Tribunal had refused to investigate allegations that Mr Rupert Murdoch and companies in the News Corporation Group had breached the ownership and control sections of the Act, because those alleging the breaches had not produced evidence which would be admissible in court. The High Court ordered the tribunal to investigate the allegations, holding that it had disregarded its statutory duty to inquire into relevant matters. The court said:

To discharge its duty the Tribunal must in an appropriate case investigate for itself the possibility of contravention, even in circumstances where there is no party before the Tribunal willing, anxious or able to pursue the issue.[28]

There has been much controversy about what information is relevant to the renewal of a licence.[29] Arguments about relevance usually start with the licensing criteria summarized earlier. Their effect has generally been to increase the scope for argument rather than to narrow it. In the reasons for its decisions, published after each licensing inquiry, the tribunal is slowly laying down a series of 'precedents' about what it considers relevant in different situations. No quantity of precedent, however, can remove fundamental differences between the licensees on the one hand and interests such as community groups and rival commercial groups on the other. The licensees try to confine the inquiry to proven breaches of the Act, the Progamme Standards and any licence conditions. Other interests argue for a full investigation of the overall quality of service provided and proposed by the licensee. In practice, the tribunal often leans towards excluding as irrelevant any evidence or submission which does not assert some specific misconduct by the licensee in the past.

OWNERSHIP AND CONTROL OF STATIONS

There would be no point in careful selection of the best applicant for a licence if the identity of that applicant could change at any time. A major change in control of a licensee company is an effective relicensing of its station; it can involve a complete personality change by the licensee. Such a change can be unfair to applicants whose application for the licence was unsuccessful and can make nonsense of the policy of local control which has lain behind the grant of nearly all commercial radio and television licences in Australia.

Until 1981 the ownership and control sections were reasonably effective in limiting oligopoly in radio and television. But in that year, major concessions towards those interested in gaining control of numbers of stations were woven into the fabric of the Act. First of all, the need for *prior* approval of the acquisition of a prescribed interest in a station was removed: a raider may now take over a licensee first, and apply for approval when the takeover is already accomplished. Secondly, a 'period of grace' was introduced. It allows many entrepreneurs who contravene the Act at least six months in which to reshuffle their shareholding portfolios so as to avoid prosecution. Thirdly, the power of the Broadcasting Tribunal to investigate concentration in control of the media was curbed, as already mentioned. The tribunal may not investigate the public interest generally. It is confined to the criteria mentioned earlier.

The licensing system makes sense only if significant changes in the ownership and control of the licensee company are subject to the same kind of scrutiny and approval as the original grant of the licence. The only scrutiny which does exist is provided by ss. 91–92U of the Act.[30] Those sections are very complex. They reflect the complex subject with which they deal, namely changes in control of companies and in management of stations. To follow the ownership and control sections, it is necessary to apply a knowledge of other legal areas, such as company law, trusts and administrative law, which are beyond the scope of this book. So a few highlights only are mentioned.

Over several decades, the ownership and control sections developed to counter virtually every legal avoidance mechanism available. They do not yet apply to public broadcasting stations, among which no monopolistic tendencies have yet appeared. Generally speaking, anybody who has a significant interest in a commercial radio or television station is treated by the Act as having a 'prescribed interest'. That is so whether that interest is through a direct shareholding in the licensee company, or through a series of interposed companies, through a trust, through a captive superannuation fund or through influence over the operations of the station. The Act regulates not changes in actual control, which would be impossible to discover or quantify in many cases, but potential control. It restricts, for example, a number of people whose shareholding is large enough to make them potential controllers of a station, regardless of whether they have been able to realize that potential.[31] The Act treats a shareholding interest representing more than 15 per cent of the voting rights or paid-up capital of a company as conferring potential control (i.e. a 'prescribed interest'). In television, where shareholdings were until recently more widely spread, a holding in excess of 5 per cent may amount to a prescribed interest in some situations. The main purpose of identifying prescribed interests is to regulate changes in control of licences already granted, but there are also maximum limits on the interests any one person or group may hold. Until 1987, the limits were eight radio stations and two television stations, with some sub-limits for states and capital cities. In that year, the Labor and National parties combined in the Parliament to remove the old television limits and replace them with a new approach, which produced revolutionary changes in control of television even before the new laws were passed. The maximum limits which a person may hold are now:

- Television licences reaching 60 per cent of the total national population
- One television licence in any capital city or territory
- A television licence for any area, plus a radio licence which is the only one serving some part of the television service area
- A television licence for any area, plus a daily newspaper with most of its circulation in the television service area
- One metropolitan radio licence in each state
- Four metropolitan stations stations in Australia
- Four radio stations in any state
- Eight radio stations in Australia
- Fifteen per cent of the interests in a television or radio licensee if the controller of those interests is a non-citizen.

There are many pages of exceptions, additions and details relating to this list. For example, the Act places restrictions on company directorships which broadly correspond with those limits. And there is a version of the old limit on numbers of television stations which still applies to multi-channel service (MCS) permits allowing their holders to provide more than one television service to a regional area. MCS permits are part of a complex legislative scheme of television 'equalization' also introduced in 1987 to accompany the new ownership rules.

Broadly, the 'equalization' scheme is a plan for the government to greatly enlarge the boundaries of regional television markets. Within those larger markets, licensees are to 'aggregate' by extending their services to cover the new boundaries, in competition with all other licensees who are within the wider boundaries. If regional television licensees wish to continue the monopolies they now hold for a period, they may in some cases obtain multi-channel service permits for the present. One of the trade-offs in an MCS permit is that, although the one licensee can provide more than one service, it is confined to its existing service area, and not allowed access to the large 'aggregated' area.

There are rules and machinery for applying the limit on 'cross ownership' of newspapers by television interests serving the same market. The Broadcasting Tribunal is required to maintain a register of the newspapers which may be affected. The limit applies only to papers in the English language which are sold, not handed out free, on at least four days in each week, and that much circulation is in the particular service area. National newspapers are therefore unlikely to be affected, because they would not have 50 per cent of circulation in any one television area. Radio stations are affected only if they have no commercial radio competitor serving a part of the television area. For example, the rule does not prevent a television group from controlling a radio station serving its area provided there is at least one other radio station serving the area. The government announced in 1987 that it planned new laws to restructure the ownership of radio along the same lines as the changes to television.

10

ACCESS TO INFORMATION

Mark Armstrong
and Michael Blakeney

Our legal system does not recognize any general right of privacy or secrecy as such.[1] The media are generally free to knock on the doors of the prominent and the powerful, to ask them questions, however disrespectful, and to follow, photograph and film them. That does not mean that the media have any special access or privilege which the law does not extend to ordinary citizens. For example, reporters, photographers and cameramen who go onto private property are subject to the law of trespass just like anyone else, and can be removed, excluded, or held liable to pay damages to the occupier to the same extent. There are many public events, press conferences and other situations where it is clearly the intention of the occupiers that the media are welcome to enter and record what happens. However, the mere fact that premises are open for business in the ordinary way does not mean that the media are invited to come and film. Unless they have the permission of the occupier, they are likely to be trespassing. This kind of situation was considered in *Lincoln Hunt* v. *Willesee*,[2] where it appeared that a film crew had accompanied the dissatisfied customer of an investment company to its office, and filmed the lobby and other parts of the premises. The judge said, in effect, that the courts have power to restrain the broadcasting of videotape obtained in that way by a trespasser, but that they are reluctant to do so unless confidential information is involved, or the person seeking the restraint can point to irreparable damage which would be suffered. In the ordinary situation, the payment of damages would be the appropriate remedy. Where goodwill of a business was damaged by such a broadcast, or exemplary damages were awarded, a media organization could be liable for a very large sum. Similar principles apply to sound recording and photography by the media.

The courts and various Acts of parliament, however, have prohibited certain grosser invasions of privacy such as 'breach of confidence', electronic bugging and phone tapping. Of course, the laws of defamation, business reputation and copyright all confer a kind of privacy protection. In New South Wales alone, a Privacy Committee established by law[3] performs a valuable role in mediating about complaints, recommending reform of law and administration, and conducting research and education. Although the Privacy Committee cannot enforce its recommendations, it can compel people to give information and produce documents to it.

The reluctance of the courts, as demonstrated by recent English decisions, to recognize any special role of the media in society shows how fortunate it is that no Australian statute gives the courts a general mandate to prevent whatever they regard as a wrongful invasion of privacy. The courts would be likely to favour personal and commercial privacy over freedom of speech. The law of breach of confidence, which the courts have developed, can severely restrict freedom of the media to publish, but the courts have shown little inclination to allow journalists to protect their own sources of information from disclosure in the witness box. The federal and Victorian Freedom of Information Acts are the first Acts of parliament for a long time to attempt any inroad into the privacy which protects the incompetent and dishonest person in public life. The inroads are minor; although the Victorian Act goes further than the federal one.

CONFIDENTIAL INFORMATION

As a general rule, individuals may not claim an exclusive right to information or ideas, apart from patentable inventions. A recently developed exception to this rule is that 'no person is permitted to divulge to the world information he has received in confidence'.[4] This protection of confidential information has developed as an adjunct of patent law, to protect trade secrets and industrial designs; but the principles established in that environment are increasingly applied to confidential information used by the media.

The remedies for breach of confidence are an injunction to prevent publication, or damages where the information has already been published. In commercial cases, it may be possible to recover from the wrongdoer the profits attributable to the breach of confidence. An action may be brought not only against the person who purloins or otherwise misuses confidential information, but also against those who acquire that information and seek to publish it.[5] In other words, the media may find themselves defending court actions when they do nothing more than try to publish information leaked by others. In *British Steel Corporation* v. *Granada Television Ltd*,[6] for example, a controversial 1981 decision, the House of Lords compelled Granada to divulge to British Steel the identity of the British Steel employee who had leaked documents which were said to show incompetence and government intermeddling at British Steel.

For a breach of confidence action to succeed, it must be established that the information was confidential; that it was communicated in circumstances imparting an 'obligation of confidence'; and that there has been an unauthorized use of the information to the detriment of the person communicating it (i.e. the plaintiff).[7] It is a defence to such an action to show that the information has already become public knowledge, or that it discloses an iniquity or serious wrongdoing.

What Information is Confidential?

When two people expressly agree that the information imparted by one will not be divulged by the other, a breach of that agreement will usually be a simple breach of contract. Here is an example: a person received news from a news agency on condition that he did not pass it on to anyone else. He was liable for breach of that contract when the news was published by a newspaper.[8] Sometimes, an obligation not to divulge information is an implied term of a contract. Thus, an employee will be prevented from divulging any of his or her employer's trade secrets. The general skills which an employee picks up as a matter of course are not usually protected in this way. Thus, an accountant who wrote a book on business management based on his employment experiences could not be prevented from publishing it, because it did not 'betray any secret of the plaintiff's business'.[9]

Outside formal contractual relationships, the law recognizes that there are certain 'relationships of confidence' within which communications are protected. Communications from within most professional relationships, such as doctor and patient, solicitor and client, banker and customer, and priest and penitent usually may not be divulged. The leading case in this area is *Prince Albert* v. *Strange*,[10] in which Prince Albert was able to prevent the publication in a book of some etchings and drawings made by himself and his family. They had entrusted the originals to a printer for the purpose of having a few copies printed for their own use. In two similar cases, photographers were restrained from publishing portraits of people taken under contract with them.[11]

Limited categories of other, non-professional, relationships have been recognized as requiring similar protection. In the celebrated *Crossman Diaries* case, the UK Attorney-General failed to obtain an injunction restraining Jonathan Cape Ltd and *The Sunday Times* from publishing the diaries of a former cabinet minister.[12] The Court of Appeal acknowledged that the principle of joint cabinet responsibility was in the public interest and would be undermined by the premature disclosure of the views of individual ministers expressed during cabinet discussions. The diaries dealt with cabinet deliberations ten years earlier, however, and disclosed nothing which should remain confidential because of any tendency to prejudice open cabinet discussions within future cabinets.

Until recently, it was thought that communications between spouses were totally protected. In 1965 the Duchess of Argyll, for example, was able to prevent the Duke of Argyll from revealing to a newspaper the story of their marriage, including secrets told by the duchess to her husband.[13] In a 1978 case involving a feature article for the *News of the World* by the first wife of the late John Lennon, the Court of Appeal distinguished between confidences in a 'normal' marriage and those in a marriage where the spouses do not have much regard for the sanctity of marriage.[14] A poster for the forthcoming *News of the World* proclaimed '"How Yoko Stole My Husband"—Cynthia Lennon Exclusive'. The Court of Appeal refused to apply the principle set down in the *Duchess of Argyll* case to suppress the article. Lord Denning explained that, because of previous revelations of marriage secrets by the Lennons themselves and by a former chauffeur:

> the relationship of these parties had ceased to be their own private affair. They themselves had put it into the public domain. They made it public to all the world themselves ... One only has to read these articles all the way through to show that each of them is making money by publishing the most intimate details about the other ... It is all in the public domain and thus not confidential.[15]

Even outside contractual relationships and the relationships of confidence which the courts have traditionally recognized, the law has more recently recognized situations where communications ought to be protected, such as discussions between inventors and potential marketers of their inventions.[16] This principle was applied in *Talbot* v. *General Television Corporation Pty Ltd*.[17] The plaintiff in that case was Robert Talbot, an independent film producer, who wanted to break into the field of Australian television production. In late 1976 he developed a concept for a new TV series to be called 'To Make a Million'. The series would depict the success stories of certain self-made millionaires that would cater for the public fascination with large amounts of money, and public enjoyment of observing the private lives of others. In the course of negotiations with Channel Nine Network executives in December 1976, Talbot disclosed the concept and handed copies of his submission and a pilot script to them. After repeated unsuccessful attempts to contact the Nine Network executives again, he became aware of a promotion for a series of *A Current Affair* segments to be broadcast by GTV Channel 9 (Melbourne). In the segment promoted, millionaires would spell out their recipes for success. The promotion posed viewers the question: 'Could you be a millionaire too?' In defence to Talbot's action for an injunction, General Television Corporation argued that there was no confidential information, since the careers of the millionaires were public knowledge. The trial judge granted the injunction, saying:

I am satisfied that what was called the 'commercial twist', or the particular slant, of the plaintiff's concept (or idea) does give it a quality which takes it out of the realm of public knowledge.[18]

Confidential Information in the Media

Talbot's case was unusual in that the Nine Network executives were the direct recipients of the confidential information which the court found they had abused. More usually, the media receive information leaked by others. The media ought not to be liable for breach of confidentiality of which they are unaware.[19] There are no cases, however, on this point. In the typical situation, the confidentiality is obvious. Bingham J, for example, granted injunctions to restrain the publication in England of the contents of tapes of telephone conversations between Prince Charles and the then Lady Diana Spencer allegedly recorded in Australia, because it was obvious that any tapes had been illicitly recorded.[20] Similarly, in the *Duchess of Argyll* case, the court granted an injunction against the newspaper because the information was obviously confidential. Even where a newspaper or station buys information innocently, and only subsequently discovers its confidentiality, it will be liable for damages if it publishes the information.[21]

Disclosure of Confidential Sources

In several chapters of this book, it has been said that the courts do not give any recognition to the special position of the media. That also applies to the obligation to answer relevant questions if called as a witness in court. To refuse to answer is a contempt of court, which can be punished by a fine or imprisonment. Yet nearly all the media recognize an ethical obligation to protect the confidentiality of their sources, as does the AJA Code of Ethics. This conflict is unresolved, so most journalists face the danger that one day they may be called upon to face embarrassment and punishment for protecting a source. The same danger can arise when the media are called on to give evidence before a tribunal, such as the Administrative Appeals Tribunal, the Broadcasting Tribunal, and many others, which has a statutory power to demand that people answer questions or produce documents. Parliamentary committees and royal commissions usually have similar powers.

McGuinness v. *Attorney-General*[22] arose from the refusal of the editor of the Melbourne *Truth* to disclose the sources for his articles which said that money was being collected to stop the passage of two bills by bribing members of parliament. The royal commission had been appointed to investigate those very allegations, with the same powers as a court to compel people to give evidence. The High Court held that he was rightly fined for his silence. Dixon J said:

No one doubts that editors and journalists are at times made the repositories of special confidences which, from motives of interest as well as of honour, they would preserve from public disclosure, if it were possible. But the law was faced at a comparatively early stage of the growth of the rules of evidence with the question how to resolve the inevitable conflict between the necessity of discovering the truth in the interests of justice on the one hand and on the other the obligation of secrecy or confidence which an individual called upon to testify may in good faith have undertaken to a party or other person. Except in a few relations where paramount considerations of general policy appeared to require that there should be a special privilege, such as husband and wife, attorney and client, communications between jurors, and by statue, physician and patient and priest and penitent, an inflexible rule was established that no obligation of honour, no duties of non-disclosure arising from the nature of a pursuit or calling, could stand in the way of the imperative necessity of revealing the truth in the witness box.[23]

Following the same approach, the Supreme Courts of New South Wales and the ACT have fined journalists who failed to answer questions about their sources in defamation cases,[24] and English journalists have been gaoled for refusal to identify their sources to an inquiry into espionage which had a statutory power to require that questions be answered.[25]

In 1980 the Law Reform Commission of Western Australia carefully examined this area, but did not recommend that the law should be changed.[26] The courts do, however, make two slight concessions. First of all, they are aware of the ethical views of the media and will only require that sources be disclosed in evidence if that really is relevant and necessary.[27] They do not relish opportunities to embarrass the media. Secondly, the media are not required to disclose their sources before the trial of a defamation or slander of title action in the course of the procedures known as answers to interrogatories and discovery.[28]

In the *British Steel* case,[29] the House of Lords demonstrated that a person or corporation suffering through breach of confidence can sometimes force the media to disclose the identity of a source by bringing a confidential information action solely for that purpose. Granada Television had been given confidential documents from the files of British Steel, disclosing alleged mismanagement of industrial relations and government interference. The Law Lords said that British Steel was not seeking disclosure merely for the gratification of curiosity about which of its employees had breached confidence; it had suffered a legal wrong for which it could not seek relief until the identity of the wrongdoer was revealed. They required Granada Television to identify the source to British Steel. In a powerful dissent from the other Law Lords, Lord Salmon argued that the freedom of the press, and 'much of the information to which the public of a free nation is entitled' would disappear if the media were not immune from disclosing sources of information.[30]

Exposure of Iniquity

It has been held that a publication exposing misconduct may legitimately be made even if it involves a breach of confidence. The leading case which established this defence was *Initial Services Ltd* v. *Putterill*.[31] It concerned an employee of a laundry who discovered in the course of his employment that his employer was involved in an illegal price-fixing arrangement. The Court of Appeal refused to prevent a newspaper publishing details of that arrangement. In a more recent case, *Allied Mills Pty Ltd* v. *Trade Practices Commissions*,[32] Sheppard J similarly refused to restrain the Trade Practices Commission from using documents taken from Allied Mills which indicated that it had been involved in price fixing in breach of the Trade Practices Act. He stressed that the public interest in the disclosure of iniquity would always outweigh the public interest in the preservation of private and confidential communications.

A very broad ambit was given to the defence of disclosure in the public interest in the recent English case *Lion Laboratories Ltd* v. *Evans*.[33] That case concerned an attempt by the manufacturer of a breath-testing device used by the police to suppress the publication in the *Daily Express* of a confidential report that the device was inaccurate. The Court of Appeal held that the public interest in maintaining the confidentiality of the plaintiff's report was outweighed by the public interest in the reliability of an approved device on which depended the liability of persons to sanctions for drink driving. One judge went so far as to say that there may be circumstances in which the media has a duty to publish confidential information even if it has been unlawfully obtained in flagrant breach of confidence.

An example of the latter was the case of *Cork* v. *McVicar*[34] which concerned the publication by the *Daily Express* of an illegally tapped telephone conversation concerning police corruption and alleged miscarriages of justice. An example on the wrong side of the line was *Francome* v. *Mirror Group Newspapers Ltd*[35] which concerned illegally tapped telephone conversations concerning race fixing. The breaches of the Jockey Club rules which the taps revealed were held not to justify breaking the law to make the recordings.

Leaked Government Documents

In *Commonwealth of Australia* v. *John Fairfax & Sons Ltd*,[36] the government sought an injunction to suppress publication of a book entitled *Documents on Australian Defence and Foreign Policy 1968–1975* and a serialization of that book in the *Age* and *Sydney Morning Herald*. The book was based on documents probably leaked to the authors by a public servant. In response to the government's claim that the information was confidential, Mason J indicated that the law would regard it as different from a claim made by a private person:

It may be a sufficient detriment to the citizen that disclosure of information relating to his affairs will expose his actions to public discussion and criticism. But it can scarcely be a relevant detriment to the government that publication of material concerning its actions will merely expose it to public discussion and criticism. It is unacceptable, in our democratic society, that there should be a restraint on the publication of information relating to government when the only vice of that information is that it enables the public to discuss, review and criticise government action.

Accordingly, the court will determine the government's claim to confidentiality by reference to the public interest. Unless disclosure is likely to injure the public interest, it will not be protected.

The court will not prevent the publication of information which merely throws light on the past workings of government, even if it be not public property, so long as it does not prejudice the community in other respects. Then disclosure will itself serve the public interest in keeping the community informed and in promoting discussion of public affairs. If, however, it appears that disclosure will be inimical to the public interest because national security, relations with foreign countries or the ordinary business of government will be prejudiced, disclosure will be restrained. There will be cases in which the conflicting considerations will be finely balanced, where it is difficult to decide whether the public's interest in knowing and in expressing its opinion, outweighs the need to protect confidentiality.[37]

He was not persuaded that the embarrassment to Australia's foreign relations which would flow from disclosure of memoranda on overseas diplomatic and political personalities justified suppression of the book, particularly because some copies had already found their way into circulation. He did ultimately grant an injunction because the verbatim reproduction of official documents in the book was a breach of commonwealth's copyright. But that copyright protection did not stop the newspapers publishing the substance of the revelations contained in the documents, since copyright protects forms of expression rather than ideas or information as such. A NSW judge applied the statements of Mason J about government secrets when refusing to suppress *Spycatcher*, written by the former M15 officer Peter Wright.[38]

ELECTRONIC INTERCEPTION AND RECORDING

Electronic eavesdropping is one area where the commonwealth and the states have made strict laws, the breach of which can attract heavy criminal penalties. Mainland states have passed similar restrictions on the use of 'bugs' to overhear or record private conversations.[39] Those Acts make it an offence to use a listening device to overhear, record, or monitor any private conversation without the consent of the parties to it. It makes no difference if the person using the device is a party to the conversation. It is also an offence to communicate or publish any information obtained from such activity. So a journalist who bases a story on an interview which he or she has secretly taped commits two offences, each of which can attract a gaol sentence.

The state Acts do not apply to use of telephones. That area is covered by the federal *Telecommunications (Interception) Act* 1979, which makes it an offence to listen to or record any communication passing over a telecommunications system provided by Telecom, or with the authority of Telecom, except by use of equipment supplied or authorized by Telecom *and* with the knowledge of the person making the communication.[40] It is also an offence to record or publish any information obtained in that way,[41] or to authorize, help or permit any other person to intercept.[42] This very wide protection for telecommunications privacy covers not just the conventional telephone conversation, but also the wide range of other Telecom services such as mobile telephones and car telephones, as well as data and facsimile transmissions over the Telecom system.

These anti-tapping laws are further supported by s. 94 of the *Telecommunications Act* 1975, which makes it an offence to attach any kind of apparatus to telecommunications equipment without Telecom authority to do so. Telecom will not allow any recording device to be used by a radio or television station unless it is used with a Telecom recorder-connector, which emits a warning tone every fifteen seconds while calls are being recorded.[43] The tone is only to alert the person speaking on the telephone, so it may be removed from the recording. The Programme Standards of the Australian Broadcasting Tribunal affect the use which can be made of tape recordings of conversations, whether obtained from telephone conversations or not. The standards say that a station may not broadcast the words of an identifiable person unless he or she has been informed before interview of the possible broadcast, or else has consented after interview but before the broadcast.[44]

The commonwealth *Wireless Telegraphy Act* 1905 attempted to limit interception of radiocommunications messages regardless of whether they were part of the Telecom system or whether they were purely private, or licensed to police, ambulance or other services. However, the commonwealth *Radiocommunications Act* 1983[45] does not place restrictions on interception of those non-Telecom messages.

'D' NOTICES

Some sensitive information about defence and espionage operations is protected by the 'D' notice system, modelled on the UK system of the same name.[46] It is based on a voluntary agreement between officials of the federal Defence Department and representatives of the major media that material outlined in 'D' notices issued from time to time will not be published. The system was so effective for many years that even its existence was not revealed by the media.

The focus of the system is the Defence, Press and Broadcasting Committee. Its executive secretary and a minority of members are provided by the government. The majority of members represent the larger media companies and media industry associations. The committee revises the small number of current 'D' notices occasionally. The notices are communicated to people holding editorial and management positions in the media. The system is a voluntary one, not based on any law, and there is no penalty for breaching it. Breaches are rare, however, and regarded with great disfavour by the Defence Department. Editors in doubt about how the terms of notices apply to particular situations are expected to obtain advice from the secretariat of the Defence, Press and Broadcasting Committee in Canberra.

In 1978 *Nation Review* published what was apparently the first full public disclosure of 'D' notices in force.[47] Those notices covered things such as technical details of military equipment, strategic military information, the address of Mr and Mrs Vladimir Petrov, details of Australian monitoring and exploitation of the communications of foreign countries, and information about the Australian Secret Intelligence Service (ASIS).

One topic which does not need the protection of any 'D' notice is the identity of officers, employees and agents of ASIO. Section 92 of the federal *Australian Security Intelligence Organisation Act* 1979 makes it a criminal offence to disclose those identities in a newspaper, on radio or on television without the written consent of the minister, or of the Director-General of ASIO.

FREEDOM OF INFORMATION

Commonwealth and state laws prohibit public servants from disclosing information to the public without approval of their superiors.[48] This creates an environment in which much deception and dishonesty by politicians and senior officials goes undetected, and in which the media can be more easily manipulated.

In 1982, the commonwealth and Victoria passed their own Freedom of Information Acts. The Victorian Act is very similar to the commonwealth one, which has attracted most litigation and use. For the sake of brevity, only the commonwealth Act will be discussed below.[49] Following the US example, it provides for access only to government organizations, leaving private organizations such as credit bureaus untouched. It was intended more to help the individual citizen to contend with the government than to help the media. As even this brief summary will show, most of the information which the media would like to obtain is excluded from the limited 'freedom' which the Act confers. The Act does not, however, impose *new* restrictions on information. Ministers, for example, retain power to give people copies of documents which they could not obtain under the Act.

The scheme of the Act is to confer a general right to information, then to list a series of major exceptions. Section 3 announces its general objects, which the courts and the Administrative Appeals Tribunal apply when interpreting it. The main object is 'to extend as far as possible the right of the Australian community to access to official information in the possession of the Government of the Commonwealth'. That is to be done first by making information about the operations of the government, its departments and authorities available; and secondly, by creating *a general right of access* to information in documentary form in the possession of ministers, departments and public authorities. The right of access is contained in s. 11, which says that 'every person has a legally enforceable right to obtain access' ... to '*a document of an agency*' and to 'an *official document of a Minister*', with the exception of 'an *exempt document*'. Much of the Act is concerned with defining and expanding those words used in s. 11.

An important feature of the right of access is that a person need have no personal or economic interest in order to exercise it. Everybody, including anyone working in the media, has the right, without any need to say why they should have the information. Section 12(2) says, in effect, that the right of access does not extend to documents from before 1977, unless they are documents which relate to the personal affairs of the person who seeks them. Officials supplying information under the Freedom of Information Act are immune from any liability for defamation, breach of confidence or infringement of copyright.[50]

Like many modern federal Acts, the Freedom of Information Act is an intersecting maze of definitions and deeming sections. As with the Copyright Act, considered in Chapter 5, a person who understands the network of terms in the Act understands most of how it works.

The first terms which need explaining are those italicized above. A *'document of an agency'* includes film, videotape, and audio tape as well as the more usual kinds of written and printed records.[51] The definition of 'agency' determines which authorities are obliged by the Act to make information available. The 'agencies' are nearly all the departments of the Australian Public Service, the statutory authorities, and some other bodies as well.[52] The exceptions are mentioned later. An *'official document of a Minister'* is a document in the minister's possession relating to the affairs of a department or other agency.[53] The amusing omission from that definition is the minister's *own* documents. The Act is careful throughout to avoid any public exposure of the personal, political or policy activities of ministers.

Exemptions

'Exempt document', the last of the key terms in the general right of access to information, opens the gates to the flood of exemptions which occupy so many pages of the Act. Apart from the ministerial documents, exempt documents are in effect those excluded by the operation of the second schedule to the Act and by ss. 32 to 47. The second schedule contains a list of twenty-three agencies or kinds of agencies *all* of the documents of which are exempt. These include the espionage agencies such as ASIS and ASIO; some agencies which must operate in the commercial arena, such as the Australian National Airlines Commission, the Commonwealth Banking Corporation and the Health Insurance Commission; and other miscellaneous agencies such as the Aboriginal Land Councils and the Auditor-General. Then the second schedule lists departments or agencies which are exempt from disclosing *particular kinds* of documents. Most of the exemptions in this list cover the competitive commercial activities (but not the other activities) of bodies such as the Wheat Board, the Dairy Corporation, Australia Post, Telecom and the OTC. The programme material of both the ABC and the SBS is excluded.

The second schedule also says that non-administrative functions of several tribunals such as the Arbitration Commission and Public Service Arbitrators are excluded. Similarly, s. 5 says that the Act applies only to the administrative activities (and not the judicial activities) of the commonwealth courts, such as the High Court, Federal Court and Family Court. Most commonwealth tribunals, including the Broadcasting Tribunal, are subject to the Act; but the exemptions mentioned below, such as the 'business affairs' exemption, still prevent many of their documents from being accessible under the Freedom of Information Act.

Specific Exemptions

Whereas the second schedule exempts some or all of the documents of named agencies, the additional specific exemptions in ss. 33–47 (Part IV of the Act) exempt any documents which fall into specified classes, regardless of who produced them. The classes are as follows:

National security, defence, international and interstate relations (ss. 33, 33A). A document is exempt if it could reasonably be expected to damage the security or defence of the commonwealth, its international relations or relations between it and any state or the Northern Territory; or if it would divulge confidential material communicated to the commonwealth by one of those governments.

Cabinet and Executive Council documents (ss. 34, 35). This exemption is probably the most disappointing to the media. It includes not only documents submitted to the cabinet and its committees, but also official records of the cabinet, documents brought into existence for the purpose of submission to cabinet, and any documents which would involve disclosure of any past deliberation or decision of the cabinet, except an official announcement of a cabinet decision. The same kind of restriction applies to Executive Council documents.

Internal Working Documents (s. 36). This important exemption covers any opinion, advice or recommendation involved in the deliberative processes of an agency, a minister, or the government, if their disclosure would be contrary to the public interest.

Law enforcement and public safety (s. 37). Among the documents exempted by this class are those which would prejudice investigation of a possible breach of the law, disclose a confidential source or a lawful means of detection of offenders, endanger the safety of those involved in law enforcement, or prejudice the fair trial or impartial adjudication of a particular case. As the Freedom of Information Act does not apply at all to state activities, it is only commonwealth law enforcement to which this exception relates.

Secrecy provisions of other Acts (s. 38). Regardless of the Freedom of Information Act, a document will not be disclosed if it is sufficiently covered by a secrecy provision in some other Act. There are said to be about 300 such provisions. An example may be s. 106A(5) of the Broadcasting and Television Act, which says that the Broadcasting Tribunal is not to make certain kinds of information available where it would be 'prejudicial to the interests of any person'. Section 16 of the Income Tax Assessment Act covers most tax records from disclosure.

Privacy (s. 41), business affairs (s. 43) and confidentiality (s. 45). A document is exempt if its disclosure would involve an unreasonable intrusion into the privacy of a person, including even a deceased person. Except for certain medical and psychiatric situations, a person cannot be denied access to a document on the ground that it would invade *his or her own* privacy. Section 43 protects trade secrets and other commercial information, the value of which could be destroyed by disclosure. It then goes on to confer very wide protection on business information the disclosure of which could unreasonably affect people in their business or profession, or which could prejudice the future supply of information to the commonwealth or an agency. Section 27 provides an opportunity for those who may be prejudiced by release of such information to make submissions objecting to its disclosure, but that opportunity is not provided for people whose personal privacy may be invaded. Section 45 says that a document is exempt if its disclosure would be 'a breach of confidence'. By those words, it incorporates the common law of confidential information discussed above. It does not mean that every document on which somebody has written the word 'confidential' is exempt.

National economy (s. 44). Financial journalists have not been forgotten. Documents are exempt if their disclosure would be against the public interest because of a substantial adverse affect on the ability of the government to manage the national economy, or could result in undue disturbance to business, or an undue benefit or detriment to any class of persons who would be receiving premature knowledge of something. This can include information about currency or exchange rates, taxes, foreign investment in Australia, and the regulation of banking and financial institutions.

Contempt of court or parliament (s. 46). This exemption applies to the law discussed in Chapters 6 and 7 of this book, without modification.

National Companies and Securities Scheme (s. 47). Certain national companies and securities scheme documents relating to the deliberations of the ministerial council which directs that scheme, or to the administration of related state and Northern Territory laws, are excluded.

Legal Professional Privilege (s. 42). A document which would be protected from disclosure in court by legal professional privilege, typically a communication between solicitor and client for the sole purpose of obtaining legal advice, is exempt.

Property interests and agency operations (ss. 39, 40). Documents which would have 'a substantial adverse affect on the financial or property interests of the Commonwealth or an agency' are exempt, as are documents which would prejudice the effectiveness of tests, examinations or audits by an agency. Other 'agency operation' exemptions include documents which would have a 'substantial adverse effect' on the industrial relations policy or negotiations of the commonwealth or an agency, or on supervision or review of an agency for efficiency or similar purposes, or on the staff management of an agency or the commonwealth. The precise meaning of this exemption, like some of the others, is not entirely clear.

The Workings of the Act

If the politicians and bureaucrats were the sole judges of when the above exemptions applied, little information might ever be released under the Freedom of Information Act. The Act, however, does make an attempt to introduce some independence into the key decisions about access, and to create an onus in favour of disclosing information. Only a few features of the complex scheme which contains those elements can be mentioned here.

Of some use to the media is s. 8, which requires publication of basic information about agencies and the information available from them. The internal organization, functions and powers of an agency are to be included, as well as the documents available from it, the information facilities which are open to members of the public and the way in which rights under the Freedom of Information Act may be exercised in relation to it. Section 9 requires publication of formerly recondite decision-making tools such as manuals and other documents containing interpretations, guidelines, precedents, and procedures for investigating breaches.

There is no great formality for requesting information under the Act, except that the request must be in writing,[54] and the prescribed fee must be paid.[55] An applicant for information must be notified about the decision on his or her request as soon as practicable, but not in any case more than sixty days after the request was received.[56] If access is denied, the applicant first seeks an internal review of the decision from the minister or the head of the agency concerned.[57] If that fails, there is then an appeal to the Administrative Appeals Tribunal,[58] which can broadly speaking remake the original decision about whether a document is exempt or not.[59] The commonwealth ombudsman may also be asked to investigate possible maladministration in any failure to supply information under the Act.[60]

A minister can ensure that a document will not be disclosed by issuing a certificate saying in effect that it ought to fall into the commonwealth security or deliberative categories of exemption mentioned above.[61] The secretary of the Department of Prime Minister and Cabinet may similarly certify that documents are cabinet documents, and the secretary of the Executive Council may certify that a document is within the Executive Council exemption.[62] One of the limits on the power of the Administrative Appeals Tribunal is that it cannot 'look behind' one of those certificates. The most it can do is refer it to the Document Review Tribunal, which exists to make decisions about whether, in its opinion, there are reasonable grounds to justify the certificate.[63] The powers of the Document Review Tribunal go no further than that. It has no power to release a document or override a certificate.

11

PRESS REGULATION

Mark Armstrong

It is generally true to say that just as the law gives no special recognition to the role of the press, so it imposes no special burdens on it. Certainly, the content of newspapers and journals is not subject to the kind of administrative control which the Broadcasting Tribunal exercises over radio and television programmes. No Australian laws require diversity in control of the press, except for some limits on television control noted in Chapter 9. The Trade Practices Act has only limited effects on concentration of press power.[1] Section 50 of that Act prohibits mergers resulting in dominance by one company in a particular market. Attempting to ensure that s. 50 is observed, the Trade Practices Commission has on occasion threatened intervention in takeovers of newspaper companies where it appeared that they would leave one company without a serious competitor in a city. Concentration in control of Victorian newspapers was the subject of a thorough report in 1981 by the Norris inquiry.[2] Sir John Norris, who conducted the inquiry, recommended a legislative scheme to counter oligopoly. It was not implemented, however, and any state scheme to affect such a national industry would face difficulties.

The three main controls which apply to print media as such are the printing and newspaper laws of the states and territories, the control of the Australian Journalists' Association over malpractice by its members, and the voluntary supervision of the Australian Press Council.

PRINTING AND NEWSPAPER LEGISLATION

Australian printing and newspaper Acts fall into two categories: the rudimentary laws of New South Wales, Queensland and the

Northern Territory; and the more detailed, onerous laws of the other jurisdictions (except South Australia), which still follow the model of Acts passed to help repress dissent in England around the time of the French Revolution.

The laws of New South Wales and Queensland impose almost identical 'imprint' requirements.[3] They require that any person who prints a document which is to be sold or distributed to the public or to a restricted number of people, or is to be publicly displayed, must print on one copy of that document the name and address of the person for whom it was printed. That copy must be retained for six months, and produced to a member of the police force on demand. In addition, the printer's name and address and *the year of printing* must appear on the front or first or last page of the document. These obligations clearly apply to a large amount of the material which is photocopied and duplicated, not just to commercial printers. The main exceptions are business cards, receipts for the sale of property, bills of exchange and some other legal documents, and documents printed for government authorities. Where the item printed is a newspaper, the only requirement is that the publisher's name and address, as well as that of the printer, must appear on the front or first or last page of each issue. It is an offence to sell or otherwise distribute to the public documents or newspapers which do not carry the required imprints, unless the document or newspaper was not printed in the state. The Northern Territory and Tasmanian laws are similar,[4] although in Tasmania basic particulars about newspapers must still be lodged with the Registrar of the Supreme Court.[5]

The Western Australian *Newspaper Libel and Registration Act* 1884 imposes imprint requirements on newspapers alone. The name and address of the printer must appear on every copy of a newspaper printed in the state, and one copy bearing the name and address of the person for whom each issue was printed and the signature of the printer must be sent to the Library Board of Western Australia. Newspaper proprietors in Western Australia who are not incorporated as companies must have their names, addresses and occupations entered on an official register, and must pay a fee for doing so. The more extensive legislation of Victoria and the ACT imposes imprint requirements broadly similar to New South Wales and Queensland, but it also requires the registration of printing presses and newspapers.[6]

The registration requirements, with their associated fees and administrative provisions, cannot be briefly summarized.

In Victoria and the Northern Territory, a bond of some hundreds of dollars is required for registration of a newspaper.[7] In the ACT, a press which is not used in accordance with the registration requirements may be seized and forfeited to the crown. In the Victorian Act there lurks a s. 29 which makes it an offence to print or publish a newspaper advertisement for employment in industry or commerce in a language other than English unless there is an accompanying English translation.

In 1982, South Australia became the first state to remove such burdens from printers and newspapers entirely.[8] The government considered the former Imprint Act ineffective and unjustified. No outbreak of defamation, obscenity or sedition in South Australian print media has been reported since it was repealed.

Section 201 of the federal *Copyright Act* 1968 requires that one copy of virtually all printed material published in Australia be sent to the National Library in Canberra. Each of the states similarly requires one copy of material published in the state for the relevant library.[9] The result is that a publisher, including even a local community group which produces a free newsletter or pamphlet, must normally send one copy to the National Library and one copy to the local state library.

THE AUSTRALIAN JOURNALISTS' ASSOCIATION

Nearly all working journalists are members of the Australian Journalists' Association (AJA), the trade union of the profession, which exercises some control over the ethics of journalism. Rule 49 of its registered rules says:

Each member of The Australian Journalists' Association shall observe the following Code of Ethics in his employment:

1 He shall report and interpret the news with scrupulous honesty.
2 He shall not suppress essential facts and shall not distort the truth by omission or wrong or improper emphasis.
3 He shall in all circumstances respect all confidences received by him in the course of his calling.
4 He shall observe at all times the fraternal obligations arising from his membership of the Association, and shall not on any occasion take unfair or improper advantage of a fellow member of the Association.
5 He shall not allow his personal interests to influence him in the discharge

of his duties nor shall he accept or offer any present, gift or other consideration, benefit or advantage of whatsoever kind if such acceptance or offer is of a character which may have the effect of so influencing or benefiting him.
6 He shall use only fair and honest methods to obtain news, pictures and documents.
7 He shall reveal his identity as a representative of the Press or of Radio or Television services before obtaining any personal interview for the purpose of using it for publication.
8 He shall do his utmost to maintain full confidence in the integrity and dignity of the calling of a journalist.

It may be seen that some items in the code are more definite than others. The rigour with which it is enforced depends largely on the AJA branch judiciary committees in the scheme outlined below. In one decision, a member who photographed a pop star in hospital after improperly gaining access to her room was suspended from membership for several years, with an obvious effect on his employment. Item 3 in the code embodies the obligation to protect confidential sources, which has occasionally brought journalists into conflict with the courts, as mentioned in Chapter 10. It would be contempt of court for a judiciary committee to discipline a member for giving evidence in court, but otherwise the committees may punish breaches of confidence which contravene the code.

Rule 49 also provides for each branch of the AJA to elect from its members a five-member judiciary committee to maintain observance of the code, as well as a three-member appeal committee. A judiciary committee is empowered by the rules to investigate alleged contraventions of the Code of Ethics, but will not receive anonymous or oral complaints. Rule 50 requires members to attend meetings of a judiciary committee when summoned, and authorizes the committees to impose fines of up to $250, and to expel members from the association. Rules 51 and 52 stipulate careful 'natural justice' and appeal requirements designed to ensure that a member accused of contravening the code has full opportunity to know the case against him or her, to be heard in defence, and to appeal first to an appeal committee and, if that fails, to the federal council of the union. Sub-rule 51(t) is one reason why the work of judiciary committees is not very well known, as it prohibits publication of their proceedings and findings except with specific authorization from the federal council or federal executive, which must 'consider the advisability of first obtaining legal advice'.

THE PRESS COUNCIL

The Australian Press Council has made considerable progress since its foundation in 1976 towards becoming the main arbiter of press ethics in the print media. It was supported and financed by the Australian Newspapers Council and other press organizations and by the AJA, which long advocated its establishment. It is a private association, lacking the endorsement of any Act of parliament and without any powers, legal or consensual, to discipline the press. That absence of disciplinary power was seen as a strength rather than a weakness. Sir Frank Kitto, its former chairman, said:

> Founded on the lines of the British Press Council, the Australian counterpart has striven to provide an effective alternative to the frequently advocated governmental authority for Press control. It has taken as self-evident truth, illustrated in many countries throughout the world, that control of the Press by any form of external authority paves the way for dictatorship, and that the only practicable defence against the agitation for control is self-regulation assisted by a system of supervision by a body formed from within the Press and operating, not by coercive effect of threatened punishment, but by the persuasive effect of constantly reiterated ethical principle.[10]

The 'constant reiteration of ethical principle' usually takes the form of adjudications on complaints made to the council. They are published in its own annual reports and also in most Australian newspapers, including newspapers which the council censures in its adjudications. The council is not solely a dispute-resolution body. Its constitution[11] gives it the much wider charter of maintaining journalistic standards and press freedom, and reporting on the ownership and control of the press, among other things.

Anyone may complain to the council. It is not necessary to have been specially affected by an offending article, and there is no prescribed form for a complaint, except that it should identify a specific complaint about the conduct of a paper or a specific item published in a newspaper; be accompanied by a copy of the paper or a cutting or photostat, or if not published an explanation of the matter complained of; state the ground of complaint; and give the name of the complainant, his or her telephone number if any, and the address to which documents for the complainant may be sent.[12]

Complaints are handled informally, and without legal representation. The council prefers that people complain directly to the editor of the paper concerned before approaching it. Otherwise, the council will itself refer the complaint to the editor on receipt. If a person is unhappy with the response of the editor, the complaint will then be referred to the complaints committee of the council for an adjudication, the result of which will be published. Where it is possible that a person complaining may have a legal claim against the paper concerned, the council will require a formal waiver of the complainant's rights against it, or else require that the legal claim be first determined by a court. This is to avoid contempt of court, and to avoid having an investigation used as a 'fishing expedition' by a plaintiff. The council does not investigate complaints about radio or television, or about print advertisements, which it refers to the Advertising Standards Council.

Although the offering of remedies to people who complain is not the prime purpose of the council, it does offer a valuable opportunity for people who have been injured by unethical press conduct to be publicly vindicated in a council adjudication. That is particularly valued by people who cannot afford or risk a defamation action, or to whom the law offers no remedy. Examples have been defamed associations, racial, political and ethnic groups, and a wide range of people and groups whose privacy has been invaded. But the largest group of complaints is about inaccuracy or misrepresentation. The council supports the AJA Code of Ethics, and has also issued its own statement of principles, which says, among other things, that rumour and unconfirmed reports should be identified as such, and not published if it would be unfair to do so; news obtained by unfair or dishonest means should not be published; newspapers are justified in advocating their own views (provided it is clear whose views are being expressed, and that these are clearly distinguishable from fact, which should not be distorted); and persons or groups should not be disparaged by reference to their sex, race, nationality, religion, colour or country of origin.[13]

The future of the council was left in doubt by a division between its members in 1987, arising from the takeover of the extensive newspaper interests of The Herald & Weekly Times Ltd by Mr Rupert Murdoch, whose companies already owned a number of Australian papers. The council was evenly divided over whether to urge the government to set up a tribunal to approve or disapprove takeovers which could cause greater concentration of press ownership.[14] The chairman, Mr H. Wooten QC (a former Supreme Court judge), resigned, as did some other members, including representatives of the AJA. Mr Wooten was reported as saying that it was terrifying for one man such as Mr Murdoch to have such a large degree of power to control the flow of information and opinion. He pointed to the power of the treasurer under the Foreign Takeovers Act to disallow the takeover, and said that at the very least the council should have issued a strong statement against the takeover. The surviving members of the council entered discussions about how to continue its functions after the resignations.[15] The result was a new membership with increased press representation.

12
ADVERTISING

Michael Blakeney

The commercial mass media were described by Humphrey McQueen as 'advertisements which carry news features, and entertainment in order to capture audiences for the advertisers'.[1] Leacock defined advertising as 'the science of arresting human intelligence long enough to get money from it'.[2] This cynicism about the role and quality both of advertising and the media which carry them has generated an equivalent cynicism about the veracity of the advertising messages that are disseminated. Since Victorian times, the courts have expressed the view that buyers should expect a considerable amount of lying by sellers eager to dispose of their products, and they developed the notion of 'puffery'. The 'mere puff', as it was called, was a term used by judges to exonerate the exaggerations employed in advertisements. The puff thus became the means by which, according to Richard Brinsley Sheridan, advertisers were able 'to inlay their phraseology with variegated chips of exotic metaphor, to clothe ideal walls with gratuitous fruits and to insinuate obsequious rivulets into visionary groves'.[3]

The late 1960s and early 1970s saw the explosion of 'consumer consciousness' in Australia. Both state and federal legislatures assumed that notwithstanding the improvement in educational standards since the demise of the Dame Schools the consumer was helpless against the importunities of the modern advertiser. Typical of contemporary legislative attitudes was the explanation of Senator Murphy when introducing the Trade Practices Bill into parliament:

The existing law is still founded on the principle known as *caveat emptor*—meaning 'let the buyer beware'. That principle may have been appropriate for transactions conducted in village markets. It has ceased to be appropriate as a general rule.

Now the marketing of goods and services is conducted on an organised basis and by trained business executives. The untrained consumer is no match for the businessman who attempts to persuade the consumer to buy goods or services on terms and conditions suitable to the vendor. The consumer needs protection by the law and this Bill will provide such protection.[4]

The *Trade Practices Act* 1974 is merely one of the several hundred statutes which have been enacted in Australia regulating unfair advertising practices. As consumerism became the nostrum of the 1970s, judges began to declare that it was for the law 'to control advertisers and not for what are claimed to be present advertising standards to mould the law'.[5] It was thought that the Trade Practices Act and the state and territory consumer protection laws would entirely change the face of advertising practice. The judges trained in the earlier era of laissez faire enterprise, however, have deprived those legislative innovations of much of their impact by interpreting them through *caveat emptor* spectacles. In the recent case *Stuart Alexander & Co. (Interstate) Pty Ltd* v. *Blenders Pty Ltd*,[6] for example, Lockhart J was obliged to consider the veracity of a television advertisement which sought to compare the price of the plaintiff's and the defendant's instant coffee. The means of comparison was a shower of silver coins into jars representing the respective products. The pile of coins in the plaintiff's jar was about twice as high as that in the defendant's, although the respective prices were much closer. Lockhart J did not consider this means of price comparison to be misleading. He said:

> A robust approach is called for when determining whether television commercials of this kind are false, misleading or deceptive. The public is accustomed to the puffing of products in advertising. Although the class of persons likely to see this commercial is wide, it is inappropriate to make distinctions that are too fine and precise.[7]

Despite this sort of judicial attitude and the abating of the protectionist tide since the halcyon days of Ralph Nader and his antipodean imitators, the sheer volume of legislation may effectively prevent a reversion to the questionable advertising practices of bygone eras. Potentially, the Trade Practices Act and the state and territory consumer protection statutes have established a fairly comprehensive regime of advertising regulation. The extent of its rigour will depend upon the way that the courts and the various watch-dog agencies approach the task of enforcement. Apart from the statutory regime, media industries have established a number of self-regulatory agencies which enforce a range of voluntary advertising codes.

ADVERTISING LAWS

Advertising in Australia is regulated primarily by statute law. In each state and territory, a proliferation of enactments, exceeding one hundred in some jurisdictions, both proscribe and prescribe the content of advertisements and the manner in which they are disseminated. The vast corpus of statute law should not obscure the fact that the common law also has an impact on advertising practice. The common law of contract regulates the nature of the promises extended by advertisments. The torts of defamation, deceit and negligent misstatement may render an advertiser liable for wrongs to consumers. The torts of injurious falsehood and passing off provide remedies to trade rivals injured by deceptive advertising.[8] The impact of the common law, however, has been made superfluous by the comprehensive code of advertising statutes.

The most important advertising statute is the Trade Practices Act. This contains a number of provisions which range from the broad prohibition in s. 52 of conduct which is misleading or deceptive, to the more specific prohibitions in s. 53 of false representations. Section 53A prohibits certain false or misleading representations in connection with the promotion of land transactions. Section 53B prohibits misleading conduct in relation to the promotion of employment opportunities. Section 53C makes it an offence not to state the cash price of a product where a statement is made in the promotion of a product as to an amount which has to be paid. Section 55 prohibits persons engaging in conduct liable to mislead the public 'as to the nature, the manufacturing process, the suitability for their purpose of any goods' and s. 55A of the Act prohibits corporations in trade or commerce engaging in conduct 'that is liable to mislead the public as to the nature, the characteristics, the suitability for their purpose of any services'. Bait advertising is prohibited by s. 56. The making of misleading statements about home-operated businesses is prohibited by s. 59(1) and the making of misleading statements about investment activities by s. 59(2).

Advertising which is misleading or deceptive attracts the civil sanctions of the Act, and contraventions of the more specific provisions carry additional criminal penalties. Criminal penalties for false or misleading advertisements are imposed by the consumer protection Acts of New South Wales, Queensland, Tasmania and Victoria.[9] In South Australia, Tasmania, Western Australia and the Northern Territory, false or misleading advertising is prohibited by specific criminal statutes.[10] In South Australia and the Australian Capital Territory, criminal sanctions are imposed for misrepresentations made in the course of trade.[11] Finally, a range of statutes are addressed to specific advertising practices. The state and territory legislation is largely cosmetic in effect because there have been very few actions brought under it. Enforcement, such as it exists, is largely by way of negotiations between advertisers and the relevant consumer protection authority.

THE TRADE PRACTICES ACT 1974

The importance of the Trade Practices Act in regulating advertising is emphasized by the volume of litigation which it has generated. In its 1981 publication, *Private Actions Under the Trade Practices Act*, the Trade Practices Commission lists some 199 court actions started by private litigants under the advertising provisions of the Act since 1975. Virtually all this litigation has been instituted by traders alleging deception of consumers in the advertising of trade rivals. The remedy being sought by these traders is an injunction to suppress the allegedly infringing advertisements. Injunctions are quickly obtainable. An interim injunction can be obtained within a couple of days to restrain objectionable advertising until a more comprehensive hearing can be convened. In exceptional circumstances, an injunction can be obtained on the application of one party within a few hours. The importance of this expeditious form of relief is obvious. An advertiser is able to preserve a market position from the inroads which a new but deceptive advertising campaign might make. An example of this use of the injunction is the Colgate-Palmolive litigation.[12] Colgate-Palmolive was able to restrain the advertising of Aim toothpaste by its rival Rexona on the basis that the latter's claim about the efficacy of Aim in inhibiting the growth of dental plaque was not substantiated and thus misleading.

Persons injured by illicit advertising may also obtain damages under the Act as well as any ancillary orders the court cares to make. The expense of private litigation is often an effective bar to consumer actions, notwithstanding apparent availability of legal aid under s. 170 of the Act. For this reason, a watch-dog agency, the Trade Practices Commission, has been created to enforce the provisions of the Act. The commission is empowered to institute criminal prosecutions under s. 79. A maximum penalty of $100 000 is imposed on companies which breach the criminal provisions of the Act and a maximum penalty of $20 000 on people who contravene them. People who aid, abet, counsel or procure or who are knowingly concerned in contravention of the Act are liable to the same penalties. Fines have been imposed on advertising agencies that have prepared contravening copy, or executive employees of defendant corporations or both, as well as on employees participating in illegal promotions.

The Trade Practices Commission may also obtain injunctions and may obtain corrective advertising or affirmative disclosure orders. Corrective advertising orders may oblige contravening advertisers to correct, through advertising, the deception which has appeared in previous advertisements. No limit is imposed by the Act as to the amount of money which has to be expended in corrective advertising. Affirmative disclosure orders can require the publication of important information which when omitted from advertisements creates a deceptive impression. The Trade Practices Act provides a range of defences to both civil and criminal actions, including a specific advertiser's defence available to those whose business it is to publish advertisements.

MISLEADING OR DECEPTIVE CONDUCT

The most general rule dealing with advertising is contained in s. 52 of the Trade Practices Act, which says: 'A corporation shall not, in trade or commerce, engage in conduct that is misleading or deceptive or is likely to mislead or deceive'. The requirement that the impugned conduct must occur in 'trade or commerce' is obviously met by most advertising. The expression 'trade or commerce' has been very broadly interpreted in the courts, and at its extremities has been held to include the placing of brochures in the foyer of a manufacturer's office,[13] a single private advertisement in a newspaper[14] and the preparation of a television documentary on the timber industry.[15]

In addition to express misrepresentations in advertisements, ambiguities from which deception results may contravene s. 52.

The courts have adopted dictionary definitions of the expression 'misleading or deceptive', namely, 'misleading: to lead astray in action or conduct; to lead into error; to cause to err. Deceptive: to cause to believe what is false; to mislead as to a matter of fact, to lead into error, to impose upon, delude, take in'.[16] Intention does not have be proved to establish a contravention of the section, but if intention is established the court will not 'be astute to say that [the respondent] cannot succeed in doing what he is straining every nerve to do'.[17] In determining whether conduct is misleading or deceptive, the court considers the audience in relation to which the conduct occurs and the standard of intelligence to be attributed to that audience.

Promises in advertising in relation to future events are deemed to be misleading where the advertiser does not have reasonable grounds for making the promise.

THE ADVERTISING AUDIENCE

No clear or consistently applied standard of audience intelligence has been enunciated by the courts. Early decisions under the Act indicated a fairly low standard of audience intelligence, reflecting the pro-consumer bias of the Act. In *World Series Cricket Pty Ltd* v. *Parish*,[18] for example, Bowen CJ observed that 'it is to be remembered that the advertisements are designed to meet a very wide audience which will include people possessing the widest possible range of knowledge or lack of knowledge about cricket and previous association or lack of association with it'.[19] Brennan J considered the relevant audience to be 'the general public' including 'the knowledgeable and those who are not, the superficial dreamer or viewer and listener as well as the profound, the gullible as well as the cautious'.[20] Franki J required the conduct to be 'likely to deceive or mislead at least a sufficient number of potential purchasers'.[21] A number of cases have adopted a statement made in *CRW Pty Ltd* v. *Sneddon*,[22] a decision under s. 32 of the *Consumer Protection Act* 1969 (NSW), where Sheldon and Sheppard JJ, referring to a newspaper advertisement, explained:

The advertiser must be assumed to know that the readers will include both the shrewd and the ingenuous, the educated and uneducated, and the experienced and inexperienced in commercial transactions. He is not entitled to assume that the reader will be able to supply for himself, or (often) herself, omitted facts or to resolve ambiguities. An advertisement may be misleading even though it fails to deceive more wary viewers.[23]

Since those early decisions, a more restrictive approach has begun to emerge. For example, in *Annand & Thompson Pty Ltd* v. *Trade Practices Commission*,[24] Franki J stated the test to be:

whether in an objective sense the conduct of the appellant was such as to be misleading or deceptive when viewed in the light of the type of person who is likely to be exposed to that conduct. Broadly speaking, it is fair to say that the question is to be tested by the effect on a person, not particularly intelligent or well informed, but perhaps of somewhat less than average intelligence and background knowledge although the test is not the effect on a person who is, for example, quite unusually stupid.[25]

Similarly, the Chief Justice of the High Court, in its most recent consideration of this issue, explained:

Section 52 does not expressly state what persons or class of persons should be considered as the possible victims for the purpose of deciding whether conduct is misleading or deceptive or likely to mislead or deceive. It seems clear enough that consideration must be given to the class of consumers likely to be affected by the conduct. Although it is true, as has often been said, that ordinarily a class of consumers may include the inexperienced as well as the experienced, and the gullible as well as the astute, the section must, in my opinion, be regarded as contemplating the effect of the conduct on reasonable members of the class. The heavy burdens which the section creates cannot have been intended to be imposed for the benefit of persons who fail to take reasonable care of their own interests.[26]

The identification of the target audience, where standard of intelligence is assessed, will depend on the nature of the advertising medium, the nature of the product advertised and the potential consumers of that product. Where the medium has wide dissemination, such as an evening newspaper, the standard of intelligence expected of the audience (or the propensity of an advertisement to mislead or deceive) will be affected by the inclusion of many people of less intelligence than possessed by readers of trade journals or even the 'quality' morning dailies. Where the electronic media are used to disseminate an advertisement, the audience will presumably include the illiterate and children. On the other hand, where the product being advertised is only relevant to one section of the medium's audience, the specialist knowledge of that section might raise the standard of intelligence. An advertisement for a woman's foundation garment in the *Women's Weekly*, for example, which has 750 000 men readers,[27] ought only to be deceptive if it is deceptive to women.

Finally, the abnormal susceptibilities of particular audiences may well be taken into account by a court weighing the deceptiveness of an advertisement. In the United States, the abnormal susceptibilities of children, parents, the sick and self-medicators, the poor, the elderly, the handicapped and particular ethnic groups have been taken into account in judging deception.[28] In the days before Betty Friedan and the crusading sisterhood, a US court even considered women to be abnormally susceptible to vanity product advertising, declaring:

... While the wise and worldly may well realize the falsity of any representations that the ... product can roll back the years, there remains 'that vast multitude' of others who, like Ponce de Leon, still seek a perpetual fountain of youth. As the [Federal Trade] Commission's expert further certified, the average woman, conditioned by talk in magazines and over the radio of 'vitamins, hormones and God knows what' might take 'rejuvenescence' to mean that this 'is one of the modern miracles' and is 'something which would actually cause her youth to be restored'.[29]

DECEPTION IN CLAIMS ABOUT PRODUCTS

Allegations of misleading or deceptive conduct under s. 52 have generated the vast majority of cases brought under the Act. Quite a few of these cases have involved claims by traders that a rival by the use of a similar name, advertising campaign, packaging, labelling or logo has attempted to pass itself off as the plaintiff. Additionally, cases have alleged deception in the manufacture of different products of a similar appearance, in the representation of price, product attributes and performance characteristics and in the representation of product histories, affiliation and novelty.[30]

DECEPTION IN THE COMMUNICATION OF PRODUCT CLAIMS

In much of the more intrusive advertising carried by the mass media, the information content of advertisements is subordinate in importance to the way that information is communicated. Thus an advertiser's claims may be boosted by celebrity endorsements or testimonials, the publication of test claims and market surveys and the use of television mock-ups and fantasy devices to enhance the advertising message. Where these techniques generate a deceptive impression about the substance of a product, the Act may be breached.

Celebrity Endorsements

The endorsement of an advertiser's product by a sports or television personality is a common advertising technique in Australia. The endorsement may be express, or implied from the use of a celebrity as presenter. The advertising message thus contains two pieces of information: any facts which the advertiser cares to disclose, and the information that the endorser approves of the product.

Endorsement by a celebrity may involve three different types of deception. Where the endorsement is unauthorized, there will be deception about the actual approval of the endorser. In *Coonan and Denlay Pty Ltd* v. *Superstar Australia Pty Ltd*,[31] for example, a manufacturer of cricket helmets successfully restrained the defendant from using photographs of test cricket players on its packaging when its helmet was not used by test stars. A celebrity endorsement may be deceptive if it implies an expertise which is untrue. The endorsement of a motor vehicle emission control device by an astronaut, for example, was held to be deceptive in the United States because the celebrity endorser did not have any expertise in motor vehicle engineering.[32] The Trade Practices Commission suggests that an endorsement outside a person's area of expertise may be a mere expression of opinion, but that an insupportable endorsement within the expert's area of competence can be an actionable statement of fact. For example, if a leading motor sports personality expresses a technical opinion about the performance, characteristics or benefits (e.g. by way of fuel consumption) of a particular motor product, the claims would need to be capable of substantiation using acceptable test criteria.[33] The American Federal Trade Commission took the view that paid celebrity endorsements were deceptive if the fact of payment were not disclosed, but more recently has required this disclosure only where the celebrity has a financial interest in the product promoted.[34]

Testimonials

The principles applying to celebrity endorsements apply with equal force to advertising which uses the testimonials of satisfied customers, or of organizations held in particular esteem by consumers. Obviously, an unauthorized testimonial will contravene the Act. A number of cases have involved the false representation of a testimonial. The leading example is *Hartnell* v. *Sharp Corporation of Australia Pty Ltd*,[35] in which the advertiser falsely represented that its goods had been tested and approved by the Standards Association of Australia.

The Trade Practices Commission recommends that:

> where technical aspects of products are endorsed by persons who, though not widely known, are represented as possessing relevant technical or professional expertise (e.g. a dietician or a food scientist), the facts presented should also be capable of substantiation using established and proven techniques of the particular field of technology.[36]

The commission has also stated that the Act will be contravened where it is falsely represented that a solicited endorsement is unsolicited.[37] The US Federal Trade Commission requires that an endorsement by an individual consumer should typify what consumers in general will experience. And, if an advertisement represents that it is the unrehearsed testimony of consumers, deception may result if actors are used.[38]

The Use of Test Results

Where test data are presented by an advertiser to present its product in a favourable light, s. 52 of the Act will be contravened if the test data draw conclusions which are not permissible, or the testing techniques are not scientifically reliable. The leading Australian case on the use of test data in advertising is *Colgate-Palmolive* v. *Rexona Pty Ltd*,[39] which concerned the claim that 'independent clinical tests have proved that, while no toothpaste can permanently rid the teeth of plaque, *Aim* with citraden slows down the regrowth of plaque dramatically' and that 'comparative tests show that *Aim* is significantly better at slowing down the regrowth of plaque than the toothpaste your family is using now'. The judge considered the scientific evidence and found that there was a real dispute on whether citraden inhibited plaque and whether the concentration of the compound in *Aim* would have inhibited plaque and reduced decay. The tests relied on by the defendant were largely unpublished and had not been independently assessed by the dental profession, all of which led the judge to find a *prima facie* case that the advertising was misleading or deceptive.

Where test results are summarized for the purposes of an advertisement, deception may result if the summary indicates erroneous product comparisons. In its *Advertising and Selling Guide*,[40] the Trade Practices Commission lists the following examples of uses of tests and surveys in advertising which may breach s. 52 of the Act:

Advertisements in which the claims made are said to be based on a statistical survey (e.g. 'Nine out of ten housewives prefer ...') when in fact such a survey has not been undertaken or the results of the survey are distorted. Advertisers should not make such claims unless supported by an objective survey, based on recognised statistical method, preferably conducted by an independent organisation. The Commission expects advertisers making such claims to be in a position to meet the Commission's request for full particulars of the survey upon which the claims are based;

claims that a product is 'tested' by an authority when only part of the product was tested, or another similar product was tested or the product failed the test

... tests showing a particular performance result has been achieved by a product when that test is not representative of what can be achieved by the average user ...;

claims that are supported by tests or surveys which suggest that they are unbiased and were conducted by an independent agency may be misleading if, in fact, the tests were carried out by a related organisation (unless the results could be confirmed by independent analysis).

Comparison Advertising

Probably the most contentious advertising technique is the comparison in an advertisement of the advertiser's product with that of a trade rival. If the comparison involves disparagement, it may fall foul of the industry bodies which restrict unfavourable comparisons in advertising.[41] False or misleading comparisons will fall foul of the Trade Practices Act. The Trade Practices Commission warns:

Consumers may be misled by 'before and after' advertisements where the comparison is distorted to deprecate the 'before' or enhance the 'after' situations or by comparisons between the advertiser's goods or services and those of a competitor which fail to compare 'like with like'.[42]

In the *Colgate-Palmolive* case, the defendant claimed that its Aim toothpaste was '50–90 per cent more effective than Australia's best known toothpastes in slowing down the growth of plaque between brushing'. The plaintiff, who held about 60 per cent of the Australian market, was able to establish a *prima facie* contravention of s. 52 of the Act because, among other things, the defendant was not able to demonstrate the superiority of the product over the plaintiff's.

Television Mock-ups

The simulation of tests or comparisons in television advertisements causes particular problems where the distorting effect of television broadcasts conveys an erroneous impression, or where the advertiser compensates for that distortion. As was pointed out in a US case:

Everyone knows that on T.V. all that glistens is not gold. On a black and white screen, white looks gray, and blue looks white: the lily must be painted. Coffee looks like mud. Real ice cream melts more quickly than that firm but fake sundae. The plain fact is, except by props and mock-ups, some objects cannot be shown on television as the viewer, in his mind's eye, knows the essence of the object.[43]

In the United States, the Supreme Court in *FTC* v. *Colgate Palmolive Co.*[44] held the use of a television mock-up to be deceptive. That case concerned an advertisement which in the voice-over declared: 'To prove Rapid Shave's super moisturizing power, we put it right from the can onto this tough, dry sandpaper'. A close-up shot focused on a razor cutting a smooth diagonal path through the lather and the purported sandpaper to the accompaniment of the commentary that it was 'apply ... soak ... and off in a stroke'. The complaint alleged that viewers were deceived because what had been shaved was not sandpaper but plexiglass on which sand had been sprinkled. The respondent argued that the mock–up was necessary because sandpaper on television looked like clear coloured paper. The Federal Trade Commission argued that the commercials were deceptive in representing that the cream enabled the immediate shaving of sandpaper, whereas it required the sandpaper to be soaked for three hours. The Supreme Court affirmed the Federal Trade Commission's order which required the respondents to desist from

Unfairly or deceptively advertising any ... product by presenting a test, experiment or demonstration that (1) is represented to the public as actual proof of a claim made for the product which is material to inducing its sale, and (2) is not in fact a genuine test, experiment or demonstration being conducted as represented and does not in fact constitute actual proof of the claim, because of the undisclosed use and substitution of a mock-up or prop instead of the product, article or substance represented to be used therein.

The Supreme Court was not hostile to mock-ups as such, only to the misleading simulation of the experiment. Where a mock-up is used for the purpose of a comparison, the problems faced by the advertiser in the *Colgate-Palmolive* case can partially be overcome by the disclosure of the simulation. As the case illustrates, however, such disclosure would not prevent falsified test results from being deceptive. The US approach to mock-ups may well be applied here.

FALSE OR MISLEADING CLAIMS IN ADVERTISEMENTS

In addition to the general prohibition in s. 52 of the Trade Practices Act of conduct which is misleading or deceptive there are, as we have seen, a number of prohibitions of various specific false representations and false or misleading statements. The most comprehensive catalogue of prohibitions is contained in s. 52 which provides:

A corporation shall not, in trade or commerce, in connexion with the supply or possible supply of goods or services or in connexion with the promotion by any means of the supply or use of goods or services:—
(a) falsely represent that goods are of a particular standard, quality, grade, composition, style or model or have had a particular history or particular previous use;
(aa) falsely represent that services are of a particular standard, quality or grade;
(b) falsely represent that goods are new;
(bb) falsely represent that a particular person has agreed to acquire goods or services;
(c) represent that goods or services have sponsorship, approval, performance characteristics, accessories, uses or benefits they do not have;
(d) represent that the corporation has a sponsorship, approval or affiliation it does not have;
(e) make a false or misleading representation with respect to the price of goods or services;
(ea) make a false or misleading representation concerning the availability of facilities for the repair of goods or of spare parts for goods;
(eb) make a false or misleading representation concerning the place of origin of goods;
(f) make a false or misleading representation concerning the need for any goods or services; or
(g) make a false or misleading representation concerning the existence, exclusion or effect of any condition, warranty, guarantee, right or remedy.

A list of the actions brought under each of the paragraphs of s. 53 will indicate the comprehensive scope of the section.

'Standard, Quality, Grade, etc.'

Section 53(a) prohibits false representations of the particular standard, quality, grade, composition, style or model or of the particular history or particular previous use of goods and s. 53(aa) prohibits false representations that services are of a particular standard, quality or grade. These are all related concepts and the cases seem to use some of them interchangeably. 'Standard' has been applied to false representations about compliance with standards of the Standards Association of Australia[45] as well as to the previous use or history of motor vehicles.[46] Claims that goods comply with non-existent standards may also contravene the Act.[47] Quality has been held to cover odometer readings of motor vehicles,[48] product composition,[49] previous use,[50] previous ownership,[51] the efficacy of a product, special features, performance capabilities,[52] or origin.[53]

A representation that a car is a particular year model, when it is of another year, obviously falls within the paragraph.[54]

'Grade' refers to recognized grades and may apply to the erroneous comparison of grades of goods or services.[55] 'Style' suggests compliance with recognized styles: Chippendale or Sheraton furniture,[56] for example. Examples of contraventions involving false representations of composition include representation of non-existent ingredients,[57] and purity.[58]

Examples of representations about the antecedents of goods likely to fall within s. 53(a) are false claims about the mileage travelled by a vehicle (usually by tampering with odometer readings),[59] misrepresentations of previous ownership,[60] the representation that a car was a 'demonstrator'[61] or 'ex-GMH Executive Car',[62] when the relevant vehicles had been used by rental companies. The offer of trucks for sale with the promise of employment as carriers has also been held to contravene s. 53(a).[63]

New Goods

The Trade Practices Commission has identified three classes of representation of newness: new in the sense of novelty or invention; new meaning not secondhand, refurbished, repaired or rebuilt; and new in the sense of recently produced or acquired.[64] These meanings were largely derived from the English Court of Appeal decision in *R* v. *Ford Motor Co. Ltd*.[65] Other suggested meanings include: current model;[66] not having suffered significant deterioration;[67] not having extensive use;[68] not significantly damaged (where repairs are able to restore the goods);[69] but it is not necessary that goods be 'in mint condition'.[70] Because of the various meanings of the word 'new', it is necessary to determine the context in which the word is used.[71]

'Sponsorship, Approval, Affiliation'

Section 53(c) prohibits false representations about the sponsorship or approval of goods or services and s. 53(d) prohibits representations that a corporation has sponsorship or approval it does not have. The false representation that the Packer cricket games were sponsored by the Australian Cricket Board was the subject of an injunction by the board.[72] Other contraventions include the false representation that microwave ovens had been tested and approved by the Standards Association of Australia;[73] that electric welders had the approval of the State Electricity Commission;[74] that a fire extinguisher had been approved by the non-existent 'Yachting Association of Australia',[75] and that electric crock-pots had been approved for use in Australia by the electrical authorities.[76] Claims of affiliation with a competitor may be implied from the use of a similar corporate name,[77] or from the use of trade names used by competitors.[78] A publisher who published a magazine as the magazine of a particular association after the association had cancelled its arrangement with the publisher was found to have breached s. 53 (c).[79]

'Performance Characteristics, Accessories, Uses, or Benefits'

Claims about the performance characteristics of goods include those on the disability, efficiency, maintenance, standard of performance and suitability for a particular purpose of goods. False representations of 'stereo amplification',[80] insect repellent facility[81] and compliance with fire efficiency tests[82] have been prohibited. The Trade Practices Commission requires that performance claims be capable of substantiation.[83] The commission has advised that the requirements of s. 53(c) are best met by stating clearly (not in fine print) the additional cost of any accessories depicted in an advertisement or accessories that are necessary, which are not included in the advertised base price.[84] An example was the advertisement which failed to explain that a gas cylinder shown attached to a gas barbecue was $25 extra.[85] Contraventions of the Act have included advertisements falsely representing that certain models of a car were fitted with 'servo-assisted brakes'[86] or that vehicles were fitted with stabilization bars.[87]

Section 53(c) prohibits false representations about the 'benefits' of goods or services. The representation that a superannuation scheme was exempt from state death duties was held to be an illegal representation of a benefit,[88] as was the incorrect claim that the use of a burglar alarm would result in insurance savings.[89] Two instances of misdescribing travel packages by overstating the duration of a tour have been held to be false representations that services had benefits they did not have.[90]

'Price'

Section 53(e) prohibits 'false or misleading statements with respect to the price of goods or services'. 'Price' is defined in s. 4(1) of the Act to include 'a charge of any description'. False or misleading statements which refer to price will obviously contravene s. 53(c).[91] Statements understood by purchasers to be related to price will also fall foul of the paragraph,[92] as well as statements which refer to the constituents of a price such as sales tax[93] or 'on road costs'.[94] A statement prescribing 'the manner in which and the time by which the obligation to satisfy the payment of the price may be discharged is ... a statement with respect to price'.[95] Misleading price comparisons or statements of price reductions will also contravene the section.

'Need'

Section 53(f) prohibits false or misleading statements 'concerning the need for goods or services'. 'Need' has not been limited to 'an imperative question or demand or necessity'[96] but applied to statements of desirability or preferability.[97] The section probably requires clear factual assertions rather than general claims about product desirability unless such claims are made by experts.[98] Contraventions of s. 52(f) have included the false claim that contributors to a medical fund needed to contribute to a particular table to have the doctor of their choice;[99] that fire extinguishers had to be 'fitted adjacent to each exit on your van';[100] and that certain car repair work was necessary.[101]

Section 53(g) 'Conditions, Guarantees, Rights or Remedies'

Examples of contraventions of the prohibition in s. 53(g) against false or misleading statements 'concerning the existence, exclusion or effect of any condition, warranty, guarantee, right or remedy' include a discrepancy between the warranty period set out in a brochure and that contained in a warranty card delivered with a calculating machine, and a failure to reveal the limits to a guarantee.[102]

SPECIFIC CATEGORIES OF FALSE OR MISLEADING ADVERTISING

In addition to the catalogue of prohibitions contained in s. 53, the Trade Practices Act specifically regulates the advertising of land, employment opportunities and investment opportunities, presumably because these have generated sufficient complaints from consumers to justify specific legislation.

Advertising of Land

Section 53A of the Trade Practices Act prohibits a corporation, in trade or commerce in connection with the sale or grant or the possible sale or grant of an interest in land or in connection with the promotion by any means of the sale or grant of an interest in land, making certain false representations or false or misleading statements or engaging in certain unfair or offensive conduct. The section prohibits a corporation representing that it has 'a sponsorship approval or affiliation it does not have', from making false or misleading statements concerning the nature of the interest in the land, the price payable for the land, the characteristics of the land, the use to which the land is capable of being put, or may lawfully be put, or the existence or availability of facilities associated with the land; or from offering gifts, prizes or other free items with the intention of not providing them or of not providing them as offered. A corporation is also prohibited from causing, or permitting a servant or agent using at a place of residence, physical force, undue harassment or coercion in connection with the sale or grant, or the possible sale or grant, of an interest in land or the payment for an interest in land.

The opening words of s. 53A refer to the 'promotion' by any means of the sale or grant of an interest in land. In *Sackville* v. *Mansard Developments Pty Ltd*,[103] Lockhart J held that the advertising of building sites or lots for sale by a general heading in a newspaper advertisement was part of a general promotion of the unsold land covered by the general description. Intention not to promote part of the land included in that general description was not relevant to a consideration of whether that land was covered in the promotion. Advertisers must clearly state the nature of the interest in land being promoted. It has been held to be misleading to suggest that a purchaser will acquire an exclusive interest in land, whereas what was being offered was an interest in an undivided portion of land to be shared with others.[104] In the absence of further explanations the use of the term 'legal title' has been suggested to be misleading.[105]

A statement prescribing the terms for the payment of land was held in *Henderson* v. *Pioneer Homes Pty Ltd*[106] to be a statement concerning the price of land. The advertised purchase scheme involved a period of temporary finance to be replaced by more expensive long-term finance. The failure of the advertisements to refer to the greater expense of the latter finance was held to contravene s. 53, but it might equally have contravened s. 53A.

Advertisements that describe the location of land are said to be less likely to mislead or deceive than an advertiser's subjective assessment of the excellence of a piece of land.[107] Advertisers using sketch maps, diagrams, artists' impressions or photographs are advised to take particular care not to mislead or deceive about the location of the land.[108] In *Videon* v. *Beneficial Finance Corporation*,[109] a developer claimed that lots advertised were adjacent to a zone subject to development restrictions, whereas the land fell within the zone. The developer and agent were convicted of misleading intending purchasers about the location of the land.

Representations about the use to which land may be put will contravene the section if legal restrictions on its use are concealed. A television commercial, for example, which showed pictures of an estate which included houses was held to be misleading because the land was zoned non-urban.[110] The section envisages statements about present and future land use[111] and will cover matters such as zoning, building regulations, restrictive covenants, easements and leases.

Finally, the section prohibits false or misleading representations concerning both the existence or availability of facilities associated with the land. In *Sackville* v. *Mansard Developments Pty Ltd*,[112] the defendant land developer advertised the sale of subdivided land as fully serviced with electricity. Only some lots were serviced, and the trial judge found the statements to be false, but on appeal the Full Federal Court ruled that the advertisement did not refer to all the lots; only to those offered for sale on the particular day.[113]

Employment Advertising

Section 53B prohibits conduct 'that is liable to mislead persons seeking ... employment as to the availability, nature, terms and conditions' of the employment. The Trade Practices Commission noted in its Information Circular No. 23, which promulgates private employment agency advertising guidelines, that employment agencies and brokers are also regulated by specific legislation in New South Wales, South Australia and Western Australia.[114] In those guidelines, the commission warned against employment advertising with the primary purpose of promoting ancillary services such as self-improvement courses, and suggested that advertising which overstated pay or other conditions of employment was false in material particulars.[115] In *Wilde* v. *Menville Pty Ltd*,[116] a company promoted the sale of trucks to potential purchasers by offering to provide them with 'permanent' positions as owner-drivers. The company, its directors, and some senior employees pleaded guilty to having contravened s. 53B.

Investment Opportunities

Section 59(1) of the Trade Practices Act prohibits a corporation in trade or commerce from:

making a statement that is false or misleading in a material particular concerning the profitability or risk or any other material aspect of any business activity that the corporation has represented is one that can be, or can be to a considerable extent, carried on at, or from a person's place of residence.

Section 59(2) prohibits similar statements where persons are asked 'by advertisement or otherwise' to invest moneys and perform work associated with the investment.

A 'material particular' for the purposes of both s. 59(1) and s. 59(2) appears to include the profitability or risk of a business venture. The Trade Practices Commission requires a full disclosure of the risks likely to be incurred by the average person carrying on the business and itemizes as matters to be disclosed the minimum amount of capital investment required by the average person to carry on the business; the annual gross expenditure likely to be incurred by the average person; the annual gross income likely to be received by the average person; the amount of time the average person would have to devote to the business to achieve that income; the market for the goods or services which may be supplied by the person carrying on that business; the number of other persons carrying on such businesses in that market and the number of persons likely to carry on business in that market; whether the person carrying on the business requires a licence or permit; and, whether the person carrying on the business may acquire supplies necessary for the conduct of the business from persons other than the advertiser or his nominees or whether that person may supply persons other than the advertiser or persons nominated by it.[117]

Penalties under the Trade Practices Act

Contraventions of state and territory consumer protection statutes attract fines of up to $10 000 for each advertising offence, in the case of the New South Wales and South Australian Acts. Contraventions of the advertising provisions in Part V of the Act, other than s. 52, as we have seen, render corporations liable to fines of up to $100 000 for each offence. In the case of non-corporate people, fines of up to $20 000 may be imposed. Individuals knowingly concerned in a contravention of the Act may, by the application of s. 5 of the federal *Crimes Act* 1914, be fined up to $20 000 for each offence and, by an application of s. 6 of that Act, they may be fined up to the same amount for aiding and abetting a contravention. Amendments to the Act in 1977 inserted ss. 79(2) and (3), which impose ceilings of $100 000 in respect of companies and $20 000 in respect of individuals for fines arising from two or more offences which 'appear to the Court to have been of the same nature or a substantially similar nature and to have occurred at about the same time'. A similar ceiling was inserted in s. 76(3) in 1978 to provide that a person should not be liable for more than one fine for the same conduct in contravention of the restrictive trade practice provisions of the Act. Smithers J held in *Ducret* v. *Colourshot Pty Ltd*[118] that to fall within the ceiling established by s. 79(2) the multiple offences had to coincide 'in time so close as to impart unity' to the offences. In this case, a fine of $95 000 was imposed on the defendant company and a fine of $35 000 on its managing director for multiple offences occurring at intervals of two months. In *Wilde* v. *Menville Pty Ltd*,[119] Smithers J fined the defendant company $75 000 and three senior employees $19 000, $18 000 and $8000, respectively, for multiple offences arising out of the same promotional campaign.

In *Hartnell* v. *Sharp Corporation of Australia Pty Ltd*,[120] in which a fine of $100 000 was imposed on the defendant, Smithers J enumerated a number of factors to be taken into account in quantifying penalties under the Act. These have been adopted in a number of subsequent cases. His Honour listed as factors to be considered:

First, the importance of untrue statements and the departure from standards; secondly, the degree of wilfulness or carelessness in the making of these statements; thirdly, the degree that the statement departs from the truth; fourthly, the degree that the statement has been disseminated.

Next, what efforts have been made to correct the situation; finally we have to look at it in the context of the Act and to consider the deterrent effect of any penalty that we must impose.[121]

DEFENCES TO CRIMINAL PROSECUTIONS

Most of the state and territory advertising statutes provide defences to prosecutions to persons who have 'exercised due diligence' to prevent the commission of offences, persons who were the victims of error or persons who had no knowledge of the relevant contraventions. The most comprehensive catalogue of defences to criminal actions arising from advertising are contained in s. 85(1) of the Trade Practices Act, which resembles the defences found in the state and territory statutes. Additionally, s. 85(3) provides a general publisher's defence available for both criminal and civil action brought under the Act. Section 85(1) provides that a person shall have a defence to prosecutions in respect of contraventions of Part V of the Act if he establishes that the contravention in respect of which the proceeding was instituted was due to reasonable mistake; to reasonable reliance on information supplied by another person; or to the act or default of another person, to an accident or some cause beyond the defendant's control and that the defendant took reasonable precautions and exercised due diligence to avoid the contravention.

Section 85(3) of the Act provides a general defence to both civil and criminal contraventions of Part V provisions committed by the publication of an advertisement:

if the defendant establishes that he is a person whose business it is to publish or arrange for the publication of advertisements and that he received the advertisement for publication in the ordinary course of business and did not know and had no reason to suspect that its publication would amount to a contravention of a provision of that Part.

The defence applies only to contraventions committed by the publication of an advertisement and is thus primarily designed for media proprietors and broadcasting licensees. The Full Federal Court in *Universal Telecasters (Qld) Pty Ltd* v. *Guthrie*[122] did not question the availability of the defence to a television station licensee. The defence is probably unavailable to advertising agencies because their business is the creation of advertisements for publication. The requirement that the advertisement be received in the ordinary course of business suggests that it is the persons who deal with the completed advertisement, rather than the agencies who deal with preliminary copy, to whom the defence is available. The cornerstone of the s. 85(3) defence is the requirement that the defendant lacked knowledge or suspicion that the advertisement contravened a provision of Part V of the Act.

The primary question which concerned the court in the *Universal Telecasters* case was whether the knowledge of an employee that an advertisement contravened the Act could be imputed to his employer. The Full Court was prepared to impute to the company only the knowledge of those people who could be said to represent the 'directing mind and will' of the company. Thus repeated complaints made to a sales manager about the legality of an advertisement televised by the company were not considered by the Full Court to attribute knowledge or suspicion to the corporation. Analysing the duties of the sales manager the Full Court, by a majority of two to one, overruled the trial judge's assumption that the sales manager exercised the powers of the company.

SELF-REGULATION OF ADVERTISING

Paralleling the regulation of advertising by the law is a complex fabric of self-regulatory, or voluntary organizations. The most important of these are the Media Council of Australia and the media approval bodies, namely, the Federation of Australian Commercial Television Stations, the Federation of Australian Radio Broadcasters; and the Australian Publisher's Bureau. Each of these bodies enforces voluntary codes of advertising standards which are imposed on advertising agencies. Additionally, a Joint Committee for Disparaging Copy hears complaints by the agencies themselves.

Media Council of Australia

The Media Council of Australia is a trade association of virtually all the non-government proprietors of mass media in Australia. The council is responsible for the accreditation of advertising agents. Accreditation entitles agents to obtain financial credit from council members provided the agents comply with and observe the voluntary codes promulgated by the council. The council has promulgated a general Advertising Code of Ethics which provides:

1. Advertisements must be truthful and shall not be misleading or liable to misinterpretation.
2. Advertisements must be clearly distinguishable as such.
3. Advertisements must comply with Commonwealth and State Law.
4. Advertisements of a controversial nature shall disclose their source.

5. Scientific, statistical or other research data quoted in advertisements shall be neither misleading nor irrelevant.
6. Testimonials used in advertisements must honestly reflect the sentiments of the individuals represented. Claims in testimonials are subject to the same rules as other advertising.
7. Advertising of goods or services must be for the purpose of genuinely selling those goods or services, and not for the purpose of selling substitute goods or services.
8. Advertisements for medicines and treatments shall be subject to the rules of the 'Guide to Advertising of Proprietary Medicines and Therapeutic Appliances' in addition to the rules of this Code.
9. The intention of an advertiser who, without making an appointment intends to call upon or send a representative to call upon any person applying for particulars or details of any product or service advertised must be clearly stated in the advertisement.
10. Advertisements shall not exploit the superstitious or unduly play on fear.
11. Advertisements shall not exploit children nor contain anything which might result in their physical, mental or moral harm.
12. Contests shall be conducted with fairness to all entrants.
13. If the word 'guarantee' is used in an advertisement the terms of the guarantee, or the place where the guarantee may be obtained must be clearly stated.
14. Mail order advertisers shall be prepared to meet any reasonable demand created by their advertising, and shall readily refund money in full to buyers with reasonable cause for dissatisfaction with their purchase or delay in delivery. The name of a mail order advertiser shall be prominently displayed in the advertisement and samples of goods advertised shall be available at the advertiser's place of business for public inspection during normal business hours.
15. Advertisements shall not disparage identifiable products, services or advertisers in an unfair or misleading way.

In addition, the Media Council of Australia has promulgated or enforces voluntary codes dealing with the advertising of therapeutic goods and services, cigarettes, alcoholic beverages, hair-piece treatments, slimming preparations and domestic insecticides, as well as a code dealing with mail order promotions.[123]

The codes are enforced by the Advertising Standards Council. On a complaint from a member of the public, an advertiser or advertising agency the council seeks comment from the relevant media approval bodies, as well as the advertiser, agency and media proprietor. If a complaint is sustained, the council may order the suspension of the accreditation of the contravening agency.[124]

Three councils have recently been formed to review and maintain the more contentious codes. These are the Tobacco Products Advertising Council, Alcoholic Beverages Advertising

Council and Therapeutic Advertising Council. At the moment these councils have a purely advisory role.

Federation of Australian Commercial Television Stations

The Australian Broadcasting Tribunal has, pursuant to the *Broadcasting and Television Act* 1942, promulgated standards relating to advertising generally and to children's television advertising in particular. These standards are paralleled and endorsed by codes promulgated by FACTS and in practice the tribunal leaves enforcement to the voluntary organization. The Commercials Acceptance Division of the federation requires all accredited advertising agencies to submit to it virtually all film and television commercials which are to be broadcast on more than one station other than ephemeral commercials, such as for grocery specials. Member stations will not televise relevant commercials until an approval number has been granted by the Commercials Acceptance Division. Its approval is dependent upon the advertisements complying with the Australian Broadcasting Tribunal's Standards, state and federal laws and with its own guidelines.

The Commercials Acceptance Division has issued some fifty-one guidelines[125] dealing with such disparate topics as children's advertising and the advertising of pet foods, real estate, motor vehicles, personal products, security and self-defence devices and election advertising. It has also issued guidelines on the manner in which advertising messages may or may not be communicated. The most important of these are its guidelines on taste and decency and the related guidelines on references to sex in advertisements, the simulation of news items and the use of impersonations, caricatures or look-alikes. Among the more controversial recent suspensions of television advertisements by the Commercials Acceptance Division were simulations of endorsements by the then Lady Diana and ex-President Nixon.[126] Where objection is taken to an advertisement approved by the Commercials Acceptance Division an appeal committee may be convened and that approval may be overruled.[127]

Federation of Australian Radio Broadcasters

All recorded radio commercials to be broadcast by more than one station must be approved by the federation, which ensures compliance of advertisements with the Australian Broadcasting

Tribunal's Broadcasting Advertising Standards mentioned in Chapter 9.

Australian Publishers' Bureau

The accreditation rules of the Media Council of Australia oblige agencies to submit to the bureau draft print advertisements to which the council's codes apply. Without an approval number from the bureau, advertisements will not be published. One of the problems with the bureau's activities is that the agency has to ascertain, in the first place, whether a code applies. An anti-smoking campaign by the Health Commission of New South Wales was suspended by the bureau because the campaign was alleged to involve the advertising of therapeutic services for which approval had not been obtained.

Joint Committee for Disparaging Copy

The committee consists of seven members drawn from television, radio, the print media, national advertisers and agencies. Acting on complaints from advertisers or advertising agencies, it is empowered to veto any advertisement which 'contains a specific and identifiable disparagement of a particular product or service advertised by a rival.'[128] Thus, an advertisement which a court may consider to involve an innocuous comparison may be held by the committee to involve disparagement.[129]

13

SALES PROMOTIONS

Michael Blakeney

The launch of a new product is frequently accompanied by a promotional price reduction as well as the offer of some non-price benefits such as gifts, trading stamps, coupon offers, bonus packs, refund vouchers or club schemes. Additionally, below-the-line promotions may be engaged in to renew interest in a static product. The offer of a 'special price' may fall within the state and federal bait advertising legislation. Prize promotions may fall foul of the Trade Practices Act; and coupon offers may attract liability under the state Trading Stamps legislation. Finally, certain marketing and distribution schemes, which may involve promotion in the mass media, have been specifically prohibited. These include inertia, referral and pyramid selling.

BAIT ADVERTISING

Advertisting goods or services at special prices, with the intention of not offering them at that price may fall foul of s. 56 of the Trade Practices Act or of the bait advertising provisions of statutes in New South Wales, Victoria and South Australia.[1] Section 56(1) of the Trade Practices Act prohibits a corporation, in trade or commerce, advertising for supply at a 'special price', goods or services that the corporation does not intend to offer for supply at that price for a period that is and in quantities that are reasonable, having regard to the nature of the market in which the corporation carries on business and the nature of the advertisment. Section 56(2) prohibits a failure to supply goods following a bait advertisement in circumstances of the sort mentioned in s. 56(1). Where there are legitimate reasons for non-supply, a defence is provided by s. 56(3).

An offer at a 'special price' is defined in s. 4(1) of the Trade

Practices Act to be either a price that is represented in the advertisement to be a special or bargain price by reference to an ordinary price or a price that a consumer would take to be a special or bargain price having regard to the usual price of the goods or services. Examples of the first category of advertisements are those which claim 'greatly reduced', 'buy while the price is low', 'below cost sale', 'anniversary special', 'opening sale prices' or 'clearance sale'.[2] Examples of the second category of advertisements are those which convey the impression that there is a special price below the normal selling price for the relevant goods or services. The New South Wales Act contains a similar definition. The Victorian and South Australian Acts require prices to be specified in the impugned advertisement.

A difficult legal problem which has arisen in the interpretation of the bait advertising statutes is whether the word 'offer' is used in its technical legal sense, as an offer to be contractually bound, or whether offers may include displays of goods which have traditionally been interpreted as mere invitations to treat, not involving any legal liability. The problem has arisen primarily because in *Reardon* v. *Morley Ford Pty Ltd*,[3] the first decision under s. 56, the trial judge adopted the technical legal definition, although he conceded that a trader might intend that an invitation to treat be regarded as an offer.[4] This problem is eschewed in the New South Wales Act which uses the expression 'make available'. The Victorian Act refers to 'offer' and the South Australian Act prevents the 'notification, sale, offer, exhibition or exposure for sale by retail' of goods subject to conditions that a minimum quantity be sold to one purchaser.

Contraventions of s. 56 are avoided if stocks are available for a reasonable period. In assessing the reasonableness of the period, regard is had to the nature of the relevant market and the nature of the advertisement. The Trade Practices Commission also refers to the 'methods of advertising, the method of distribution of any goods and their rate of turnover in the market of their normal selling price and, in the case of services, the frequency at which persons acquire the services at their normal selling price'.[5] The commission suggests that expressions such as 'while stocks last' or 'limited offer' will not prevent a contravention, but should be qualified by some indication of likely availability.[6]

The commission advises that quantities may be unreasonable where an advertiser fails to stock enough goods to meet the expected demand, or where undisclosed limits are placed on the number of goods to be obtained by a consumer, or where undisclosed conditions are placed, for example, on the minimum number which must be acquired before the special price can be obtained.[7]

The most difficult aspect of the offence for a prosecutor to establish is that goods were offered with the requisite intention of not supplying them as offered. Non-supply may not be sufficient to establish a contravention, although persistent non-supply may be sufficient circumstantial evidence.[8] Other evidence may be persistent disparagement of the 'bait' offer,[9] rejection of consumer proposals to purchase the bait and their 'switching' to a more expensive alternative product,[10] and any policy of underordering or failure to take steps to meet the demand for the bait.[11]

An extreme example of the bait advertising technique is provided by the 1958 US case of *People* v. *Glubo*,[12] which involved the advertising of sewing machines for $29.50 from which customers were encouraged to 'step up' to more expensive models, once a sale contract had been signed on the cheaper model. The judge explained:

In pursuance of their agreement to 'kill' the sale of the advertised machine and to 'step up' the customer, defendants conducted instruction sessions or clinics for the salesmen. The sales pitch and selling methods used ... in attempting to switch the prospective customers from the advertised machine to the higher priced machine were numerous. For example the advertised machine was rigged so that when it was demonstrated it would operate for the salesman but would jam up for the customer. The customer would be told that his television set would have to be turned off when the advertised machine was demonstrated, otherwise the television tube or fuses would blow out. The customer would be told that the machine would have to be oiled every few minutes; that a five-pound can of grease would be needed to pack the bearings; that the customer could lose an eye if the machine jammed and the needle broke; or that the customer had a heavy foot for sewing. The salesmen were specifically instructed that they could not sell the $29.50 advertised machine. After the customer had been discouraged from purchasing the $29.50 machine, the salesmen would undertake to sell the higher priced machine.[13]

To meet the problem of inadvertent non-supply, the Trade Practices Act allows a supplier to offer substitute goods or services whether or not the consumer accepts such offers. The defence allows a supplier to offer equivalent goods or to find another person to offer equivalent goods at the advertised price. The New South Wales Act contains similar defences and exonerates suppliers who establish that they have exhausted the specified quantity by supplying it at the advertised price.[14] The

South Australian Act contains a limited defence when goods are in short supply.[15]

PRIZE PROMOTIONS

Section 54 of the Trade Practices Act prohibits the deceptive offering of 'gifts, prizes or other free items' in connection with the supply or promotion of the supply of goods or services. A similar prohibition is contained in s. 53A(1)(c) in respect of the sale, grant or promotion of an interest in land. These sections do not prohibit the making of such offers. They do prohibit the making of offers with the intention of not providing them or not providing them as offered. The sections may thus be contravened by offers where charges were made for the 'gift', or where there are limits on the availability of gifts or where the offer simply does not intend to provide the gift. The true nature of prizes should be stated. The Trade Practices Commission, for example, advises that a ticket in a $20 000 lottery should not be described as $20 000 worth of prizes.[16] Other sections of the Act also affect prize promotions. Where the price of an item is inflated to cover the cost of the prize, s. 53(e) may be contravened. If the promotion involves misleading or deceptive conduct, s. 52 will be contravened.

As with the prohibition of bait advertising, by the Act, the intention of the promoter not to offer the prize must be established. The meaning of the word 'offer' must also be settled to determine whether it is used in its technical or colloquial sense. The concluding words 'other free items' suggest that the sections apply only to items that are free. If 'item' is interpreted to mean tangible goods, then prizes in the nature of holidays or the receipt of services may be outside its scope. The requirement that items are 'free' may exonerate schemes involving a proof of purchase.

TRADING STAMPS

Where a trader wishes to make the receipt of gifts or benefits in a sales promotion dependent on the purchase of his products, the trader may enforce proof of purchase by specifying that gifts be exchanged for labels or coupons supplied with the product or that the customer must complete an application form in a newspaper or periodical. If the receipt of a benefit in a trade promotion is dependent on the production of coupons, labels, packages, stamps or other documents, this may be a prohibited trading stamp scheme. The states and territories prohibit those schemes where a third party supplies the trading stamps to retailers and provides the benefits to consumers.[17] In New South Wales, the ACT and the Northern Territory, schemes where the retailer both issues stamps and redeems them are expressly permitted.[18] Permission is implied in Tasmania.[19] The South Australian Act applies only to third-party schemes and exempts stamps supplied by the print media and by manufacturers or vendors of goods or services to which the trading stamp relates.[20] Advertising or otherwise promoting such schemes is prohibited in all jurisdictions.[21] Details of the regulatory schemes vary from one state to the next.[22]

INERTIA SELLING

The practice of sending unordered goods to a consumer with a statement that unless they are returned within a specified period the consumer will be taken to have agreed to purchase them is regulated by the common law, although that law is unclear on the liability of the people who receive the goods.[23] Section 64(1) of the Trade Practices Act, and state and Northern Territory[24] Acts prohibit assertion of a right to payment for unsolicited goods or services. The Trade Practices Act also prohibits such an assertion for unordered directory entries and unsolicited credit cards. The Trade Practices Act provides exceptions for goods or services supplied to trade customers, and all the statutes provide a defence of reasonable belief of entitlement to payment. Finally, this legislation settles the question of the liability of the recipients of unsolicited goods.

A corporation is taken to have asserted a right to payment for goods in five situations:

(a) a demand for payment or assertion of a present or prospective right to payment amount to an assertion (the demand or assertion need not accompany the goods);
(b) a threat to bring any legal proceedings with a view to obtaining payment;
(c) placing, causing to be placed, or threatening to place the recipient's name on a list of defaulters or debtors with a view to obtaining payment;

(d) invoking or threatening to invoke any collection procedure with a view to obtaining payment;
(e) it is an assertion to send an invoice or other document stating the amount of the payment or setting out the price of the goods if the sender does not also state as prominently that no claim is made to payment.[25]

The Trade Practices Act defines 'unsolicited goods' and 'unsolicited services' as those supplied to a person 'without any request made by him or on his behalf'.[26] The state legislation adopts similar definitions, but in New South Wales goods or services must also be 'prescribed'. Books, periodicals and other publications, gramophone records or other goods are prescribed under the Act.[27] In the state and federal Acts, the assertion of a right to payment for unsolicited directory entries 'from any person of a charge for the making in a directory of an entry relating to the person or his profession, business, trade or occupation'[28] is also prohibited. The purpose of this prohibition was illustrated in *Wells* v. *John R. Lewis (International) Pty Ltd*,[29] where the defendant company was prosecuted for sending invoices to people it had included in its 'International Telex Directory'. Finally, s. 63A of the Trade Practices Act prohibits a corporation sending a credit card to a person except in response to a request in writing from that person or in renewal, replacement or substition of an existing card.

Under the Trade Practices Act and the state statutes (excluding New South Wales), it is a defence to a prosecution if the sender establishes that it had a reasonable cause to believe that there was a right to payment. The New South Wales Act will find the offence proved only if the sender knew that the goods were not solicited. The payment of one annual subscription has been held to be inadequate evidence of a reasonable cause to believe that a subscriber will take out another.[30] The defence probably embraces honest errors.[31] The Trade Practices Act also exempts a corporation asserting a right to payment for unsolicited goods or services if the recipient ordinarily uses them 'in the course of his profession, business, trade or occupation'.[32]

The Trade Practices Act and the New South Wales and Western Australian Acts provide that a recipient is not liable for loss or damage to the unsolicited goods other than that resulting from the doing by him of a wilful and unlawful act. The Victorian, Queensland, Tasmanian and Northern Territory Acts exonerate a recipient for loss or injury to the goods other than those arising from his wilful and unlawful disposal, destruction or damage. Additionally, the statutes make the recipient the owner of the unsolicited goods, free from all charges or liens, by passage of time. Under all the Acts, the prescribed time is three months after receipt of the goods. If the recipient gives a prescribed notice to the sender, requesting that it take possession of the goods, the goods will become the recipient's within one month, unless the recipient unreasonably refuses to permit the sender or owner to take possession within the relevant period, or unless the recipient knew, or might reasonably have been expected to know, that the goods were not intended for him.

REFERRAL AND PYRAMID SELLING

Referral selling is an arrangement whereby a purchaser is induced to acquire goods or services from a person on the understanding that the purchaser will receive a rebate, commission or benefit in return for giving the vendor the names of prospective purchasers, that rebate, commission or benefit being contingent on an event occurring after the contract is made. The contingent event is usually a purchase by the prospective purchaser. The saturation of the market place makes the contingency unlikely.[33] Referral selling is prohibited both by s. 57 of the Trade Practices Act and by state legislation.[34] The Act's prohibition of referral selling is addressed to inducements to consumers. The contingent event in the state legislation is the providing of names of prospective purchasers; it does not require that those prospective purchasers actually buy goods or services from the defendant.[35]

Pyramid selling is similar to referral selling and has been defined as:

> an arrangement whereby one is induced to buy upon the representation that he can not only regain his purchase price, but also earn profit by selling the same program to the public. It thus involves the purchase of the right to sell the same right to sell. A pyramid type practice is similar to a chain letter operation. Such a program is inherently deceptive for the seemingly endless chain must come to a halt insomuch as growth cannot be perpetual and the market becomes saturated by the number of participants. Thus, many participants are mathematically barred from ever recouping their original investments, let alone making profits.[36]

The practice is regulated by s. 61 of the Trade Practices Act and by legislation in the states and the ACT.[37] The Trade

Practices Act prohibits a promoter of a trading scheme inducing a person to make payments on the understanding that such payments entitled the person to recruit others to the trading scheme.[38] The ACT legislation is similar to the federal Act. The state legislation sets out the elements of prohibited schemes which resemble those of the Trade Practices Act, but they provide for specific exclusion of the prescribed schemes. The New South Wales and Queensland Acts empower the minister and a statutory committee, respectively, to declare schemes to be prohibited.[39] The scope of the South Australian Act can be extended by regulation.[40] Each state makes provision for the recovery of payments from persons convicted of pyramid selling offences.

14

COMPETITIONS

Michael Blakeney

Competitions conducted in the mass media which involve the offer of a prize with the winner determined by lot or chance may be considered to be lotteries and so fall foul of a range of state and territory legislation which regulates their conduct. The concern of lotteries legislation, according to Lord Widgery in *Reader's Digest Association Ltd* v. *Williams*,[1] decided in 1976, is to protect those 'poor people with only a few pence to feed their children [who] would go and put those few pence into a lottery and lose it', which 'sociologically was a bad thing'.[2] Despite this 'sociological' vice of lotteries, legislatures in every jurisdiction in which lotteries are prohibited have made laws permitting gambling at race courses and betting shops, the conduct of soccer pools, chocolate wheels, lotto, poker machines, bingo or government lotteries. In some jurisdictions, private lotteries are permissible provided a licence is obtained. In this context, it is not inappropriate to recall Blackstone's observation that 'our laws against gaming are not so deficient as ourselves and our magistrates in putting those laws into execution'.[3]

CHANCE

At common law, a lottery is defined as 'a distribution of prizes by lot or chance'.[4] Where a competition involves the exercise of a degree of skill by a participant, the scheme will not be a lottery.[5] In England, the view has frequently been put that if 'there is any degree of skill involved there will be no lottery'.[6] But in Australia, the High Court has expressed the view that 'a competition might be a lottery although some element of skill was involved'.[7] The Australian common law position probably requires that 'skill is the final determining factor in ascertaining the prize winner'.[8]

In most jurisdictions, the common law definition of 'lottery' has been modified by statute to take account of the presence of elements of skill in addition to chance. Thus, in New South Wales, a lottery is defined to include a competition:

> the nature, scheme or conduct of which, though a certain degree of skill on the part of the competitors is required, is such as in the circumstances of the case, to preclude the fair consideration of the answers of the competitors, or render the correctness of entries a matter of chance.[9]

In Queensland, any distribution of property determined 'wholly or partly by chance' is a lottery.[10] In South Australia, a lottery is defined to include any competition where the disposal of property 'depends at any stage of the scheme, competition or device, upon an element of chance, notwithstanding that such disposal or distribution also depends at some stage of such scheme, competition or device, upon a genuine or purported display of knowledge or skill'.[11] A similar approach is taken in Victoria, where 'lottery' is defined as including 'any scheme in which at any stage the persons eligible to receive the prizes or to participate further are determined by any mode of chance, notwithstanding that at any earlier stage or later stage a test of knowledge or skill is or may be required to be passed by any person in order to qualify him to receive a prize or participate further in the scheme'.[12] The Tasmanian legislation does not define the term 'lottery', and thus the common law definition applies.[13] In Western Australia, the common law position appears to be imported into the statutory definition: 'lottery' is any competition 'the nature or conduct of which (though skill on the part of entrants or competitors is required) is such as in the circumstances of the case to preclude the fair consideration of the answers of the entrants or competitors'.[14] Similarly, in the territories, 'lottery' is defined as any scheme by which prizes are gained by any mode of chance or by reference to any event or contingency depending upon chance.[15]

PROHIBITED CONTESTS

The following competitions conducted in Australia were held to be lotteries because they involved no real element of skill:

(a) the completion of a limerick, principally because the competitors 'must have known that the prizes would in reality

be distributed not according to merit but according to fancy or to some temporary rule which the editor might choose to adopt';[16]
(b) the random selection of customers buying cabinets of cutlery on credit to be released from the obligation to pay the full price;[17]
(c) a competition in which contestants ranked in order of merit six recorded pop songs, where the ranking had to correspond with that of three judges selected by the promoters of the contest;[18]
(d) a spot-the-ball contest, notwithstanding the argument that 'an accurate observer may draw inferences from the position of a player', knowing the idiosyncracies of the relevant player;[19]
(e) the publication of random selections of car registration numbers in which contestants had to recognize their own number to win a prize;[20]
(f) a contest in which prize tokens were inserted in packets of soap powder,[21] and a similar contest in which the contestants had to spell the name of the drink producer from letters of the alphabet printed under bottle tops.[22]

Despite differences in the laws regulating lotteries in the United Kingdom[23] and New Zealand,[24] contests similar to the examples above have been held to be lotteries. A critical feature where skill is alleged to be present in a competition is whether the principles according to which that skill is to be exercised are known to the contestants. Thus a crossword puzzle, in which there are several possible answers to a number of clues,[25] or the submission of solutions to accord with those of judges, will be lotteries if the principles by which the judges proceed are not known to the contestants.[26] Even where there is the possibility of some skill being applied, a contest will be a lottery if the judges receive so many entries that they cannot evaluate the skills applied.[27]

GRATUITOUS ENTRY

In addition to the element of chance, the common law definition of 'lottery' requires that contestants pay to participate. Where a contest is conducted in association with a trade promotion, courts have held that mere purchase of the goods constituted payment for participation in the lottery.[28] Even where participation in a competition does not require the purchase of an item at common law, the scheme may still be considered a lottery. In *Willis* v. *Young and Stembridge*,[29] the proprietors of a newspaper distributed medals gratuitously among members of the public, each bearing a distinctive number. Winning numbers were arbitrarily selected and published in the newspaper. Buying a newspaper was not a requirement of the scheme, but the court found that during the scheme, the circulation of the newspaper rose by 20 per cent, attributable to people buying it to discover the winners of the prizes offered. Lord Alverstone CJ found on these facts that 'the persons who receive the medals therefore contribute collectively (though each individual may not contribute) sums of money from which the profits of the newspaper, and also the money for the prize winners in this competition come'.[30] This decision was followed in New South Wales,[31] South Australia[32] and Victoria.[33] The common law position is modified in New South Wales, Queensland, Western Australia and the territories, where even if it involves gratuitous entry, a competition will be deemed a lottery;[34] but in South Australia and Tasmania, the common law position applies.

PERMITTED COMPETITIONS

In some jurisdictions, even where a competition may be characterized as a lottery, permits may be obtained from the relevant government department on the payment of a fee. In New South Wales, provided that no fee is charged to enter the competition and no prize consists of liquor or tobacco,[35] a permit is readily obtainable.[36] A similar approach is taken in the Northern Territory and Tasmania.[37] In Victoria, South Australia and Queensland, contests where no entry fee is charged are permissible, provided there is no proof of purchase requirement.[38] In the ACT, a lottery is permitted provided it is authorized or conducted in accordance with the law of any state,[39] which would suggest that a lottery permissible in only one other state would make it permissible in the ACT. Western Australia obliges all lotteries to be conducted with a permit.[40] A recent amendment to the Victorian Act permits trade promotion lotteries by permit.[41]

Finally, it should be noted that a promotion involving the disposition of property by chance may also fall foul of the Trade Practices Act if the prizes are not intended to be offered as advertised or if the scheme is otherwise misleading or deceptive.[42]

REFERENCES

2. Defamation

[1] For defamation law generally, see P. Lewis, *Gatley on Libel and Slander*, 8th ed., London, 1981; C. Duncan, *Duncan and Neill on Defamation*, 2nd ed., London, 1983; J. G. Fleming, *The Law of Torts*, 6th ed., Sydney, 1983, Chapter 24; H. Luntz, D. Hambly and R. Hayes, *Torts: Cases and Commentary*, Sydney, 1980, Chapter 15. For defamation law in a media context, see G. Sawer, *A Guide to Australian Law for Journalists, Authors, Printers and Publishers*, 3rd ed., Melbourne, 1984, Chapter 7; J. F. Burrows, *News Media Law in New Zealand*, 2nd ed., Wellington, 1980, Chapters 2 and 3; G. Robertson and A. Nicol, *Media Law*, London, 1984, Chapter 2.
[2] *Luckman* v. *Hart* (1904) 2 Nicholls and Stop's Reports 190.
[3] Report No. 11, Sydney, 1979.
[4] Report No. 11, Chapter 3, 'Defamation in a Changing Society', 1979.
[5] See *Wrongs Act* 1958–1981 (Vic.); *Wrongs Act* 1936–1983 (SA). For the ACT see *New South Wales Act Application Ordinance* (ACT) No. 41, 1984, Schedule 2, Parts 11 and 12 which contain and apply the *Defamation Act* 1901 (NSW) and the *Defamation (Amendment) Act* 1909 (NSW) to the ACT. The *New South Wales Acts Application (Amendment) Ordinance* (ACT) No. 58, 1984 amends the *Defamation (Amendment) Act* 1909 (NSW) as it applies to the ACT. The Northern Territory ordinances, proclaimed between 1938 and 1976, are now contained in an ordinance entitled the *Defamation Act* (NT).
[6] *Defamation Law of Queensland* (53 Vic. No. 12) 1889 together with the *Criminal Code Act* 1899 (Qld) Ch. XXXV, ss. 365–89.
[7] *Defamation Act* 1957 (Tas.).
[8] The *Criminal Code Act* 1913 (WA). The Act, s. 5, states that 'when, by the Code, any act is declared to be unlawful, no action can be brought in respect thereof'. The Act contains, as a schedule, the Criminal Code of Western Australia (the code). Some sections of Chapter XXXV of the code, which deals with defamation, provide that certain publications are 'lawful'. Section 357 provides that it shall be a 'lawful excuse' if material is published on certain occasions of qualified privilege. The effect of these provisions, and of Chapter XXXV generally, on the *civil* law of defamation in Western Australia has been the subject of controversy for many years. Since the decision of the High Court in *Western Australian Newspapers Ltd* v. *Bridge* (1979) 23 ALR 257, however, it is now clear that the defence of qualified privilege provided in s. 357 does not apply to civil defamation. Qualified privilege in Western Australia is thus governed by the common law in a civil action. In addition to the defence of qualified privilege, it now appears clear that the common law governs the following matters in the civil law of defamation in Western Australia: the definition of defamation; the distinction between libel and slander (so that the distinction remains alive in that state); the defence of truth (so that truth alone is a sufficient defence to a civil action in that state); the defence of absolute privilege. The defence of fair report in s. 354 of the Criminal Code applies to civil actions; it appears, however, that common law of qualified privilege is not excluded in this area by the

Criminal Code. Similarly, the defence of fair comment (s. 355) which applies to civil actions would not appear to exclude a defendant from relying on the common law on this matter in addition to his or her statutory defence. The *Newspaper Libel and Registration Act* 1884–1957 is also a source of defamation law relevant to the media in Western Australia. For a complete discussion of the difficulties concerning the source of civil defamation law in Western Australia see Law Reform Commission of Western Australia, Report on Defamation, Project No. 8, 1979.

9 Australian Law Reform Commission, *Unfair Publication: Defamation and Privacy*, Report No. 11, Sydney, 1979.
10 In New South Wales separate causes of action still exist but slander is actionable without special damage in the same way as libel (*Defamation Act* 1974 s. 8). The distinction has been abolished in Queensland (The Criminal Code, s. 368), Tasmania (*Defamation Act* 1957 s. 6) and the Australian Capital Territory (by virtue of the *Defamation Act* 1901 (NSW) s. 3(2)). The distinction survives in Victoria, South Australia, Western Australia and the Northern Territory.
11 [1936] 2 All ER 1237 at 1240.
12 (1840) 6 Meeson and Welsby's Reports 105 at 108.
13 (1934) 50 TLR 581 at 584, adopting the earlier language of Cave J in *Scott* v. *Sampson* [1882] 2 QBD 491 at 503.
14 [1936] 2 All ER 1237 at 1240.
15 (1934) 50 TLR 581 at 587.
16 *Slatyer* v. *Daily Telegraph* (1908) 6 CLR 1 at 7 per Griffith CJ.
17 *Gardiner* v. *John Fairfax and Sons Pty Ltd* (1942) 42 SR (NSW) 171 at 172 per Jordan CJ; *Consolidated Trust Company Limited* v. *Browne* (1948) 49 SR (NSW) 86 at 88 per Jordan CJ.
18 *Criminal Code* (Qld) s. 366; *Defamation Act* 1957 (Tas.) s. 5.
19 *Gardiner* v. *John Fairfax and Sons Pty Ltd* (1942) 42 SR (NSW) 171 at 172 per Jordan CJ; *Boyd* v. *Mirror Newspapers Ltd* (1980) 2 NSWLR 449 at 452 per Hunt J.
20 [1926] VLR 115.
21 [1926] VLR 115 at 122.
22 [1970] 1 All ER 1095 at 1104 per Lord Pearson.
23 (1980) 31 ALR 624.
24 P. Lewis, *Gatley on Libel and Slander*, 8th ed., London, 1981, p. 29.
25 [1980] 2 NSWLR 449.
26 *Ratcliffe* v. *Evans* [1892] 2 QB 524.
27 *Hall-Gibbs Mercantile Agency Limited* v. *Dun* (1910) 12 CLR 84. Decided in respect of the *Criminal Code* (Qld) s. 366 but recognizing implicitly that such a statement would not be defamatory at common law.
28 *Sungravure Pty Limited* v. *Middle East Airlines Airliban SAL* (1975–6) 134 CLR 1. Decided in relation to the now repealed *Defamation Act* 1958 (NSW) s. 5 but recognizing implicitly that such a statement would not be defamatory at common law.
29 *Dawson Bloodstock Agency Pty Ltd* v. *Mirror Newspapers Ltd* [1979] 1 NSWLR 16.
30 *Grappelli* v. *Derek Block (Holdings) Ltd* [1981] 1 WLR 822 at 824 per Lord Denning.
31 *Mentone Racing Club* v. *Victorian Railways Commissioner* (1902) 28 VLR 77.
32 Australian Law Reform Commission, *Unfair Publication: Defamation and Privacy*, Sydney, 1979, pp. 47–8; *Criminal Code* (Qld) s. 366; *Defamation Act* 1957 (Tas.) s. 5.
33 *Yarwood* v. *Mirror Newspapers Ltd* [1968] 1 NSWLR 720.
34 (1936) 82 *Federal Reporter* (2d) 154. See also *Cook* v. *Ward* (1830) 6 Bingham's Reports 409; *Dunlop Rubber Co. Ltd* v. *Dunlop* [1921] AC 367.
35 *Emerson* v. *Grimsby Times & Telegraph Co. Ltd* (1926) 42 TLR 258.
36 *Plumb* v. *Jeyes, The Times*, 15 April 1937.
37 *Mazati* v. *Acme Products Ltd* [1930] 4 DLR 601.
38 *Cook* v. *Ward* (1830) 6 Bingham's Reports 409.
39 Lewis, *Gatley on Libel and Slander*, op. p. 17 fn. 23.
40 *Morosi* v. *Mirror Newspapers Ltd* [1977] 2 NSWLR 749.
41 *Massey* v. *New Zealand Times* [1911] NZLR 929; *Vander Zalm* v. *Times Publishers* [1980] 109 DLR (3d) 531.
42 *Youssoupoff* v. *Metro-Goldwyn-Mayer Pictures Ltd* (1934) 50 TLR 581 at 587.
43 *Middle East Airlines* (1975–6) 134 CLR 1 at 24 per Mason J.
44 [1974] 1 NSWLR 323 at 341.
45 *Boyd* v. *Mirror Newspapers Ltd* [1980] 2 NSWLR 449; *Dawson Bloodstock Agency Pty Ltd* v. *Mirror Newspapers Ltd* [1979] 1 NSWLR 16. The matter is not, however, finally

settled and reference should also be made to: *Middle East Airlines* (1975–6) 134 CLR 1 at 13–18 per Stephen J and 23–4 per Mason J; *Mirror Newspapers Limited* v. *World Hosts Pty Ltd* (1978–9) 23 ALR 167 at 171 per Mason and Jacob JJ; *Sergi* v. *Australian Broadcasting Commission* [1983] 2 NSWLR 669 at 675 per Glass JA.
46 [1968] 1 All ER 497 at 504.
47 *Reader's Digest Services Pty Ltd* v. *Lamb* (1982) 38 ALR 417 at 421 per Brennan J.
48 *Mirror Newspapers Limited* v. *World Hosts Pty Ltd* (1978–9) 23 ALR 167 at 173 per Mason and Jacobs JJ.
49 [1971] 2 All ER 1156 at 1162–3.
50 *Mirror Newspapers Ltd* v. *Harrison* (1982) 56 ALJR 808 at 811 per Mason J.
51 *Ainsworth Nominees Pty Ltd* v. *Hanrahan* [1982] 2 NSWLR 823; *Sergi* v. *Australian Broadcasting Commission* [1983] 2 NSWLR 669.
52 [1939] 1 KB 467 at 479.
53 *Potts* v. *Moran* (1976) 16 SASR 284 at 303 per Bray CJ.
54 *Slatyer* v. *Daily Telegraph* (1908) 6 CLR 1 at 7 per Griffith CJ.
55 *Gardiner John* v. *Fairfax and Sons Pty Ltd* (1942) 42 SR (NSW) 171 at 172 per Jordan CJ; *Consolidated Trust Company Limited* v. *Browne* (1948) 49 SR (NSW) 86 at 88 per Jordan CJ.
56 [1937] 2 All ER 204. Followed in *Blair* v. *Mirror Newspapers Ltd* [1970] 2 NSWR 604.
57 An unreported case cited in Australian Law Reform Commission, *Unfair Publication: Defamation and Privacy*, p. 47 fn. 41.
58 [1949] SASR 98.
59 [1983] 2 NSWLR 682. See also *Krahe* v. *TCN Channel Nine Pty Ltd* [1986] 4 NSWLR 536.
60 [1983] 2 NSWLR 682, 694.
61 [1983] 2 NSWLR 708.
62 *Farquhar* v. *Bottom* [1980] 2 NSWLR 380; *Gordon* v. *Amalgamated Television Services Pty Ltd* [1980] 2 NSWLR 410.
63 [1981] 2 NSWLR 474.
64 *Morosi* v. *Broadcasting Station 2GB Pty Ltd* [1980] 2 NSWLR 418.
65 [1971] 2 All ER 1156 at 1184.
66 (1985) 60 ALJR 10. (Privy Council). Context was also important in *John Fairfax & Sons Ltd* v. *Hook* (1983) 47 ALR 477.
67 *David Syme & Co. Ltd* v. *Lloyd* [1984] 3 NSWLR 346, at 359 per Priestley JA (NSW Court of Appeal).
68 *John Fairfax & Sons Ltd* v. *Punch* (1980) 31 ALR 624 at 635 per Brennan J.
69 (1980) 31 ALR 624.
70 *John Fairfax & Sons Ltd* v. *Punch* (1980) 31 ALR 624 at 636.
71 [1929] 2 KB 331.
72 The actual name of Cassidy's companion appeared in the *Mirror* but was omitted in the report of the case by the court.
73 [1910] AC 20.
74 An unreported case mentioned in P. F. Carter-Ruck, *Libel and Slander*, London, 1972, p. 22.
75 *Sims* v. *Wran* [1984] 1 NSWLR 317.
76 *McWhirter* v. *Manning*, The Times, 30 October 1954.
77 (1974) 22 FLR 181.
78 *Renouf* v. *Federal Capital Press of Australia Pty Ltd* (1977) 17 ACTR 35 at 58.
79 *Morgan* v. *Odhams Press Ltd* [1971] 2 All ER 1156 at 1164 per Lord Morris.
80 (1934) 51 CLR 276.
81 [1974] 2 NSWR 348.
82 *Steele* v. *Mirror Newspapers* [1974] 2 NSWR 348 at 364 per Hutley J.
83 [1944] 1 All ER 495 at 499.
84 (1918) 25 CLR 234.
85 [1974] 1 NSWLR 436. See also *Martyn* v. *Australian Consolidated Press Ltd* (1982) 55 FLR 342.
86 *London Computer Operators Training Ltd* v. *British Broadcasting Corporation* [1973] 2 All ER 170.
87 [1981] 1 NSWLR 9.
88 *Bognor Regis Urban District Council* v. *Campion* [1972] 2 All ER 61; *National Union of General and Municipal Workers* v. *Gillian* [1946] KB 81.
89 The code definition of defamatory matter in Queensland and Tasmania provides relevantly, that 'any imputation concerning any person, or any member of his

family, whether living or dead, by which the reputation of that person is likely to be injured ... is defamatory'. *Criminal Code* (Qld) s. 366, *Defamation Act* 1957 (Tas.) s. 5. Although there are no decided cases resolving the matter, the better view is that the code definition requires an imputation concerning the plaintiff or a member of his family, living or dead, by which the *living* plaintiff is likely to be damaged. Thus construed the definition does not alter the common law and permit a defamation action to lie in the hands of the relatives of a deceased person for a statement that impugnes his reputation.

90 The Australian Law Reform Commission has recommended that close relatives or the legal personal representative of a deceased person be permitted to obtain a correction order, declaration or injunction (but not damages) to vindicate the reputation of that person within a three-year period of his or her death. The Australian Law Reform Commission, *Unfair Publication: Defamation and Privacy*, pp. 54–6.

3. Defamation: Defences and Remedies

1. J. G. Fleming, *The Law of Torts*, 6th ed., Sydney, 1983, p. 525.
2. *Alexander v. N. E. Railway* (1865) 6 Best & Smith's Reports 340.
3. *Weaver v. Lloyd* (1824) 1 Carrington & Payne's Reports 295.
4. *Defamation Act* 1974 (NSW) s. 16; *Defamation Act* 1957 (Tas.) s. 8.
5. *Jackson v. John Fairfax & Sons Pty Ltd* [1981] 1 NSWLR 36.
6. The Australian Law Reform Commission has recommended that truth alone should be a defence to defamation and that a separate law of privacy be enacted to protect people from 'the distressing and unfair disclosure of personal information, whether true or not and whether defamatory or not'. Australian Law Reform Commission, *Unfair Publication: Defamation and Privacy*, Report No. 11, Sydney, 1979, p. 66.
7. *Criminal Code* (Qld) s. 376; *Defamation Act* 1957 (Tas.) s. 15; ACT: *Defamation Act* 1901 (NSW) s. 6.
8. *Defamation Act* 1974 (NSW) s. 15.
9. (1928) 29 SR (NSW) 125.
10. (1928) 29 SR (NSW) 125 at 137.
11. *Rajski v. Carson* [1986] 4 NSWLR 735.
12. *Huntley v. Ward* (1859) 6 Common Bench, New Series 517.
13. *Adam v. Ward* [1917] AC 309 at 334 per Lord Atkinson.
14. *Arnold v. The King-Emperor* (1914) 30 TLR 462 at 468.
15. [1977] 2 NSWLR 749.
16. [1977] 2 NSWLR 749 at 792.
17. [1917] AC 309.
18. [1917] AC 309 at 343.
19. (1938) 59 CLR 503.
20. (1938) 59 CLR 503 at 512.
21. *Sinclair v. Bjelke-Petersen* [1984] 1 Qd R 484.
22. [1979] 26 ALR 55.
23. [1979] 26 ALR 50 at 59.
24. *Morosi v. Mirror Newspapers Ltd* [1977] 2 NSWLR 749 at 797.
25. [1977] 1 NSWLR 697.
26. *Austin v. Mirror Newspapers Ltd* (1986) 60 ALJR 3.
27. *Criminal Code* (Qld) s. 377(8); *Defamation Act* 1957 (Tas.) s. 16(h).
28. *Calwell v. Ipec Australia Limited* (1975) 135 CLR 321.
29. (1973) 22 FLR 181.
30. The Australian Law Reform Commission has criticized the extent of the protection afforded to the media by the code defence and has recommended that the law of qualified privilege should confer no greater rights on the media than are conferred presently by the common law and the *Defamation Act* 1974 (NSW). Australian Law Reform Commission, *Unfair Publication: Defamation and Privacy*, pp. 76–8.
31. The defence is governed by statute in New South Wales (*Defamation Act* 1974 ss. 29–35), Queensland (*Criminal Code* s. 375), Tasmania (*Defamation Act* 1957, s. 14) and the Northern Territory (*Defamation Act* s. 6A). In Western Australia, the common law and the *Criminal Code* (WA), s. 355, relating to fair comment, appear to

apply concurrently. In Victoria, South Australia and the ACT, the common law applies. The text discusses the basic concepts and principles of fair comment applicable to all jurisdictions.
32 *Slim* v. *Daily Telegraph* (1968) 2 QB 170 at 175 per Lord Denning.
33 (1958) 2 All ER 516.
34 *Clarke* v. *Norton* (1910) VLR 494 at 499 per Cussen J.
35 *Myerson* v. *Smith's Weekly* (1923) 24 SR (NSW) 20 at 26 per Ferguson J.
36 (1969) 43 ALJR 242.
37 (1908) 2 KB 309 at 310.
38 (1970) 45 ALJR 59. For an example of a television current affairs programme mingling fact and opinion see *Comalco Ltd* v. *Australian Broadcasting Corporation* (1985–1986) 64 ACTR 1.
39 (1970) 45 ALJR 59 at 60.
40 (1950) 1 All ER 449 at 474.
41 (1932) 47 CLR 279.
42 (1932) 47 CLR 279 at 303–4.
43 *Kemsley* v. *Foot* [1952] AC 345.
44 *Mangena* v. *Wright* [1909] 2 KB 958.
45 *Cawley* v. *Australian Consolidated Press Ltd* [1981] 1 NSWLR 225; *Australian Consolidated Press Ltd* v. *Bond* 56 ACTR 14. Note, however, that the *Defamation Act* 1974 (NSW) s. 32(2) says that the defence is only defeated if 'the comment did not represent the opinion of the defendant'. It is not finally settled whether this section leaves room for defeat of comment in New South Wales on the ground that the comment was distorted by malice. On this see *Hawke* v. *Tamworth Newspaper Co. Ltd* [1983] 1 NSWLR 699; *David Syme & Co. Ltd* v. *Lloyd* [1984] 3 NSWLR 346; *Bob Kay Real Estate Pty Ltd* v. *Amalgamated Telvision Services Pty Ltd* [1985] 1 NSWLR 505.
46 (1958) 2 All ER 516 at 518.
47 *Lyon and Lyon* v. *Daily Telegraph* (1943) 2 All ER 316 at 319 per Scott LJ.
48 (1969) 2 All ER 193 at 198.
49 The Australian Law Reform Commission has recommended the abandonment of the requirement that comment be on a matter of public interest having regard to its proposal for the separate protection of privacy. Australian Law Reform Commission, *Unfair Publication: Defamation and Privacy*, p. 69.
50 (1928) 29 SR (NSW) 125 at 137 per Ferguson J.
51 The more important provisions are those contained in *Defamation Act* 1974 (NSW) ss. 24–6; *Wrongs Act* 1958–1981 (Vic.) ss. 3–5; *Wrongs Act* 1936–1983 (SA) ss. 6–7; *Criminal Code* (Qld) s. 374; *Defamation Act* 1957 (Tas.) s. 13; *Criminal Code* (WA) s. 354. For ACT, see *Defamation (Amendment) Act* 1909 (NSW) s. 5, as amended by the *New South Wales Application (Amendment) Ordinance* (ACT) 1984; *Defamation Act* (NT) ss. 5–6.
52 In view of the unmethodical and inconsistent protections provided to reporting by the present laws, the Australian Law Reform Commission has recommended a new law of defamation operating uniformly throughout Australia and including a separate defence of 'fair report' based on a comprehensive list of protected public proceedings. It has also recommended that such a defence be expanded to include a report of a statement made by a person on a topic of public interest. The proposed defence would require the media, among other things, to name the maker of the statement and provide a person defamed by the statement with an opportunity to reply. Australian Law Reform Commission, *Unfair Publication: Defamation and Privacy*, pp. 79–97.
53 The common law requires that a report be fair and accurate before privilege is accorded. The statutes use the term 'fair and accurate' or 'fair'. No significant practical consequences result from the differences in terminology: to be 'fair' a report must achieve a standard of accuracy.
54 (1971) 1 NSWLR 773 at 780.
55 (1980) 26 SASR 286.
56 The article published in the *Truth* carried Bunker's full name, age, address and occupation. We have omitted these details to protect his privacy.
57 The *Wrongs Act* 1958 (Vic.) s. 5, *Wrongs (Defamation) Act* 1979 (Vic.) s. 2, *Wrongs (Defamation) Act* 1981 (Vic.) s. 2, *Wrongs Act* 1936–1983 (SA) ss. 6–7 and *Defamation Act* (NT) ss. 5–6 all employ the term 'privileged' to describe the protection afforded. 'Malice' is the test of defeasance in these provisions. In all other jurisdictions the 'fair report' formula is employed and the test is that of 'good faith'.

[58] *Waterhouse* v. *Broadcasting Station 2GB Pty Ltd* [1985] 1 NSWLR 58.
[59] The geographical extent of common law privilege and that of the protection afforded by some of the various state statutory provisions is uncertain. It has been suggested, for example, that a report published in South Australia concerning proceedings in the Queensland parliament may not receive the protection of South Australian law. This lamentable uncertainty has been resolved in New South Wales, Victoria and Western Australia. These states provide protection for the publication of a report concerning any Australian parliament: *Defamation Act* 1974 (NSW) s. 24, Sch. 2, para. 2(1); *Wrongs Act* 1958–1981 (Vic.) s. 3A; *Criminal Code* (WA) s. 354(1) and (2).
[60] *Defamation Act* 1974 (NSW) s. 24, Sch. 2, para. 2(1); *Wrongs Act* 1958–1981 (Vic.) s. 3A; *Criminal Code* (WA) s. 354(1); *Criminal Code* (Qld) s. 374(1); *Defamation Act* 1957 s. 13(1)(a); ACT: *Defamation (Amendment) Act* 1909 (NSW) s. 5 (applying to a newspaper report only); *Defamation Act* (NT) s. 6(1)(ba) (applying to a newspaper report only). The *Wrongs Act* 1936–1983 (SA) s. 7(1)(ab) and (c) provides privilege for a newspaper, radio and television report of the proceedings of either house of parliament and of a select committee of either house.
[61] *Defamation Act* 1974 (NSW) s. 25; *Constitution Act Amendment Act* 1958 (Vic.) s. 65; *Wrongs Act* 1936–1983 (SA) s. 12(3); *Criminal Code* (Qld) s. 374(2); *Defamation Act* 1957 (Tas.) s. 13(1)(b); ACT: *Defamation (Amendment) Act* 1909 (NSW) s. 5A; *Criminal Code* (WA) s. 354(2).
[62] Absolute privilege is accorded by *Wrongs Act* 1958–1981 (Vic.) s. 4; *Newspaper Libel and Registration Act* 1888 (WA) s. 6 (applying to a newspaper report only); *Defamation Act* (NT) s. 5 (applying only to a newspaper report published contemporaneously with proceedings). Qualified privilege only is accorded by *Defamation Act* 1974 (NSW) ss. 24–6; *Wrongs Act* 1958–1981 (Vic.) ss. 3A–4; *Criminal Code* (Qld) s. 374(3); *Wrongs Act* 1936–1983 (SA) s. 6 (applying to a newspaper, radio or television report published contemporaneously with proceedings); *Criminal Code* (WA) s. 354(3); *Defamation Act* 1957 (Tas.) s. 13(1)(c); ACT: *Defamation (Amendment) Act* 1909 (NSW) s. 5 (applying to a newspaper report only).
[63] *Gobbart* v. *West Australian Newspapers* (1968) WAR 113.
[64] (1968) 3 NSWLR 642.
[65] (1981) 26 SASR 286.
[66] (1981) 26 SASR 286 at 289 per Zelling J.
[67] *Defamation Act* 1974 (NSW) ss. 24–6; *Wrongs Act* 1958–1981 (Vic.) s. 3A; *Criminal Code* (Qld) s. 374(4); *Wrongs Act* 1936–1983 (SA) s. 7(1)(c) (applying to a newspaper, radio or television report of proceedings of a royal commission or select committee of either house of parliament); *Criminal Code* (WA) s. 354(4); *Defamation Act* 1957 (Tas.) s. 13(1)(d); *Defamation Act* (NT) s. 6(1)(c) (applying only to a newspaper report of a meeting in the Territory of any royal commission or select committee of either house of federal parliament); ACT: *Defamation (Amendment) Act* 1909 (NSW) s. 5(f) (applying to a newspaper report only).
[68] *Allbutt* v. *General Council of Medical Education and Registration* (1889) 23 QBD 100.
[69] (1932) 2 KB 431.
[70] *Defamation Act* 1974 s. 24, Sch. 2, cl. 2(7).
[71] *Defamation Act* 1974 (NSW) s. 28; *Wrongs Act* 1936–1983 (SA) s. 7; *Criminal Code* (Qld) s. 374(5); *Criminal Code* (WA) s. 354(5); *Defamation Act* 1957 (Tas.) s. 13(1)(f); *Defamation Act* (NT) s. 6(1); ACT: *Defamation (Amendment) Act* 1909 (NSW) s. 5(g) (applying to newspapers only). This category does not receive statutory protection in Victoria. It may, however, be covered by the common law in that state: see *Boston* v. *W. S. Bagshaw and Sons and Another* (1966) 1 WLR 1126.
[72] *Campbell* v. *Associated Newspapers Ltd* (1948) 48 SR (NSW) 301; *John Fairfax & Sons Ltd* v. *Hook* (1983) 47 ALR 477. Note, however, *Defamation Act* 1974 (NSW) s. 28(3).
[73] *Forster* v. *Watson* (1944) 44 SR (NSW) 39 at 403 per Jordan CJ.
[74] [1973] NZLR 1. See also *Morosi* v. *Mirror Newspapers Ltd* [1977] 2 NSWLR 749 at 782–5.
[75] *Gannon* v. *White* (1886) 12 VLR 29 at 35 per Williams J.
[76] *Defamation Act* 1974 (NSW) s. 24, Sch. 2, para. 2(9); *Wrongs Act* 1936–1983 (SA) s. 7(1)(a); *Criminal Code* (Qld) s. 374(7); *Criminal Code* (WA) s. 354(7); *Defamation Act* 1957 (Tas.) s. 13(1)(h); *Defamation Act* (NT) s. 6(1)(a) (applying to a newspaper report only). In Western Australia, there is, in addition, absolute privilege for newspaper reports of state or municipal ceremonials and political, municipal or public meetings: *Newspaper Libel and Registration Act* 1888 s. 6. Further note that with

the exception of the *Defamation Act* 1974 (NSW) s. 24 and the *Newspaper Libel and Registration Act* 1888 (WA) s. 6, each of these provisions requires the meeting to be lawful so that, for example, a report of a speech delivered at a rally which is held in contravention of a local government ordinance will not be protected.

77 The *Defamation Act* 1974 (NSW) contains no express protection for the report of a local council meeting. But s. 24(2) and Sch. 2, para. 2(a), which confer protection on the report of proceedings of a public meeting relating to a matter of public interest and open to the public have been interpreted as conferring protection on the report of a local council meeting in New South Wales. *Cassel* v. *Gold Coast Publications Pty Ltd* [1984] 1 NSWLR 11. For other jurisdictions see *Wrongs Act* 1958–1981 (Vic.) s. 5 (applying to a newspaper report only); *Wrongs Act* 1936–1983 (SA) s. 7(1)(b); *Criminal Code* (Qld) s. 374(6); *Criminal Code* (WA) s. 354(6); *Defamation Act* 1957 (Tas.) s. 13; ACT: *Defamation (Amendment) Act* 1909 (NSW) s. 5(h) (applying to a newspaper report only); *Defamation Act* (NT) s. 6(1)(b) (applying to a newspaper report only).

78 *Wrongs Act* 1936–1983 (SA) s. 7(1)(d); *Defamation Act* (NT) s. 6(1)(d) (applying to a newspaper report only).

79 *Defamation Act* 1974 (NSW) s. 25, Sch. 3, para. 4.

80 *Reis* v. *Perry* (1895) 64 Law Journal Reports, Queen's Bench 566.

81 ss. 36–45.

82 *Mirror Newspapers* v. *Fitzpatrick* [1984] 1 NSWLR 643. For other apology procedures see: *Wrongs Act* 1958–1981 (Vic.) s. 7; *Defamation Law of Queensland* 1889 s. 22; *Wrongs Act* 1936–1983 (SA) s. 10; *Defamation Act* 1957 (Tas.) s. 23; ACT: *Defamation Act* 1901 (NSW) s. 5. A Western Australian ordinance of 1847 (10 Vic. No. 8) adopts the apology procedure provided by the *Libel Act* 1843 (UK) for that state.

83 The common law defence is still available in New South Wales. The codes make no specific provision for a defence of consent. They do provide, however, for qualified privilege where 'the publication is made in good faith on the invitation or challenge of the person defamed': *Criminal Code* (Qld) s. 377(6); *Criminal Code* (WA) s. 357(6); *Defamation Act* 1957 (Tas.) s. 16(1)(f).

84 *Mundey* v. *Askin* [1982] 2 NSWLR 369.

85 *Defamation Law of Queensland* 1889 s. 20; *Defamation Act* 1957 (Tas.) s. 9(2). These provisions apply only in the case of oral defamation. The provision applying in the ACT, *Defamation Act* 1901 (NSW) s. 4, is not thus limited.

86 (1977) 2 NSWLR 749 at 799–801.

87 56 ACTR 14.

88 (1967) 117 CLR 118.

89 *Uren* v. *John Fairfax & Sons Ltd* (1966) 117 CLR 118. Punitive damages for defamation have been abolished in New South Wales: *Defamation Act* 1974 (NSW) s. 46(3).

90 *Unfair Publication: Defamation and Privacy*, pp. 139–43.

91 *Stocker* v. *McElhinney (No. 2)* (1961) 79 WN (NSW) 541.

4. Protecting Business Reputation

1 *South Hetton Coal Company Ltd* v. *North Eastern News Association Ltd* [1894] 1 QB 153.

2 *Dawson Bloodstock Agency Pty Ltd* v. *Mirror Newspapers Ltd* [1979] 1 NSWLR 16.

3 (1978) 32 FLR 360.

4 (1984) 55 ALR 25.

5 See J. D. Heydon, *Economic Torts*, 2nd ed., London, 1978, p. 81.

6 (1975–76) 134 CLR 1.

7 See *Australian Newspaper Co.* v. *Bennett* [1894] AC 284.

8 [1975] 1 WLR 972.

9 *De Beers Abrasive Products Ltd* v. *International Electric Co. of New York Ltd* [1975] 1 WLR 978.

10 [1895] AC 154.

11 *Western Counties Manure Co.* v. *Lawes Chemical Manure Co.* (1874) 9 Law Reports, Exchequer Division 218.

12 *Thorley's Cattle Food Co.* v. *Massam* (1880) 14 Ch D 763.

13 *Linotype Co. Ltd* v. *British Empire Type-Setting Mechanic Co. Ltd* (1898) 79 Law Times Reports 8.

REFERENCES 255

14 *Lyne* v. *Nicholls* (1906) 23 TLR.
15 [1975] 1 WLR 978.
16 See *Swimsure (Laboratories) Pty Ltd* v. *McDonald and Another* [1979] 2 NSWLR 796.
17 FACTS Commercials Acceptance Division, Guideline 35, November 1980.
18 Australian Boradcasting Tribunal, Re: *Advertisements Produced for Television on Behalf of the Health Commission of New South Wales*, Decision and Reasons, 9 October 1981.
19 Australian Broadcasting Tribunal, Re: *An Advertisement Produced by the Campaign Palace for Sanyo Australia Pty Ltd for the product Betacord, Communications Law Bulletin*, vol. 1, no. 7, 1981, p. 7.
20 Joint Committee for Disparaging Copy, *Annual Report* 1980, Appendix A.
21 *Colgate-Palmolive Pty Ltd* v. *Rexona Pty Ltd* (1981) 37 ALR 391.
22 *Stuart Alexander & Co. (Interstate) Pty Ltd and Another* v. *Blenders Pty Ltd* (1981) 37 ALR 161.
23 *Clement* v. *Maddick* (1859) 1 Gifford's Reports 98.
24 *Television Broadcasters Ltd* v. *Home Guide Publication Co.* [1982] FSR 505.
25 *B. M. Auto Sales Pty Ltd* v. *Budget Rent A Car System Pty Ltd* (1977) 51 ALJR 254, 257–8.
26 [1970] SASR 207.
27 *South Australian Telecasters Ltd* v. *Southern Television Corporation Limited* [1970] SASR 211.
28 *Maxwell* v. *Hogg* (1967) 2 Chancery Appeal Cases 307.
29 *George Outram and Co. Ltd* v. *London Evening Newspapers Co. Ltd* (1911) 27 TLR 231.
30 *Bradbury* v. *Beeton* (1869) 21 LT 323.
31 *Borthwick* v. *Evening Post* (1888) 4 TLR 234.
32 *Norman Kark Publications Ltd* v. *Odhams Press Ltd* [1962] 1 WLR 380.
33 For example, *Rolls Razor Ltd* v. *Rolls Lighters Ltd* (1949) 60 RPC 299; *Dunlop Pneumatic Tyre Co.* v. *Dunlop Motor Co. Ltd* [1907] AC 430; *Electromobile Co. Ltd* v. *British Electromobile Co. Ltd* (1908) 25 RPC 149.
34 *Gramophone Co's Application* [1910] 2 Ch 423.
35 *Samuelson* v. *Producer's Distributing Co. Ltd* [1932] 1 Ch 201.
36 *Willard King Organization Pty Ltd* v. *United Telecasters Sydney Ltd* [1981] 2 NSWLR 547.
37 *Hexagon Pty Ltd* v. *Australian Broadcasting Commission* (1975) 7 ALR 233.
38 *Sykes* v. *John Fairfax & Sons Ltd* [1977] 1 NSWLR 415.
39 *Forbes* v. *Kemsley Newspapers Ltd* [1951] 2 TLR 656.
40 [1981] FSR 89.
41 *Miss World (Jersey) Ltd* v. *James Street Productions Ltd* [1981] FSR 309.
42 *Miss World* case [1981] FSR 310.
43 (1948) 65 RPC 58.
44 *Wombles Ltd* v. *Wombles Skips Limited* [1975] FSR 488.
45 *Taverner Rutledge Limited* v. *Trexapalm Limited* [1975] FSR 479.
46 (1960) 60 SR (NSW) 576.
47 *Totalizor Agency Board* v. *Turf News Pty Ltd* [1967] VR 605.
48 [1981] 1 NSWLR 273.
49 (1980) 32 ALR 387.
50 *Cadbury Schweppes Pty Ltd* v. *Pub Squash Co. Pty Ltd* (1980) 32 ALR 390.
51 *Pub Squash* case (1980) 32 ALR 393.
52 [1967] RPC 581.
53 (1982) 42 ALR 177.
54 [1977] FSR 364.
55 [1964] RPC 202.
56 [1982] FSR 1.
57 [1980] RPC 343.
58 (1981) 35 ALR 494.
59 *Dairy Vale Metro Cooperative Ltd* v. *Brownes Dairy Ltd* (1981) 35 ALR 498.
60 (1982) ATPR 40–274.
61 *Philip Morris Inc.* v. *Adam P. Brown Male Fashions Pty Ltd* (1981) 55 ALJR 120.
62 (1982) ATPR 40–287.
63 *Hanimex Pty Ltd* v. *Kodak Australasia Pty Ltd* (1982) ATPR, 43–597.
64 *Hornsby Building Information Centre Pty Ltd* v. *Sydney Building Information Centre Ltd* (1978) 140 CLR 212.
65 (1978) 2 ATPR 40–085.
66 (1980) 33 ALR 394.
67 *Snoid* v. *CBS Records Australia Ltd* (1981) 38 ALR 383.

68 *Rolls-Royce Motors Ltd* v. *D. I. A. (Engineering) Pty Ltd* (1981) 3 ATPR 40–219.
69 *Pinetrees Lodge Pty Ltd* v. *Atlas International Pty Ltd* (1981) 3 ATPR 40–248.
70 (1981) 3 ATPR 40–211.
71 (1979) 26 ALR 419.
72 (1981) 3 ATPR 40–216.
73 *The Terrace Times Pty Ltd* v. *Brock* (1981) 3 ATPR 43–414.
74 (1981) 37 ALR 161.
75 *Dairy Industry Marketing Authority* v. *Southern Farmers Cooperative Ltd* (1982) ATPR 40–274.
76 *Dairy Vale Metro Cooperative Ltd* v. *Brownes Dairy Ltd* (1981) 35 ALR 494.
77 (1982) 42 ALR 1.
78 (1980) 3 ATPR 40–191.
79 See *Rolls-Royce Motors Ltd* v. *D. I. A. (Engineering) Pty Ltd* (1981) 3 ATPR 40–219.
80 *McWilliam's Wines Pty Ltd* v. *McDonalds System of Australia Pty Ltd* (1980) 33 ALR 394.
81 (1982) ATPR 40–308.
82 (1977) 29 ALR 336.
83 *Weitmann* v. *Katies Ltd* (1977) 29 ALR 343.
84 (1981) 3 ATPR 40–217.
85 See *Maxim's Ltd* v. *Dye* (1977) FSR 364.
86 (1981) 33 ALR 383.
87 See *Hornsby Building Information Centre Pty Ltd* v. *Sydney Building Information Centre Ltd* (1978) 140 CLR 212.

5. Copyright

1 See J. A. L. Sterling and G. E. Hart, *Copyright Law in Australia*, Sydney, 1981, p. 45.
2 *John Fairfax & Sons Pty Ltd* v. *Consolidated Press Ltd* [1960] SR (NSW) 413.
3 [1964] 1 WLR 273.
4 *Ladbroke (Football) Limited* v. *William Hill (Football) Ltd* [1964] 1 WLR 289.
5 *University of London Press Ltd* v. *University Tutorial Press Pty Ltd* [1916] 2 Ch 601, 608.
6 *Walter* v. *Steinkopff* [1892] 3 Ch 489.
7 *Lamb* v. *Evans* [1893] 1 Ch 218.
8 *Mander* v. *O'Brien* [1934] SASR 87.
9 *Portway Press Ltd* v. *Hague* [1957] RPC 426.
10 *Football League* v. *Littlewoods Pools Ltd* [1959] Ch 637.
11 *Canterbury Park Race Course Co. Ltd* v. *Hopkins* (1932) 49 WN (NSW) 27.
12 (1863) 1 Hay and Marriott's Reports 603, 607.
13 *H. Blacklock and Co. Limited* v. *C. Arthur Pearson Limited* [1915] 2 Ch 376.
14 *Lamb* v. *Evans* [1893] 1 Ch 218.
15 *Thomas* v. *Turner* (1886) 33 Ch D 292.
16 [1981] 2 All ER 495.
17 [1940] AC 112.
18 *Ladbroke (Football) Ltd* v. *William Hill (Football) Ltd* [1964] 1 WLR 273, 286.
19 Sterling and Hart, *Copyright Law in Australia*, p. 48.
20 *Metzler and Co. (1920) Ltd* v. *J. Curwen & Sons Ltd* (1928–35) Macg Cop Cas 127, 134.
21 [1959] RPC 57.
22 [1963] VR 719.
23 *Cuisenaire* v. *Reed* [1963] VR 729.
24 *Copyright Act* 1968 s. 22(3).
25 See J. Lahore, *Intellectual Property Law in Australia, Copyright*, Sydney, 1977, pp. 61–2.
26 See M. Armstrong, *Broadcasting Law & Policy in Australia*, Sydney, 1982, para. 109.
27 *Copyright Act* 1961 s. 223.
28 (1937) 58 CLR 479.
29 (1984) ATPR 40–453.
30 *Copyright Act* 1968 s. 92.
31 *Springfield* v. *Thame* (1903) 19 TLR 650.
32 [1892] 3 Ch 483.
33 See also, G. Sawer, *A Guide to Australian Law for Journalists, Authors, Printers and Publishers*, 2nd ed., Melbourne, 1968, p. 76.

REFERENCES 257

[34] See *Commonwealth* v. *Walsh and Munster* (1981) 32 ALR 500.
[35] *Copyright Act* 1968 s. 33(2).
[36] *Copyright Act* 1968 s. 33(3), (4).
[37] *Copyright Act* 1968 s. 33(2).
[38] *Copyright Act* 1968 s. 212.
[39] *Copyright Act* 1968 s. 220(3).
[40] *Copyright Act* 1968 s. 93.
[41] *Copyright Act* 1968 s. 90.
[42] *Copyright Act* 1968 s. 223.
[43] *Copyright Act* 1968 s. 95(1).
[44] *Copyright Act* 1968 s. 224.
[45] *Copyright Act* 1968 s. 96.
[46] *Copyright Act* 1968 s. 34(1).
[47] *Copyright Act* 1968 s. 34(2).
[48] *Copyright Act* 1968 s. 10.
[49] *Copyright Act* 1968 s. 80.
[50] *Copyright Act* 1968 s. 180(1).
[51] *Copyright Act* 1968 s. 180(2).
[52] *Copyright Act* 1968 s. 180(3).
[53] *Copyright Act* 1968 s. 223.
[54] *Copyright Act* 1968 ss. 181, 234, 235.
[55] See *Francis Day and Hunter* v. *Feldman & Co.* [1914] 2 Ch 728.
[56] *Copyright Act* 1968 s. 35(2).
[57] [1938] Ch 106.
[58] (1903) 89 LT 242.
[59] *Donoghue* v. *Allied Newspapers Ltd* [1938] Ch 106, 109–10.
[60] *Walter* v. *Lane* [1900] AC 539.
[61] See *Pollock* v. *J. C. Williamson Ltd* [1923] VLR 225.
[62] See *A. & C. Black Ltd* v. *Claude Stacey Ltd* [1929] 1 Ch 177.
[63] *Copyright Act* 1968 s. 213(7).
[64] *Copyright Act* 1968 s. 35(6).
[65] (1928) 28 SR (NSW) 473.
[66] [1913] 2 Ch 279.
[67] (1953) 93 CLR 561.
[68] *Zuijs* v. *Wirth Brothers Pty Ltd* (1953) 93 CLR 571.
[69] [1973] 1 All ER 241.
[70] See *Commonwealth of Australia* v. *John Fairfax & Sons Ltd and Others* (1980) 32 ALR 485; *Commonwealth of Australia* v. *Walsh and Munster* (1980) 32 ALR 500; *Commonwealth of Australia* v. *Ipec Holdings Ltd and Another* (1980) 32 ALR 503.
[71] See *A-G for NSW* v. *Butterworth & Co. (Australia) Ltd* (1937–8) 38 SR (NSW) 195.
[72] See *Universities of Oxford and Cambridge* v. *Eyre & Spottiswoode Ltd* [1964] Ch 736.
[73] *Copyright Act* 1968 s. 97.
[74] *Copyright Act* 1968 s. 98.
[75] *Copyright Act* 1968 s. 197.
[76] The rights of a copyright owner are listed in s. 31 of the *Copyright Act* 1968.
[77] Sterling and Hart, *Copyright Law in Australia*, p. 31.
[78] [1974] 1 WLR 1308.
[79] [1975] 1 WLR 61.
[80] *Clifford Davis Management Ltd* v. *WEA Records Ltd* [1975] 1 WLR 64.
[81] *Copyright Act* 1968 ss. 47, 70, 107.
[82] See Lahore, *Intellectual Property Law in Australia, Copyright*, pp. 329–44.
[83] [1980] RPC 193.
[84] See *Elanco Products Ltd* v. *Mandops (Agrochemical Specialists) Ltd* [1979] FSR 46.
[85] (1975) 6 ALR 193.
[86] [1934] Ch 593.
[87] *University of London Press Ltd* v. *University Tutorial Press Ltd* [1916] 2 Ch 601, 610.
[88] [1963] 1 Ch 587.
[89] [1941] AC 417.
[90] [1905] 1 Ch 519.
[91] *Haufstaeng* v. *W. H. Smith and Sons* [1905] 1 Ch 524.
[92] For example, *Kelly* v. *Morris* (1866) 1 Law Reports, Exchequer Division 697.
[93] 239 Federal Reporter 2d 532 (1956).
[94] 137 Federal Supplement 348 (1955).

[95] (1980) 32 ALR 485.
[96] *Commonwealth of Australia* v. *John Fairfax & Sons Ltd* (1980) 32 ALR 497.
[97] *Hubbard* v. *Vosper* [1972] 2 QB 84.
[98] See Sterling and Hart, *Copyright Law in Australia*, pp. 151 ff.
[99] *Copyright Agency Ltd and Others* v. *Haines* [1982] 1 NSWLR 182.
[100] *Haines* v. *Copyright Agency Ltd and Others* (1982) 42 ALR 549.
[101] (1980) 32 ALR 485.
[102] *Commonwealth of Australia* v. *John Fairfax & Sons Ltd* (1980) 32 ALR 495.
[103] *Fairfax* case (1980) 32 ALR 496.
[104] *Fairfax* case (1980) 32 ALR 496.
[105] See Sterling and Hart, *Copyright Law in Australia*, Ch. 10.
[106] (1981) 55 ALJR 120.
[107] (1981) 37 ALR 161.
[108] See S. Barnes and M. Blakeney, *Advertising Regulation*, Sydney, 1982, pp. 264–6.
[109] *Beecham Group Ltd* v. *Bristol Laboratories Pty Ltd* (1968) 118 CLR 618, 623.
[110] [1972] 2 QB 84.
[111] See *Anton Piller K.G.* v. *Manufacturing Processes Ltd* (1976) 2 FSR 129.
[112] For example, *EMI (Australia) Ltd* v. *Bay Imports Pty Ltd* (1980) 6 FSR 328.
[113] *Interfirm Comparison (Australia) Pty Ltd* v. *Law Society of New South Wales* (1975) 6 ALR 445, 446–7.
[114] *P. J. Holdings Australia Pty Ltd* v. *Hughes and Others* (1979) 25 ALR 538.
[115] See *Colbeam Palmer Ltd* v. *Stock Affiliates Pty Ltd* (1968) 122 CLR 25, 32.
[116] See *John Lane The Bodley Head Ltd* v. *Associated Newspapers Ltd* [1936] 1 KB 715.
[117] *Copyright Act* 1968 ss. 190, 194.
[118] *Copyright Act* 1968 ss. 192, 194.
[119] *Copyright Act* 1968 ss. 191, 194.
[120] *Crimes Act* 1914 s. 86(1).
[121] See *Jaybeam Ltd* v. *Abru Aluminium Ltd* [1975] FSR 334.

6. Sub Judice Publications

[1] For contempt law generally, see: Australian Law Reform Commission, *Contempt and the Media* (Discussion paper No. 26), Sydney, 1986; C. J. Miller, *Contempt of Court*, London, 1978; *Borrie & Lowe's Law of Contempt*, 2nd ed., London, 1983; A. Arlidge and D. Eady, *The Law of Contempt*, London, 1982.
[2] *DPP* v. *ABC* [1986] ACLD 078.
[3] *DPP* v. *Wran* [1987] ACLD 079.
[4] *Hinch and Macquarie Broadcasting Holdings Ltd* v. *A-G* (hereafter *Hinch* case) Supreme Court of Vic. (Full Court) 11 December 1986 (not yet reported, and subject to appeal to High Court).
[5] *Brych* v. *The Herald & Weekly Times Ltd* [1978] VR 727 at 735.
[6] *Victoria* v. *Australian Building Construction Employees' and Builders Labourers' Federation* (1982) 41 ALR 77 (hereafter *BLF* case) at 88 per Gibbs CJ.
[7] *BLF* case (1982) 41 ALR 77, 88.
[8] (1912) 13 CLR 577.
[9] *Packer* v. *Peacock* (1912) 13 CLR 577, 588.
[10] [1946] VLR 486.
[11] [1974] AC 273.
[12] *Sunday Times* case [1974] AC 273, 300.
[13] *R* v. *Evening Standard* (1924) 40 TLR 833.
[14] *Victoria* v. *Australia Building Construction Employees' and Builders Labourers' Federation* (1982) 41 ALR 71 (*BLF* case).
[15] *BLF* case at 121.
[16] *BLF* case at 121.
[17] *BLF* case at 121–2, 150; *Waterhouse* v. *ABC* (1986) 68 ALR 75.
[18] *BLF* case at 122 per Mason J; *Hammond* v. *Commonwealth* (1982) 42 ALR 327.
[19] *A-G (NSW)* v. *Fairfax and Bacon* (1985) 6 NSWLR 695.
[20] *Waterhouse* v. *ABC* (1986) 6 NSWLR 733, 735–6.
[21] *BLF* case at 151 per Wilson J.
[22] *BLF* case at 89 per Gibbs CJ.

REFERENCES 259

23 *BLF* case at 90, 123 respectively.
24 *BLF* case at 90 per Gibbs CJ, at 124–5 per Mason J, at 151 per Wilson J.
25 *BLF* case at 90.
26 *A-G* v. *John Fairfax & Sons* [1980] 1 NSWLR 362 at 372.
27 *A-G* v. *John Fairfax & Sons* [1980] 1 NSWLR 362 at 372.
28 *A-G* v. *Times Newspapers Ltd* (hereafter *Sunday Times* case) [1974] AC 273 at 309; but see *A-G* v. *Fairfax and Bacon* (1985) 6 NSWLR 695 at 709 per McHugh JA.
29 [1960] 2 QB 188.
30 *Sunday Times* case [1974] AC at 310 per Lord Diplock.
31 *Re William Thomas Shipping Co.* [1930] 2 Ch 368.
32 *Waterhouse* v. *ABC* (1985) 6 NSWLR 695 at 739 per Mahoney JA.
33 [1981] 2 NSWLR 554.
34 For example, *Sunday Times* case [1974] AC 273 at 296 per Lord Diplock; *R* v. *Arrowsmith* [1950] VLR 78; *Ex parte Kear*; *Re Consolidated Press* (1954) 54 SR (NSW) 95 at 98–9; *A-G* v. *Mirror Newspapers Ltd* [1980] 1 NSWLR 374.
35 *BLF* case (1982) 41 ALR 71, 91.
36 *BLF* case at 125.
37 *BLF* case at 151–2.
38 *A-G* v. *Mirror Newspapers Ltd* [1962] SR (NSW) 421.
39 *Ex parte Bread Manufacturers Ltd*; *Re Truth & Sportsman Ltd* (1937) 37 SR (NSW) 242.
40 *Ex parte Bread Manufacturers Ltd* (1937) 37 SR (NSW) 242, 249–50.
41 *Ex parte Bread Manufacturers Ltd* (1937) 37 SR (NSW) 242, 251.
42 *John Fairfax & Sons Pty Ltd* v. *McRae* (1955) 93 CLR 351.
43 *Consolidated Press Ltd* v. *McRae* (1955) 93 CLR 325 at 333.
44 *John Fairfax & Sons Pty Ltd* v. *McRae* (1955) 93 CLR 351 at 370.
45 *Registrar of Court of Appeal* v. *Willesee* (hereafter 'second *Willesee* case') (1985) 3 NSWLR 650 at 661, 680–1.
46 *A-G* v. *Willesee* [1980] 2 NSWLR 143 (discussed in this chapter under 'Responsibility').
47 *R* v. *David Syme* [1982] VR 173 (discussed in this chapter under 'Responsibility').
48 *Brych* v. *The Herald & Weekly Times Ltd* [1978] VR 727 (discussed in this chapter under 'Stop Writs').
49 *Thomson* v. *Times Newspapers* [1969] 3 All ER 648 at 651 per Salmon LJ.
50 Australian Law Reform Commission, *Unfair Publication: Defamation and Privacy*, Sydney, 1979, pp. 29–31.
51 *John Fairfax & Sons Pty Ltd* v. *McRae* (1955) 93 CLR 351 at 370–1. See also the *BLF* case (1982) 41 ALR 71 at 184–5 per Brennan J.
52 *Sunday Times* case [1974] AC 273, 301.
53 *Brych* v. *The Herald & Weekly Times Ltd* [1978] VR 727.
54 [1976] VR 707. *Burton* v. *Harris* [1979] Qd R 548, esp. at 551, suggests that *Watts* v. *Hawke* was unduly restrictive.
55 (1963) 109 CLR 593.
56 *James* v. *Robinson* (1963) 109 CLR 593, 606.
57 *R* v. *Crew* [1971] VR 78.
58 *James* v. *Robinson* (1963) 109 CLR 593 at 618 per Windeyer J; *R* v. *Andrews* [1973] 1 All ER 857.
59 *In re Crown Bank* (1890) 44 Ch D 649.
60 *Ex parte Dawson*; *Re Consolidated Press Ltd* [1961] SR (NSW) 573 at 574.
61 *Ex parte Dawson*; *Re Consolidated Press Ltd* [1961] SR (NSW) 573 at 574; *DPP* v. *Wran* [1987] ACLD 079.
62 *Rigby* case (1955) 93 CLR 351 at 371.
63 Second *Willesee* case; *DPP* v. *Wran* [1987] ACLD 079; *Hinch* case (above).
64 *Rigby* case (1955) 93 CLR 351 at 372; second *Willesee* case (above).
65 *R* v. *David Syme* [1982] VR 173 at 177.
66 *R* v. *Scott & Downland Publications* [1972] VR 663; *R* v. *Regal Press* [1972] VR 67; second *Willesee* case (above).
67 *R* v. *David Syme & Co Ltd* [1982] VR 173.
68 *A-G* v *Willesee* [1980] 2 NSWLR 143.
69 *A-G* v. *Willesee* at 154.
70 [1956] VLR 544.
71 *R* v. *Pacini* [1956] VLR 544 at 547–8.
72 *Ex parte Auld*; *Re Consolidated Press* (1936) 36 SR (NSW) 596.
73 *Administrative Appeals Tribunals Act* 1975 (Cth) s. 63.

[74] *Trade Practices Act* 1974 (Cth) s. 162.
[75] *Royal Commissions Act* 1902 (Cth) s. 60.
[76] [1950] VR 78.
[77] *A-G* v. *Mirror Newspapers Ltd* [1980] 1 NSWLR 374.
[78] [1981] AC 303.
[79] Australian Law Reform Commission, *Contempt* (Report No. 35), AGPS, Canberra, 1987.

7. Courts and Parliaments: Criticizing and Reporting

[1] *Ambard* v. *A-G for Trinidad & Tobago* [1936] AC 322 at 335.
[2] (1935) 53 CLR 434.
[3] *R* v. *Dunbabin; Ex parte Williams* (1935) 53 CLR 434, 442.
[4] *R* v. *Dunbabin* at 448.
[5] *R* v. *Dunbabin* at 442.
[6] [1936] AC 322.
[7] *Ambard* v. *A-G for Trinidad & Tobago* [1936] AC 332, 335.
[8] [1950] VLR 226.
[9] [1968] AC 150.
[10] [1972] 2 NSWLR 887.
[11] *A-G* v. *Mundey* [1972] 2 NSWLR 887, 912–13.
[12] *A-G* v. *Mundey* (1972) 2 NSWLR 887, 916.
[13] *Gallagher* v. *Durack* (1982) 44 ALR 477.
[14] *Gallagher* v. *Durack* (1983) 45 ALR 53.
[15] *Wade* v. *Gilroy* (1986) 83 FLR 14.
[16] [1963] 1 QB 696. See also *Australian Building Construction Employees' and Builders Labourers' Federation* v. *Minister for Industrial Relations* (1982) 43 ALR 189; *Watson* v. *Collings* (1944) 70 CLR 51, 58–9 per Rich J; *R* v. *Wright (No. 1)* [1968] VR 164.
[17] *Registrar, Court of Appeal* v. *Collins* [1982] 1 NSWLR 682; *Prothonotary* v. *Collins* [1985] 2 NSWLR 549.
[18] *Re Nicol* [1954] 3 DLR 690.
[19] *R* v. *Ivens* (1920) 51 DLR 38.
[20] (1912) 12 CLR 280.
[21] *R* v. *Nicholls* (1912) 12 CLR 280, 288.
[22] *Journal Printing Co.* v. *McVeity* (1915) 7 Ontario Weekly Notes 633, 634.
[23] *Re Dunn* [1932] St R Q 1.
[24] *Ex parte Tubman; Re Lucas* (1970) 72 SR (NSW) 555.
[25] *Daubeny* v. *Cooper* (1829) 1 Barnewall & Creswell's Reports 237 at 240.
[26] *R* v. *Sussex Justices; Ex parte McCarthy* [1924] 1 KB 256 at 259.
[27] [1979] AC 440, 450. For a summary of the history and principles of open justice, see *Raybos Australia Pty Ltd* v. *Jones* [1985] 2 NSWLR 47 at 50–3 per Kirby P.
[28] [1915] AC 417.
[29] See also *R* v. *P* (1978) 43 Canadian Criminal Cases (2d) 197.
[30] *David Syme* v. *General Motors-Holdens* [1984] 2 NSWLR 294.
[31] Contrast *Wallersteiner* v. *Moir* [1974] 3 All ER 217, 229 with *Re de Beaujeu* [1949] 1 All ER 439.
[32] For example, *Children's Court Act* 1973 (Vic.) s. 18(1); *Children's Services Act* 1965 (Qld) s. 27; *Children's Protection and Young Offenders Act* 1979 (SA) s. 92(1). The *Child Welfare Act* 1947 (WA) merely empowers the court to exclude the public, without requiring it automatically.
[33] Australian Law Reform Commission, *Child Welfare*, Report No. 18, Sydney, 1981, p. 120.
[34] *Raybos* v. *Jones* [1985] 2 NSWLR 47; G. Sawer, 'Privilege' in Australian Press Council, *To Name or Not to Name*, Sydney, 1980, pp. 10–14.
[35] *Raybos* v. *Jones* [1985] 2 NSWLR 47 at 59–61.
[36] *R* v. *Socialist Worker Printers & Publishers Ltd; Ex parte A-G* [1975] QB 637.
[37] *P* v. *P* (1985) 2 NSWLR 401.
[38] *Evidence Act* 1929 ss. 69–71a, discussed in *R* v. *Wilson; Ex parte Jones* [1969] SASR 405 and *G* v. *The Queen* (1984) 35 SASR 349 before major amendments in 1984.
[39] *Evidence Act* 1910 (Tas.) s. 103A, 104.
[40] *Wrongs Act* 1958 (Vic.) s. 4.
[41] *Evidence Ordinance* 1971 (ACT) s. 83.
[42] [1979] AC 440.

REFERENCES 261

43 *Cain* v. *Glass (No. 2)* (1985) 3 NSWLR 230, 233–4.
44 *Fairfax* v. *Police Tribunal* (not yet reported) NSW Court of Appeal 30 July 1986.
45 *R* v. *Socialist Worker* [1975] QB 637 and *A-G* v. *Leveller* [1979] AC 440.
46 *A-G* v. *Leveller* [1979] AC 440, 450.
47 *R* v. *Wealdstone News* (1925) 41 TLR 508.
48 Australian Law Reform Commission, *Contempt and the Media* (Discussion paper No. 26), Sydney, 1986, pp. 83–92.
49 Australian Law Reform Commission, *Contempt and the Media*, pp. 83–92.
50 *Juries Act* 1967 (Vic.) s. 69A (enacted in 1985).
51 *A-G* v. *New Statesman* [1981] 1 QB 1, 8.
52 *Ex pàrte Fisher; Re Associated Newspapers Ltd* (1941) 41 SR (NSW) 272 at 278 per Jordan CJ.
53 *Hughes* v. *West Australian Newspapers Ltd* (1940) 43 WALR 12.
54 *Home Office* v. *Harman* [1982] 1 All ER 532.
55 *Home Office* v. *Harman* [1982] 1 All ER 532.
56 *Administrative Appeals Tribunal Act* 1975 (Cth) s. 35; *Broadcasting Act* 1942 (Cth) s. 19, discussed in *Swan Television* v. *Australian Broadcasting Tribunal* (1985) 61 ALR 319.
57 (1937) 37 SR 255, 257–8.
58 *Minister for Justice* v. *West Australian Newspapers Ltd* [1970] WAR 202.
59 *R* v. *Scott* [1972] VR 663.
60 *R* v. *Scott* [1972] VR 663.
61 (1937) 37 SR (NSW) 255, 259.
62 (1937) 37 SR (NSW) 255, 259.
63 (1937) 37 SR (NSW) 255, 259.
64 (1937) 37 SR (NSW) 255, 259.
65 [1970] WAR 202.
66 (1868) 4 Law Reports, Queen's Bench 73, 93–4.
67 *Cook* v. *Alexander* [1973] 1 QB 279, esp. at 288–9.
68 21 April 1978, p. 12; 22 April 1978, p. 3.
69 J. A. Pettifer (ed.), *House of Representatives Practice*, Canberra, 1981, pp. 464–8; J. R. Odgers, *Australian Senate Practice*, 5th ed., Canberra, 1976, pp. 250–3.
70 See, generally, E. Campbell and H. Whitmore, *Freedom in Australia*, 2nd ed., Sydney, 1973, pp. 316–23; E. Campbell, *Parliamentary Privilege in Australia*, Melbourne, 1966, pp. 1–27, 46–58, 109–41; Pettifer, *House of Representatives Practice*, pp. 653–67, 786–813; Odgers, *Australian Senate Practice*, pp. 647–58; J. Dickie (ed.), *Press, Parliament and Privilege*, Eighth Summer School of Professional Journalism, Sydney, 1972; D. C. Pearce, 'Contempt of Parliament: Instrument of Politics or Law', *Federal Law Review*, vol. 3, 1968–69, p. 241; 'The Privileges Committees of the Australian Parliament', *Federal Law Review*, vol. 6, 1975, p. 269.
71 *R* v. *Richards, Ex parte Fitzpatrick & Browne* (1955) 92 CLR 157.
72 House of Representatives Committee of Privileges, Report relating to a Printed Reference in the *Sydney Daily Mirror* of Wednesday 2 September 1981, Canberra, 1981, p. 4.
73 Senate Committee of Privileges, Report upon Articles in the *Sunday Australian* and the *Sunday Review* of 2 May 1971, Canberra, 1971.
74 *Commonwealth Parliamentary Debates* (Senate) 14 May 1971, vol. 48, p. 1935.
75 Senate Committee of Privileges, *First Report*, Canberra, 1984 (Parliamentary paper No. 298/1984), discussed in S. Walker, 'The Media and Parliament: the *National Times* case') (1986) 9 University of NSW Law Journal 27.
76 *Commonwealth Constitution* s. 49; *Constitution Act* 1975 (Vic.) s. 19; *Constitution Act* 1934 (SA) s. 38.
77 *Constitution Act* 1867–1978 (Qld) s. 45; *Parliamentary Privileges Act* 1891 (WA) s. 8; *Parliamentary Privileges Act* 1858 (Tas.) s. 3.
78 Joint Select Committee on Parliamentary Privilege, *An Exposure Report for the Consideration of Senators and Members*, Canberra, 1984 (Parliamentary paper No. 87/1984).
79 *Parliamentary Privileges Bill* 1986 (Cth). It was passed in May 1987.

8. Obscenity, Blasphemy and Sedition

1 On these topics generally, see E. Campbell and H. Whitmore, *Freedom in Australia*, 2nd ed., Sydney, 1973, pp. 247–69, 324–30; G. Flick, *Civil Liberties in Australia*, Sydney, 1981, pp. 224–44.

2 *Bowman* v. *Secular Society* [1917] AC 406, 466.
3 *R* v. *Gott* (1922) 16 Criminal Appeal Reports 86.
4 P. O'Higgins, *Censorship in Britain*, London, 1972, p. 22.
5 O'Higgins, *Censorship in Britain*, p. 22.
6 *R* v. *Lemon*; *R* v. *Gay News Ltd* [1979] 1 All ER 398, 900.
7 (1868) 3 Law Reports, Queen's Bench 360, 371.
8 See G. Robertson, *Obscenity*, London, 1979, pp. 45–80 for the problems of definition.
9 [1948] VLR 445.
10 (1968) 121 CLR 375, 392.
11 *Bradbury* v. *Staines* [1970] Qd R 76, 83.
12 *A-G* v. *Huber* (1971) 2 SASR 167; *Robertson* v. *Samuels* (1973) 4 SASR 465.
13 *Cullen* v. *Mecklenburg* [1977] WAR 1.
14 (1972) 2 SASR 529.
15 See also R. G. Fox, 'Depravity, Corruption and Community Standards', *Adelaide Law Review*, vol. 7, 1980, p. 65.
16 *R* v. *Sharp* (1964) 82 WN (NSW) 129; *R* v. *Neville* (1966) 83 WN (NSW) 501; *Mackinlay* v. *Wiley* [1971] WAR 3.
17 *R* v. *Anderson* [1971] 3 WLR 939.
18 *DPP* v. *Whyte* [1972] AC 849.
19 *Shaw* v. *DPP* [1962] AC 220.
20 *Knuller (Publishing, Printing & Promotions) Ltd* v. *DPP* [1973] AC 435.
21 [1962] AC 233.
22 The relevant legislation includes: *Indecent Articles and Classified Publications Act* 1975 (NSW) s. 6; *Police Offences Act* 1958 (Vic.) ss. 166, 168, 168A, 169; *Summary Offences Act* 1966 (Vic.) s. 17; *Vagrants, Gaming and Other Offences Act* 1913–1978 (Qld) ss. 7, 7A, 12; *Criminal Code* 1899–1980 (Qld) s. 228; *Indecent Publications and Articles Act* 1902–1974 (WA) s. 2; *Police Act* 1892–1978 (WA) s. 66(5); *Criminal Code* 1913–1980 (WA) s. 204; *Police Offences Act* 1953–1980 (SA) ss. 33, 35; *Criminal Law Consolidation Act* 1935–1982 (SA) s. 270; *Police Offences Act* 1935 (Tas.) s. 26; *Criminal Code* 1924 (Tas.) s. 138; *Police Offences Ordinance* 1930 (ACT) s. 17; *Classification of Publications Act* 1979 (NT) ss. 33, 34; *Police and Police Offences Act* (NT) s.53.
23 For example, *Indecent Publications and Articles Act* 1902–1974 (WA) s. 5; *Police Offences Act* 1958 (Vic.) s. 180.
24 For example, *Indecent Artices and Classified Publications Act* 1975 (NSW) s. 24; *Classification of Publications Act* 1979 (NT) s. 49.
25 The relevant legislation is: *Indecent Articles and Classified Publications Act* 1975 (NSW); *Police Offences Act* 1958 (Vic.); *Objectionable Literature Act* 1954–1967 (Qld); *Indecent Publications and Articles Act* 1902–1974 (WA); *Classification of Publications Act* 1973–1982 (SA); *Restricted Publications Act* 1979 (Tas.); *Classification of Publications Act* 1979 (NT). There is no classification Ordinance in the ACT.
26 Discussed in Campbell and Whitmore, *Freedom in Australia*, pp. 257–62.
27 Australian Broadcasting Tribunal, Brisbane, Queensland Public Broadcasting Station Licence Renewal Inquiries Dec. 1981–Jan. 1982, Sydney, 1982, pp. 71–3.
28 *Customs (Cinematograph Films) Regulations*, r. 13.
29 (1704) 14 State Trials (Old Series) 1096.
30 *R* v. *Tutchin* (1704) 14 State Trials (Old Series) 1128.
31 Unreported, discussed in R. C. Smith, *Press Law*, London, 1978, pp. 86–7.
32 For a politico-legal discussion of those cases, see M. Head, 'Sedition: Is the Star Chamber Dead?', *Criminal Law Journal*, vol. 3, 1979, p. 89; for analysis of sedition law in Australia generally, see Campbell and Whitmore, *Freedom in Australia*, pp. 324–9.
33 *Criminal Code* (Qld) ss. 44–52; *Criminal Code* (WA) ss. 44–52; *Criminal Code* (Tas.) s. 68.
34 (1949) 79 CLR 101.
35 *Schneiderman* v. *US* (1942) 320 United States Reports 156.
36 (1961) 105 CLR 177.
37 Campbell and Whitmore, *Freedom in Australia*, p. 329.

REFERENCES 263

9. Radio and Television

1. The main texts are: the Australian Broadcasting Tribunal *Manual*, a looseleaf collection of Tribunal rules, standards, practice notes and other material provided free to public libraries; Armstrong, Grey, Hitchens and Orr, *Communications Law and Policy in Australia*, Butterworths, Sydney (hereafter 'Armstrong, *Communications Law*'); Durie & Catterns, *Broadcasting Law & Practice*, Law Book Co., Sydney (both looseleaf services commencing in 1987).
2. Broadcasting Act s. 124.
3. Armstrong, *Communications Law*, para. 3030.
4. (1985) 10 *Commonwealth Record*, p. 1194.
5. ABC Act s. 78; Broadcasting Act s. 64.
6. Broadcasting Act s. 104.
7. Broadcasting Act ss. 78A, 105A; ABC Act s. 78(5).
8. *Victoria Park Racing Co.* v. *Taylor* (1937) 58 CLR 479.
9. ABC Act s. 11.
10. M. Armstrong, 'The Deregulation of Radio', (1986) 41 *Media Information Australia*.
11. Australian Broadcasting Tribunal, Report on 4ZZZ (Brisbane) licence renewal, 1981; Report on 6PR (Perth) licence renewal, 1983.
12. Broadcasting Act ss. 16(5)–(6), 99(2A).
13. (1986) 11 Commonwealth Record 154.
14. Television Advertising Condition 5; Children's Advertising Standards 18–32A.
15. Television Advertising Condition 6.
16. Television Advertising Condition 8.
17. Television Programme Standard 21.
18. Armstrong, *Communications Law*, para. 1530.
19. Armstrong, *Communications Law*, para. 1620.
20. Armstrong, *Communications Law*, para. 1635.
21. The law and conduct of inquiries are discussed in Armstrong, *Communications Law*, paras 8300 ff.
22. Armstrong, *Communications Law*, paras 4000 ff.
23. *R* v. *Australian Broadcasting Tribunal; Ex parte 2HD Pty Ltd* (1979) 27 ALR 321.
24. The sections which state criteria relating to particular kinds of application are: s. 83(5)–(9) for grant of licences; ss. 84–5 for imposition of licence conditions; ss. 86(10)–(11C), 87 for renewal of licences; s. 88(1) for suspension and revocation of licences 87; s. 89A(1A)–(1D) for licence transfers; ss. 89A(1), (3) for participation in licence benefits; ss. 90JA, 92FAA for changes in control of licences.
25. Australian Broadcasting Tribunal, Perth television licence grant report (1986), vol. 1, pp. 54–8.
26. (1978) 19 ALR 425.
27. (1980) 29 ALR 289.
28. (1980) 29 ALR 289 at 304.
29. Armstrong, *Communications Law*, paras 6015–6205.
30. Armstrong, *Communications Law*, paras 6700–7285.
31. *The Herald & Weekly Times Ltd* v. *The Commonwealth* (1966) 115 CLR 418 at 436 per Kitto J.

10. Access to Information

1. *Victoria Park Racing Co.* v. *Taylor* (1937) 58 CLR 479; J. Fleming, *The Law of Torts*, 6th ed., 1983, pp. 568–75; Australian Law Reform Commission, *Unfair Publication: Defamation and Privacy*, Report No. 11, Sydney, 1979, pp. 109–35.
2. (1986) 4 NSWLR 457; see also *Church of Scientology* v. *Trans Malia Productions*, Gazette of Law & Journalism, July 1987, p. 3.
3. Privacy Committee Act 1975 (NSW).
4. *Fraser* v. *Evans* [1969] 1 QB 349, 361 per Lord Denning MR.
5. J. Stuckey, 'Innocent Third Parties and Breach of Confidence', *University of New South Wales Law Journal*, vol. 4, 1981, p. 73.
6. [1981] 1 All ER 417.

7 *Coco* v. *A. N. Clark (Engineers) Ltd* [1969] *Reports of Patent Cases* 41, 47–8.
8 *Exchange Telegraph Co. Ltd* v. *Gregory* [1894] 1 QB 147.
9 *Stevenson, Jordan & Harrison Ltd* v. *Macdonald and Evans* [1952] 1 TLR 101.
10 (1849) 1 De Gex & Smale's Reports 652; 41 ER 1171.
11 *Pollard* v. *Photographic Co.* (1889) 40 Ch D 345; *Stedall* v. *Houghton* (1901) 18 TLR 126.
12 *A-G* v. *Jonathan Cape Ltd* [1976] 1 QB 752.
13 *Argyll* v. *Argyll* [1967] Ch 302.
14 *Lennon* v. *News Group Newspapers Ltd* [1978] FSR 573.
15 *Lennon* v. *News Group Newspapers Ltd* [1978] FSR 573, 574–5.
16 For example, *Seager* v. *Copydex Ltd* [1967] 2 All ER 415; *Deta Nomines Pty Ltd* v. *Viscount Plastic Products Pty Ltd* [1979] VR 167.
17 [1980] VR 224.
18 *Talbot* v. *General Television Corporation Pty Ltd* [1980] VR 224, 231.
19 Stuckey, 'Innocent Third Parties and Breach of Confidence', p. 73.
20 *The Times* 4 July 1981.
21 *Stevenson, Jordan & Harrison Ltd* v. *Macdonald Evans* [1952] 1 TLR 101, 195.
22 (1940) 63 CLR 73.
23 *McGuinness* v. *Attorney-General (Vic.)* (1940) 63 CLR 73, 102–3.
24 *Re Buchanan* (1964) 65 SR (NSW) 9; *Hewitt* v. *West Australian* (1976) 17 ACTR 15.
25 *A-G* v. *Clough* [1963] 1 QB 773; *A-G* v. *Mulholland* [1963] 2 QB 477.
26 Law Reform Commission of Western Australia, *Report on Privilege for Journalists (Project No. 53)*, Perth, 1980.
27 For example, *A-G* v. *Mulholland* [1963] 2 QB 477 at 489–90 per Lord Denning MR, at 492 per Donovan LJ. In the UK, s. 10 of the *Contempt of Court Act* 1981 says disclosure may be compelled only 'in the interests of justice or national security or for the prevention of disorder or crime'.
28 *McGuinness* v. *Attorney-General (Vic.)* (1940) 63 CLR 73 at 104 per Dixon J; *Broadcasting Council of New Zealand* v. *Alex Harvey Industries Ltd* [1980] 1 NZLR 163.
29 [1981] 1 All ER 417 now applied in *John Fairfax & Sons* v. *Cojuangco*, Gazette of Law & Journalism, April 1987, p. 17.
30 *British Steel* case [1981] 1 All ER 417, 467–75, esp. at 475.
31 [1968] 1 QB 396.
32 (1981) 34 ALR 105.
33 (1984) 3 IPR 276.
34 *The Times*, Oct. 1984.
35 [1984] 1 WLR 892.
36 (1980) 32 ALR 485.
37 *Commonwealth* v. *John Fairfax & Sons Ltd* (1980) 32 ALR 485, 492–3.
38 *A-G (UK)* v. *Heinemann Publishers* Gazette of Law and Journalism, April 1987, p. 18; appeal pending to higher court.
39 *Listening Devices Act* 1984 (NSW); *Listening Devices Act* 1969 (Vic.); *Invasion of Privacy Act* 1971 (Qld) ss. 41–50; *Listening Devices Act* 1978 (WA); *Listening Devices Act* 1972 (SA).
40 Ss. 6, 7, considered in *R* v. *Miglorini* (1981) 38 ALR 356.
41 S. 7(4).
42 S. 7(1)(b)–(c).
43 Telecom recording requirements reproduced in Australian Broadcasting Tribunal, *Annual Report 1981–82*, p. 210.
44 Radio Programme Standard 7; TV Programme Standard 17.
45 Armstrong, Grey, Hitchens and Orr, *Communications Law and Policy in Australia* (loose-leaf service), Sydney, Butterworths, paras 10,065 ff.
46 E. Campbell and H. Whitmore, *Freedom in Australia*, 2nd ed., Sydney, 1973, pp. 331–3.
47 'The "D" Notice System: What the Press Isn't Saying', *Nation Review*, 9–15 February 1978, vol. 8, no. 17, p. 15; ' "D" Notices Part Two: Blank Spaces', *Nation Review*, 16–22 February 1978, vol. 8, no. 18, p. 6.
48 Campbell and Whitmore, *Freedom in Australia*, pp. 346–57.
49 For a fuller discussion, see D. C. Pearce, *Australian Administrative Law Service*, Sydney, paras 601 ff.
50 *Freedom of Information Act* 1982 ss. 91–2.
51 *Freedom of Information Act* 1982, definition of 'document' in s. 4(1).
52 *Freedom of Information Act* 1982 s. 4(1), definitions of 'agency', 'department', and 'prescribed authority'.

[53] S. 4(1) definition.
[54] S. 15.
[55] Ss. 18, 94; *Freedom of Information (Charges) Regulations*.
[56] S. 19.
[57] S. 54.
[58] Ss. 55–6.
[59] S. 58.
[60] *Ombudsman Act* 1976 (Cth); *Freedom of Information Act* 1982 s. 57.
[61] Security: s. 33(2)–(7); deliberative: s. 36(3)–(10).
[62] Cabinet: s. 34(2)–(5); deliberative: s. 36(3)–(10).
[63] Ss. 58(4)–(5), 66–90.

11. Press Regulation

[1] S. Walker, 'The Trade Practices Act 1974 and Mergers in the Newspaper Industry', *Australian Business Law Review*, vol. 9, 1981, p. 322 G. de Q. Walker, 'Product Market Definition in Competition Law' (1980) 11 *Federal Law Review*, p. 386.
[2] Hon. J. G. Norris, Report of the Inquiry into the Ownership and Control of Newspapers in Victoria: Report to the Premier of Victoria (1981), discussed in L. Carlyon, *Paper Chase: The Press under Examination*, Melbourne, 1982, and P. Thomas (ed.), *The Press Gang: How Australia's Big Papers are Run*, Sydney, 1982.
[3] *Printing and Newspapers Act* 1973 (NSW); *Printing and Newspapers Act* 1981 (Qld).
[4] *Printers and Newspapers Act* 1984 (NT).
[5] *Printers and Newspapers Act* 1911 (Tas.).
[6] *Printers and Newspapers Act* 1958 (Vic.); *Printing and Newspapers Ordinance* 1961 (ACT).
[7] S. 21 (Vic.); s. 21 (NT).
[8] *Imprint Act (Repeal) Act* 1982 (SA).
[9] *Copyright Act* 1879 (NSW) ss. 5–7; *Library Council of Victoria Act* 1965 ss. 12–13; *Libraries Act* 1943 (Qld) s. 23A; *Copyright Act* 1895 (WA) s. 7; *Libraries Act* 1982 (SA), s. 35; *Libraries Act* 1984 (Tas.) s. 22.
[10] Australian Press Council, *Annual Report No. 6*, Sydney, 1982, p. 5.
[11] Australian Press Council, *Aims and Practices*, Sydney, 1977, pp. 13–16.
[12] Australian Press Council, *Aims and Practices*, p. 9.
[13] Australian Press Council, *Aims and Practices*, pp. 6–7.
[14] 'Takeovers Tribunal Plan Splits Press Council', *Sydney Morning Herald*, 13 December 1986, p. 3.
[15] 'Wootten Slams Govt Inaction Over Murdoch Bid for HWT', *Sydney Morning Herald*, 17 December 1986, p. 4.

12. Advertising

[1] H. McQueen, *Australia's Media Monopolies*, Melbourne, 1977, p. 10.
[2] S. Leacock, *Collected Works*, Chicago, 1936, p. 102.
[3] R. B. Sheridan, *The Critic*, Act 1 Scene i.
[4] *Commonwealth Parliamentary Debates* (Senate) 27 September 1973, p. 1013.
[5] *CRW Pty Ltd* v. *Sneddon* (1972) 72 AR (NSW) 17, 37 per Sheldon and Sheppard JJ.
[6] (1981) 37 ALR 161.
[7] *Stuart Alexander and Co. (Interstate) Pty Ltd* v. *Blenders Pty Ltd* (1981) 37 ALR 164–5.
[8] For a comprehensive discussion, see S. Barnes and M. Blakeney, *Advertising Regulation*, Sydney, 1982, Ch. 2.
[9] *Consumer Protection Act* 1969 (NSW) s. 32; *Consumer Affairs Act* 1972 (Vic.) s. 13; *Consumer Affairs Act* 1970–1974 (Qld) ss. 31–3; *Consumer Affairs Act* 1970 (Tas.) s. 9B.
[10] *Unfair Advertising Act* 1970–1981 (SA); *Trade Descriptions and False Advertising Act* 1936–1981 (WA); *Advertisements (Terms of Purchase) Act* 1973 (Tas.); *False Advertising Act* 1970 (NT).
[11] *Misrepresentation Act* 1971–1972 (SA); *Law Reform (Misrepresentation) Ordinance* 1977 (ACT).
[12] *Colgate-Palmolive Pty Ltd* v. *Rexona Pty Ltd* (1981) 37 ALR 391.
[13] *Larmer* v. *Power Machinery Pty Ltd* (1977) 14 ALR 243.

[14] *Smologonov* v. *O'Brien* (1982) ATPR 40-312.
[15] *Glorie* v. *WA Chip & Pulp Co. Pty Ltd* (1981) 3 ATPR 40-259.
[16] For a summary of the authorities see *Henderson* v. *Pioneer Homes Pty Ltd* (*No. 2*) (1980) 43 FLR 276, 292 per Franki J.
[17] *Slazenger and Sons* v. *Feltham and Co.* (1889) 6 RPC 531, 538 per Lindley LJ cited with approval in *Puxu Pty Ltd* v. *Parkdale Custom Built Furniture Pty Ltd* (1979) 27 ALR 387, 397 per Keely J.
[18] *World Series Cricket Pty Ltd* v. *Parish* (1977) 18 ALR 181.
[19] (1977) 18 ALR 189.
[20] *World Series* case (1977) 18 ALR 202.
[21] *World Series* case (1977) 18 ALR 195.
[22] See *CRW Pty Ltd* v. *Sneddon* (1972) 72 AR (NSW) 17.
[23] *CRW Pty Ltd* v. *Sneddon* (1972) 72 AR (NSW) 31.
[24] (1979) 40 FLR 165.
[25] (1979) 40 FLR 176.
[26] *Parkdale Custom Built Furniture Pty Ltd* v. *Puxu Pty Ltd* (1982) 42 ALR 1, 6.
[27] See *World Series Cricket Pty Ltd* v. *Parish* (1977) 18 ALR 181.
[28] See Barnes and Blakeney, *Advertising Regulation*, Ch. 4.
[29] *Charles of the Ritz Distributors Corp.* v. *FTC* 143 Federal Reporter 2d 676, 680 (1944).
[30] See Barnes and Blakeney, *Advertising Regulation*, Chs 4-8.
[31] (1981) 37 ALR 155.
[32] *Re Leroy Gordon Cooper Jr* discussed in M. E. Jones, 'Celebrity Endorsements: A Case of Alarm and Concern for the Future', *New England Law Review*, vol. 15, pp. 521, 532.
[33] Trade Practices Commission, *Advertising and Selling*, 1981, para. 334.
[34] See *General Guides Applicable to All Endorsements* 16 Code of Federal Regulation 255 (18 January 1980) reproduced in *Antitrust Law Journal*, vol. 49, 1980, p. 823.
[35] (1975) 5 ALR 493.
[36] See Trade Practices Commission, *Advertising and Selling*, para. 335.
[37] Trade Practices Commission, *Advertising and Selling*, para. 336.
[38] See *General Guides, Antitrust Law Journal*, vol. 49, 1980, p. 823.
[39] (1981) 37 ALR 391.
[40] See Trade Practices Commission, *Advertising and Selling*, para. 210.
[41] See M. Blakeney and S. Barnes, 'Industry Self-Regulation: An Alternative to Deregulation? Advertising—A Case Study', *University of New South Wales Law Journal*, vol. 5, 1980, p. 133.
[42] See Trade Practices Commission, *Advertising and Selling*.
[43] *Carter Products, Inc.* v. *FTC* 323 F 2d 523, 525 (1963) per Wisdom J.
[44] 380 US 374 (1965).
[45] *Hartnell* v. *Sharp Corporation of Australia Pty Ltd* 5 ALR 165; *Given* v. *Snuffa Pty Ltd* (1978) 2 ATPR 40-083.
[46] *Eva* v. *Southern Motors Box Hill Pty Ltd* (1977) 30 FLR 213; *Eva* v. *Preston Motors Pty Ltd* (1977) 1 ATPR 40-048.
[47] *Larmer* v. *Power Machinery Pty Ltd* (1977) 29 FLR 490; *Larmer* v. *Dome Lighting Products* (1978) 2 ATPR 40-070.
[48] *Given* v. *C. V. Holland Holdings Pty Ltd* (1977) 29 FLR 212; *Finger* v. *Malua Motors Pty Ltd* (1978) 2 ATPR 40-061.
[49] *Thompson* v. *Magnamail Pty Ltd* (*No. 1*) (1977) 1 ATPR 40-032; *Thompson* v. *Magnamail Pty Ltd* (*No. 2*) (1977) 1 ATPR 40-033; *Thompson* v. *Riley McKay Pty Ltd* (*No. 3*) (1980) 43 FLR 293; *Doolan* v. *Waltons Ltd* (1981) 39 ALR 408.
[50] *Thompson* v. *J. T. Fossey* (*No. 1*) (1978) 20 ALR 496.
[51] *Thompson* v. *J. T. Fossey* (*No. 1*) (1978) 20 ALR 496; *Wise* v. *Greenslade and C. L. M. Holdings Pty Ltd* (1977) 1 ATPR 40-035.
[52] *Doolan* v. *Magnamail Pty Ltd* (1982) ATPR 40-276.
[53] For example, *World Series Cricket Ltd* v. *Parish* (1977) 16 ALR 181.
[54] *Ransley* v. *Spare Parts and Reconditioning Co. Pty Ltd* (1975) 1 ATPR 40-055.
[55] *MacFarlane* v. *John Martin & Co. Ltd* (1977) 1 ATPR 40-034.
[56] *Wise* v. *Greenslade and C. L. M. Holdings Pty Ltd* (1977) 1 ATPR 40-035.
[57] *Thompson* v. *Magnamail Pty Ltd* (*No. 1*) (1977) 1 ATPR 40-032; *Thompson* v. *Magnamail Pty Ltd* (*No. 2*) (1977) 1 ATPR 40-033; *Thompson* v. *Riley McKay Pty Ltd* (*No. 3*) (1980) 43 FLR 293.
[58] *Doolan* v. *Waltons Ltd* (1981) 39 ALR 408.
[59] *Finger* v. *Malua Motors Pty Ltd* (1978) 2 ATPR 40-013.

[60] *Eva* v. *Southern Motors Box Hill Pty Ltd* (1977) 30 FLR 213; *Wise* v. *Greenslade and C. L. M. Holdings Pty Ltd* (1977) 1 ATPR 40–035.
[61] *Thompson* v. *J. T. Fossey (No. 1)* (1978) 20 ALR 496.
[62] *Eva* v. *Southern Motors Box Hill Pty Ltd* (1977) 30 FLR 213; see also, *Eva* v. *Preston Motors Pty Ltd* (1977) 1 ATPR 60–048.
[63] *Wilde* v. *Menville Pty Ltd* (1981) 3 ATPR 40–195.
[64] Trade Practices Commission, Information Circular No. 10, 1975, para. 5.9.
[65] [1974] 1 WLR 1220, 1227.
[66] *Henderson* v. *Bowden Ford Pty Ltd* (1979) 2 ATPR 40–129.
[67] *McGrath Motors (Canberra) Pty Limited* v. *Applebee* (1963–1964) 110 CLR 656.
[68] *Andrews Brothers (Bournemouth) Limited* v. *Singer & Co. Limited* (1934) 1 KB 27; *Anderson* v. *Scrutton* [1934] SASR 10.
[69] *R* v. *Ford Motor Co. Ltd* [1974] 1 WLR 1220.
[70] *R* v. *Ford Motor Co. Ltd* [1974] 1 WLR 1220.
[71] *Annand and Thompson Pty Ltd* v. *Trade Practices Commission* 189–90 per Fisher J.
[72] *World Series Cricket Ltd* v. *Parish* (1977) 16 ALR 181.
[73] *Hartnell* v. *Sharp Corporation of Australia Ltd* (1975) 5 ALR 493.
[74] *Larmer* v. *Power Machinery Pty Ltd* (1977) 29 FLR 490.
[75] *Given* v. *Snuffa Pty Ltd* (1978) 2 ATPR 40–083.
[76] *Larmer* v. *Dome Lighting Products* (1978) 2 ATPR 40–070.
[77] *Taco Bill Pty Ltd* v. *Taco Company of Australia Inc.* (1982) ATPR 40–277.
[78] 'Monte Carlo Circus', *Michael Edgley International Pty Ltd* v. *Ashton's Nominees Pty Ltd* (1979) 26 ALR 419; Cf 'Saint Germain', *Weitmann* v. *Katies Ltd* (1977) 29 FLR 336; 'Lego', *Lego Australia Pty Ltd* v. *Pauls (Merchants) Pty Ltd* (1982) ATPR 40–275.
[79] *Green* v. *Ford* (1985) ATPR 40–603.
[80] *Doolan* v. *Magnamail Pty Ltd* (1982) ATPR 40–276.
[81] *Doolan* v. *Magnamail Pty Ltd* (1982) ATPR 40–276.
[82] *Given* v. *Snuffa Pty Ltd* (1978) 2 ATPR 40–083.
[83] Trade Practices Commission, Information Circular No. 12.
[84] Trade Practices Commission, Information Circular No. 4.
[85] Trade Practices Commission, Information Circular No. 4.
[86] *Eva* v. *Mazda Motors (Sales) Pty Ltd* (1977) 1 ATPR 40–020.
[87] *Ducret* v. *Nissan Motors Co. (Australia) Pty Ltd* (1979) 38 FLR 126.
[88] *De Jong* v. *Prudential Assurance Co. Ltd* (1977) 14 ALR 694.
[89] *Given* v. *Optional Extras Pty Ltd* (1976) 10 ALR 627.
[90] *Doolan* v. *Air New Zealand Ltd* (1978) 2 ATPR 40–082; *Dawson* v. *World Travel Headquarters Pty Ltd* (1981) 3 ATPR 40–240.
[91] For example, *Sully* v. *Darwin Bakery Pty Ltd* (1981) 3 ATPR 40–230.
[92] *Guthrie* v. *Metro Ford Pty Ltd* (1977) Trade Practices Reporting Service 304–93.
[93] *Universal Telecasters (Qld) Ltd* v. *Guthrie* (1978) 18 ALR 531, 547 per Franki J.
[94] *Wise* v. *M. R. G. Automotive Services Pty Ltd* (1981) 3 ATPR 40–239.
[95] *Henderson* v. *Pioneer Homes Pty Ltd* (1980) 29 ALR 597, 610 per Franki J.
[96] *Keehn* v. *Medical Benefits Fund of Australia Ltd* (1977) 14 ALR 77, 82.
[97] *Dawson* v. *Motor Tyre Service Pty Ltd* (1981) 3 ATPR 40–223.
[98] Trade Practices Commission, *Advertising and Selling*, 1981, para. 346.
[99] *Keehn* v. *Medical Benefits Fund of Australia Ltd* (1977) 14 ALR 77.
[100] *Given* v. *Snuffa Ltd* (1978) 2 ATPR 40–083.
[101] *Dawson* v. *Motor Tyre Service Pty Ltd* (1981) 3 ATPR 40–223.
[102] *Ballard* v. *Sperry Rand Australia Ltd* (1975) 6 ALR 696.
[103] (1981) 3 ATPR 40–222.
[104] For example, *TPC* v. *Sterling* (1980) 28 ALR 497.
[105] See Trade Practices Commission, Information Circular No. 18.
[106] (1980) 29 ALR 597.
[107] Trade Practices Commission, *Advertising and Selling*, 1980, paras 355–7.
[108] Trade Practices Commission, *Advertising and Selling*, para. 355.
[109] (1981) 3 ATPR 40–246.
[110] *Given* v. *Pryor* (1979) 2 ATPR 40–109.
[111] See *TPC* v. *C. G. Smith Pty Ltd* (1978) 3 TPC 156.
[112] (1981) 3 ATPR 40–222.
[113] *Mansard Developments Pty Ltd* v. *Sackville* (1981) 3 ATPR 40–255.
[114] *Industrial Arbitration (Employment Agencies) Amendment Act* 1975 (NSW); *Employees Registry Offices Act* 1915–1966 (SA); *Statute Law Revision Act* 1973 (SA); *Employment Agencies Act* 1976 (WA).

[115] Trade Practices Commission, Information Circular No. 23, paras 4.1–4.4, 6.1, 6.2.
[116] (1981) 3 ATPR 40–195.
[117] Trade Practices Commission, Information Circular No. 10, para. 15.3.
[118] (1981) 35 ALR 503.
[119] (1981) 3 ATPR 40–195.
[120] (1975) 5 ALR 493.
[121] *Hartnell* v. *Sharp Corporation of Australia Pty Ltd* (1975) 5 ALR 497.
[122] (1978) 18 ALR 531.
[123] The codes are reproduced in Barnes and Blakeney, *Advertising Regulation* and Australian Advertising Industry Council, *Self-Regulation in Australian Advertising*, 3rd ed., Sydney, 1982.
[124] See Blakeney and Barnes, 'Industry Self Regulation', *University of New South Wales Law Journal*, vol. 5, 1980, p. 133.
[125] The Commercials Acceptance Division Guidelines are reproduced in Barnes and Blakeney, *Advertising Regulation*, Appendix N.
[126] See *Re an Advertisement Produced by the Campaign Palace for Sanyo Australia Pty Ltd for the Product Betacord*, Communications Law Bulletin, vol. 3, no. 7, 1981.
[127] See Australian Broadcasting Tribunal, *Re: Advertisements Produced for Television on Behalf of the Health Commission of New South Wales*, 9 October 1981.
[128] Joint Committee for Disparaging Copy, *Annual Report*, 1969, p. 3.
[129] For example, *Stuart Alexander & Co. (Interstate) Pty Ltd* v. *Blenders Pty Ltd* (1981) 37 ALR 161, discussed in M. Blakeney, 'Comparison Advertising', *Communications Law Bulletin*, vol. 2, no. 3, 1982.

13. Sales Promotions

[1] *Consumer Protection Act* 1969 (NSW) s. 29A; *Prices Act* 1948–1980 (SA) s. 33a–33e; *Consumer Affairs Act* 1972 (Vic.) s. 13(2a).
[2] Trade Practices Commission, Information Circular No. 10, para. 13.3.
[3] (1980) 33 ALR 417.
[4] *Reardon* v. *Morley Ford Pty Ltd* (1980) 33 ALR 432.
[5] Trade Practices Commission, Information Circular No. 10, para. 13.5.
[6] Trade Practices Commission, Information Circular No. 10, para. 13.4.
[7] Trade Practices Commission, Information Circular No. 10, para. 13.5.
[8] For example, *Reardon* v. *Morley Ford Pty Ltd* (1980) 33 ALR 417, 433.
[9] See *People* v. *Globo* 174 New York State Reports 2d 159 (1958).
[10] See *Tashof* v. *FTC* 437 Federal Reporter 2d 707 (1970).
[11] *Reardon* v. *Morley Ford Pty Ltd* (1980) 33 ALR 417, 433.
[12] See *People* v. *Globo* 174 New York State Reports 2d 159 (1958).
[13] *People* v. *Globo* 174 New York State Reports 2d 163 (1958).
[14] *Consumer Protection Act* 1969 (NSW) s. 29A(3).
[15] *Prices Act* 1948–1980 (SA) s. 33a(3).
[16] Trade Practices Commission, Information Circular No. 10, para. 12.1
[17] See: *Trading Stamp Act* 1972 (NSW); *Consumer Affairs Act* 1972, Part II, Division I (Vic.); *Trading Stamps Abolition* Act 1900 (Tas.); *Trading Stamp Act* 1980 (SA); *Trading Stamp Act* 1981 (WA); *Trading Stamp Ordinance* 1972 (ACT); *Trading Stamp Act* 1904 of SA (NT).
[18] NSW s. 2(2); NT s. 7; ACT s. 3(2).
[19] Tas. s. 2 definition of trading stamp refers only to redemption by a trading stamp company.
[20] SA, s. 4(2).
[21] NSW s. 3(2)(d); SA s. 5(3); Vic. s. 11(5); WA s. 4(3).
[22] See S. Barnes and M. Blakeney, *Advertising Regulation*, Sydney, 1982, para. 10.1.3.
[23] See D. K. Srivastava, 'Every Man's Castle or Every Trader's Dumping Ground', *Monash University Law Review*, vol. 2, 1976, p. 195.
[24] Relevant legislation is the *Unsolicited Goods and Services Act*: NSW 1974; Qld 1973–1974; SA 1972; Tas. 1973; WA 1973; NT 1972; *Consumer Affairs Act* 1972 (Vic.) Pt II, Div. 4.
[25] For example, *Trade Practices Act* 1974 s. 64(5).
[26] *Trade Practices Act* 1974 s. 4(1).
[27] *Unsolicited Goods and Services Act* 1974 (NSW) s. 3(1).

REFERENCES 269

[28] For example, *Trade Practices Act* 1974 s. 64(3).
[29] (1975) 25 FLR 194.
[30] *Wells* v. *John R. Lewis (International) Pty Ltd* (1975) FLR 200.
[31] *The Reader's Digest Association Ltd* v. *Pirie* [1973] SLT 170.
[32] *Trade Practices Act* 1974, s. 64(2) and (2B).
[33] See *Sherwood and Roberts-Yakima Inc.* v. *Leach* 409 Pacific Reporter 2d 160, 163 (1965).
[34] *Referral Selling Act* 1974 (NSW); *Pyramid Sales Act* 1973 (SA) s. 9; *Consumer Affairs Act* 1972 (Vic.) s. 32F; *Pyramid Sales Act* 1973–1975 (WA).
[35] *Referral Selling Act* 1974 (NSW) s. 3(2); *Consumer Affairs Act* 1972 (Vic.) s. 32F(1); *Pyramid Sales Act* 1973 (SA) s. 9(2).
[36] *Kugler* v. *Koscot Interplanetary Inc.* 293 American Reports 2d 682, 690–1 (1972) per Mehler J.
[37] *Pyramid Sales Act* 1974 (NSW); *Pyramid Selling Schemes (Elimination) Act* 1973 (Qld); *Pyramid Sales Act* 1973 (SA); *Pyramid Selling Act* 1974 (Tas.); *Consumer Affairs Act* 1972 (Vic.) ss. 32A–32E; *Pyramid Sales Scheme Act* 1973–1975 (WA); *Pyramid Selling Ordinance* 1973 (ACT).
[38] *Trade Practices Act* 1974 s. 61.
[39] *Pyramid Sales Act* 1974 (NSW) s. 4; *Pyramid Selling Schemes (Elimination) Act* 1973 (Qld) s. 13.
[40] *Pyramid Sales Act* 1973 (SA) s. 7.

14. Competitions

[1] [1976] 1 WLR 1109.
[2] *Reader's Digest Association Ltd* v. *Williams* [1976] 1 WLR 113.
[3] W. Blackstone, *Commentaries on the Laws of England*, 1765 ed., London, Bk IV, c. 13.
[4] *Taylor* v. *Smetten* (1883) 11 QBD 207; *Hall* v. *Cox* [1889] 1 QB 198, followed by the High Court in *Mutual Loan Agency* v. *Attorney-General for New South Wales* (1909) 9 CLR 79.
[5] For example, see *News of the World* v. *Friend* [1973] 1 WLR 248, 251.
[6] *Whitebread and Co. Ltd* v. *Bell* [1970] 2 All ER 64, 66.
[7] *Sobye* v. *Levy* (1909) 9 CLR 496, 501.
[8] G. Sawer, 'Competitions Involving Chance and Skill', *Australian Law Journal*, vol. 11, 1937, pp. 114, 116.
[9] *Lotteries and Art Unions Act* 1901 (NSW) s. 3(6).
[10] *Art Unions and Amusements Act* 1976 (Qld) s. 7(1).
[11] *Lottery and Gaming Act* 1936–1980 (SA) s. 4.
[12] *Lotteries, Gaming and Betting Act* 1966 (Vic.) s. 3.
[13] *Racing and Gaming Act* 1952 (Tas.).
[14] *Lotteries (Control) Act* 1954–1972 (WA) s. 4.
[15] ACT: *Lotteries Ordinance* 1964, s. 5(1); NT: *Lottery and Games Ordinance* 1940 s. 8.
[16] *Ex parte Levy* (1909) 9 SR (NSW) 688.
[17] *Ex parte British Products Pty Ltd; Re Willard* (1935) 35 SR (NSW) 152.
[18] *Ex parte Associated Newspapers Ltd; Re Lewis* (1957) 57 SR (NSW) 550.
[19] *Church* v. *News Ltd* [1953] SASR 71.
[20] *Ampol Petroleum Ltd* v. *O'Sullivan* [1960] SASR 137.
[21] *Lord* v. *Re* [1968] VR 411.
[22] *Wyatt* v. *Tarax Drinks Holdings Ltd* [1960] VR 626.
[23] See R. G. Lawson, *Advertising Law*, London, 1978, pp. 180–202.
[24] See J. F. Burrows, *News Media Law in New Zealand*, Wellington, 1974, Ch. 12.
[25] *Coles* v. *Odhams Press Ltd* [1936] 1 KB 416.
[26] *Hobbs* v. *Ward* (1929) 45 TLR 373.
[27] *Blyth* v *Hulton* (1908) 24 TLR 719.
[28] For example, *Taylor* v. *Smetten* (1883) 11 QBD 207.
[29] [1907] 1 KB 448.
[30] *Willis* v. *Young and Stembridge* [1907] 1 KB 455.
[31] *Ex parte British Products Pty Ltd; Re Willard* (1935) 35 SR (NSW) 152.
[32] *Ampol Petroleum Products Pty Ltd; Re Willard* (1935) 35 SR (NSW) 152.
[33] *Lord* v. *Re* [1968] VR 411.
[34] NSW: *Lotteries and Art Unions Act* 1901 s. 3(6); Qld: *Art Unions and Amusements Act* 1976 s. 7; Vic.: *Lotteries, Gaming and Betting Act* 1966 s. 5(4)(b); WA: *Lotteries (Control)*

Act 1954–1972 s. 4; ACT: *Lotteries Ordinance* 1964 s. 5: NT: *Lottery and Gaming Ordinance* 1940 s. 8; SA: *Lottery and Gaming Act* 1936–1981 s. 4.

[35] *Lotteries and Art Unions Act* 1901 s. 4B.
[36] See D. Shannon, *Sales Promotion in Australia, Law and Practice*, Sydney, 1981, p. 30.
[37] *Lottery and Gaming Ordinance Act* (NT) s. 25A; *Racing and Gaming Act* 1952 (Tas.) s. 85.
[38] *Lotteries, Gaming and Betting Act* 1966 (Vic.) s. 5(4)(b); *Lottery and Gaming Act* 1936–1981 (SA) s. 9(d); *Art Unions and Amusements Act* 1976 (Qld) s. 27.
[39] *Lotteries Ordinance Act* 1964 (ACT) s. 6(1).
[40] *Lotteries (Control)* Act 1954–1972 (WA) s. 12.
[41] *Trade Practices Act* 1974 ss. 52, 54.
[42] *Trade Practices Act* 1974 ss. 52, 54.

Index

abbreviations ix–x, 5–6
accessories in advertisements 225
accreditation of advertising agencies 232–5
Administrative Appeals Tribunal 139, 192, 198, 203
admission of guilt, reporting 108–9, 123–4
advertisements 5, 211–43
  Acts regulating 211–15
  broadcasting 172–5
  claims made in 218–29
  comparison 221
  copyright 96,
  criminal liability 213–15, 231–2
  disparagement 61–6, 221, 235
  employment 228–9
  land 227–9
  misleading 72, 215–32
  passing off 66–71, 73
  penalties 230
  sales promotion 236–43
  Standards Association of Australia 217, 224
  trade practices law 71–5, 211–43
  see also Trade Practices Act
Advertising Standards Council 208, 233
Age tapes case 99, 117
anonymous works, copyright 83
appeals 3–4
  comment on 109–10, 121–2
artistic works, copyright 79, 82
associations, defamation of 31–2, 210

audience 99
  advertisements 211, 216–18
  defamation 19–22, 26, 213
Australian Broadcasting Commission 87, 99, 142, 155–66, 179, 200
Australian Broadcasting Corporation 156, 165
Australian Broadcasting Tribunal 64, 139, 149–51, 156–74, 177, 178–85, 193, 197, 200
Australian content in broadcasts 161, 175–6, 181
Australian Journalists' Association 119–20, 193, 205, 207–8
Australian Law Reform Commission
  Children's Courts 136
  contempt 127–8
  defamation 8–10, 15, 59
Australian Press Council 205, 208–10
Australian Publishers' Bureau 235
Australian Security Intelligence Organisation (ASIO) 196, 198
authors
  copyright 84–5
  false authorship claims 97–8
  joint works 83

Bacon case 107, 117
bait advertising 236–9
'bare facts' in crime reporting 103
Barrier Reef case 182, 186
benefits claimed in advertisements 235
Bill of Rights, US 4
blasphemy 145–7, 149–51, 170

271

BLF *see Builders Labourers* case
Bradley case   112–13, 117
Bread Manufacturers case   113–14, 117–19, 128
British Steel case   189, 193
broadcasting, radio and television   155–86
  contempt, special dangers   101, 102–3, 116, 121, 123, 124–5
  control of licence ownership   183–6
  copyright   79–81, 83, 87, 89–90
  defamation   10, 27–8, 162–3
  offensive matter   166–71
  programme standards   166–8
  public inquiries   178–83
  taste and decency   147–52
  who can advertise   172–5
  see also advertisements, and programmes
Brych case   101, 117–19
bugging   188, 191–2, 194–6
Builders Labourers (BLF) case   102, 104–6, 108–9, 112, 116–17
business reputation   31–2, 61–75, 136
  defamation   13–15, 61–2
  imitation   66–75
  injurious falsehood   62–4
  passing off   66–71
  slander of goods   61, 62–4

Carleton case   42–3
cartoons
  copyright   86, 92
  defamation   17, 38
case reports   2–3
cassettes, copyright   78
  see also music, and sound recordings
Cassidy case   25–6, 57
celebrity endorsements in advertising   218–19
censorship
  broadcasting   147–51, 164–76
  film   151–2
  print media   148–9
children's broadcasts   168, 176–7, 234
children's courts   136

cigarette advertisements   64–5, 174–5
civil cases, prejudicial comment   121–2
claims in advertisements   218–29
codes, defamation   9, 12
  Media Industry   64–6
Colgate-Palmolive case   66, 214, 220–2
Colonel 'B' case   137, 142
commercial broadcasting   156–60, 166–78
  see also broadcasting
companies, defamation   31–2, 36, 61–6,
comparisons in advertisements   62–4, 221
competitions   244–7
confidential information   188–95
  concept of   191
  contracts   190–2
  'D' notices   197
  Freedom of Information Act   197–203
  journalists' source   192–4
  marriage secrets   190–1
consent to defamation   56–7
contempt   5, 99–144
  definition   100
  of court   207–9
  reforming the law   128
  see also Australian Law Reform Commission, broadcasting, crime reports, criticism, dormant cases, 'fair and accurate' reports, 'fair comment', headlines, identification, injunctions, parliaments, photographs, printers, publication, royal commissions, *sub judice*, and tribunals
contracts
  confidential information   188–95
  copyright   84, 89
control of broadcasting   178–85
Coonan (cricket helmet) case   96, 219
copying   91
copyright   76–98
  assignment   87, 88–9

breach of 90–8
concept of 76
compensation 97–8
Crown 83–4, 86–7
definitions of 76–81
expiry of 81–4
fair dealing 92–5
infringement of 90–3, 96–8
injunctions 96–7
international protection 95–6
licences 88–90
originality 76–81, 84–8, 90–2
owners 84–8
penalties 96–8
remedies 80, 96–8
trade practices actions 95–8
Copyright Tribunal 90
coroners, prejudicial contempt 127
courts
  access to 134–6
  bias accusations 129–34
  copyright 95
  criticism of 129–34
  defamation 36, 50–6
  'gag' orders 136–8
  media access 134–6
  prejudicial publications 99–128
  restrictions on reporting 136–9
  role of 3–5
  sub judice issues 99–128
crime reports
  contempt 102–9, 113–16, 120–2, 124–5
  defamation 21, 30, 49
criticism
  contempt 132–3
  copyright 94–5
  courts 129–34
  defamation 45–50
  parliament 141–4, 152–4

'D' notices 197
dance, copyright 78
dead, defamation of 32
deception 71–3, 74–5
defamation 7–60
  damages 58–9
  defences 33–58
  definitions 7–8, 10–12
  history of 8–10

injunctions 59–60
justification 33–6
liability 26–9, 36–58
meaning of words 18–26, 32
privilege 35, 36–44, 49–50, 53–5
public interest 35–8, 41–5, 49–50
radio and television transcripts 162–3
remedies 58–60
'shun and avoid' 18
state laws 5, 9–10, 206
truth 33–6, 48–9
see also broadcasting, business reputation, codes, criticism, 'defamatory', disparagement, 'fair and accurate' reports, 'fair comment', identification, journalists, malice, parliament, publication, retraction, and royal commissions
'defamatory', meaning of 11–18, 21–6
dictionaries, copyright 92
disparagement
  in advertising 61–6, 219
  in defamation 12–16, 21–2, 26, 61–6
  media industry codes on 64–6, 235
dormant cases, contempt 122
dramatic works, copyright 78, 81–2
Duchess of Argyll case 190–2
Dunbabin case 129–30

editions, copyright 81, 83
editors, contempt 101, 103–25, 129–30
election
  broadcasts 161–2, 177–8
  defamation 162
employment
  advertisements 228–9
  copyright 85–6
  defamatory references 36–7
ethics of journalism 205–8

'fair and accurate' reports
  contempt 139–42
  defamation 50–6

'fair comment'
  contempt 111, 134
  defamation 44–50
'fair dealing' in copyright 93–5
Family Court 133, 136, 200
federal laws 4–5
Federation of Australian Commercial Television Stations (FACTS) 64–5, 151, 168, 174–5, 232, 234
  Commercial Acceptance Division of 234
Federation of Australian Radio Broadcasters (FARB) 65, 151, 174–5, 177, 230, 234–5
films
  censorship 151–2
  contempt 112–13
  copyright 79–80, 82–3, 87
  defamation 18
foreign law 4
freedom of information 197–203
  cabinet documents 200
  exemptions 199–202
  federal Act 188, 197–9, 202–3
  minister's documents 197
  right to 105, 113–14
  Victorian Act 188, 198
  see also Press regulation 204–10
freedom of speech
  contempt 101, 105–16, 118, 130–33
  defamation 10–11, 19–20, 121
  government documents 193–4
  parliamentary privilege 141–4
  restrictions on programme makers 168–72

'gag' orders 136–8
'gagging' writs 118–20
Gallagher case 132–3
Gay News case 146–7
'get-up' of products 67, 73–4
Gordon case 117, 123–4
Gorton case 28–9, 44
government
  broadcasting powers 155–85
  secrets of 194–5, 200–2
  sedition cases 152–4
groups, defamation of 31–2, 209
guarantees and warranties 224

Hardiman case 182
'hatred and contempt' 11–13, 18
headlines,
  contempt 100, 103, 106–7, 109, 113, 119, 139, 141
  defamation 23, 48
health advertisements 64–5, 174–5, 233–4
Hicklin test 147
Hinch case 100, 117
humour, defamation 16–17

ideas, copyright 76
identification
  contempt 112–13, 123–5, 136
  defamation 29–32
imitation
  copyright 90–3, 96
  passing off 66–71, 73–5
'imprint' laws 204–5
indecency 145, 147–52, 168–72
inertia selling 234, 240–2
information
  access to 187–8
  confidential 188–95
  freedom of 197–203
  see also confidential information
'inherent tendency', contempt 122
injunctions
  contempt 103–4
  interlocutory 59
  permanent 60
  Trade Practices Commission 212–13
injurious falsehood 62–4
innocent publication of defamation 56
innuendo 19–20, 25, 34
inquiries of tribunals
  broadcasting 178–85
  defamation 54
  sub judice 104–5, 119, 125–8
  see also tribunals
interception of communication 188, 191–2, 195–6
'investigative' reporting 104
investment opportunities in advertising 229

Joint Committee for Disparaging Copy 235

INDEX

journalists 2
  Australian Journalists' Association 119–20, 192, 204, 206–7
  copyright 85–6
  defamation 27–32, 37–8, 55, 188
  responsibilities of 101, 103, 105–7, 116, 123–5, 132
  restrictions on 136–9, 204–9
  rights of 37–8, 134–6
  sources 29, 50–3, 188, 193–5
judges
  criticism 129–34
  influencing 108–11
  role of 3–4
judicial proceedings, defamation 53–4
juries
  influencing 99–100, 104, 106–9, 121–2, 133
  intimidating 134
  material withheld from 138
jurors, confidentiality of 138–9
'justification' in defamation 33–6

land advertisements 227–8, 239
laws
  complexity 1–2
  sources of 1–6
leaks 143, 188–90, 193–4
liability in defamation 26–9, 36–58
libel 10
libraries
  copying in 91, 94
  printer's copies for 205
licences
  broadcasting inquiries 179–83
  broadcasting ownership 183–5
  copyright 88–90
literary work, copyright 77–8, 81–2
local content
  advertising laws 173
  broadcast programmes 161, 175–6
lotteries 242–5

malice in defamation 40–1, 53, 140
marketing
  see trade practices and advertising
marriage secrets 189, 191

Media Council of Australia 64, 126, 232–4
medical advertisements 64–5, 174–5, 233–4
meetings, defamation 55
Middle East Airlines case 18, 62
misleading advertisements 215–32
Moccona case 66, 73, 212
monopoly in broadcasting 179–85
Morosi case 17, 23, 37, 57
movies
  see films
Mundy case 131–2
music, copyright 78–9, 81–2, 88–9

names
  copyright 78
  defamation 26–9
  passing off 66–71
  trade practices 72–5
national broadcasting service 155–66
National Literature Board of Review 149
'natural justice', 182
'need' for advertised goods 226
'newness' claimed in advertisements 224
news
  broadcasting press reports 178
  copyright 81, 84, 95
  defamation 26–7, 36–8, 41
newspapers
  blasphemy 146–7
  defamation 26–9, 36–8, 41–53
  registration and imprint laws 205–6
  takeovers 204, 209
  see also press regulation, publication
Norris inquiry 204
notice
  international copyright © 95
  Phonograms Convention ℗ 96

'obloquy', public 110–11
obscenity 145, 147–52
  broadcasts 149–51, 166–71
  films 151–2
  print media 148–9

offensive broadcasts   166–71
official notices, defamation   54–5
oligopoly
  broadcasting   182–5
  newspaper ownership   204
open justice   129–41
  see also freedom of speech
opinions, defamatory   44–50
organizations, defamation of   31–2
Othello case   46–7
ownership
  of broadcasting stations   178–83
  of copyright   84–8

Packer v. *Peacock*   102–3, 117
parliament
  contempt of   142–4
  defamation   36, 38–9, 50–3
  disrespect for   142–3
  law-making role   4–5
  leaks   143
  reports of   141–4
  sedition against   152–4
parodies,
  copyright   2–3, 86
parties in cases
  influence on   110–11, 136
  intimidation   111, 113–14
passing off   66–71
performance claims in advertising   223
performance rights   88
phone tapping   188, 192–3, 195–6
photocopying   91, 94
  see also 'fair dealing'
photographs
  contempt   112–13, 123, 125
  copyright   79, 82
  defamation   16–17
'piracy', record   97
planning of broadcasting   155–60
police, contemptuous information from   125
political broadcasts   161–4, 177–8
prejudice
  see sub judice publications
'prejudicial' contempt   101–5, 121, 126–7, 130
Press Council   204, 208–10
Press regulation   204–10
prices, advertised   225–6

printers
  contempt   123
  defamation   27
  'imprint' laws   205
  registration   205–6
privacy   186–7
  Freedom of Information Act   188, 197–204
  marital   189, 191
  Press Council   204, 208–10
  Privacy Committee (NSW)   187
  sporting events   80, 164
privilege
  absolute   35, 50–1
  abuse of   40–1
  legal professional   201
  parliamentary   141–4
  qualified   36–44, 55
  statutory modifications   41–3
prizes
  competitions   242–7
  promotions   239
products
  claims in advertising   216–30
  identity of   66–71
programmes, broadcast   149–51, 155–78
  Australian content   161, 175–6, 181
  children's   176–7
  contempt, special dangers   101–3, 121–5
  copyright   79–81, 83, 87, 89–90
  defamation   10, 28–9, 42–3, 162–3
  electoral   177–8
  laws affecting   160–78
  political broadcasts and current affairs   161–4
  press reports   178
  protection of a concept   190
  religion   178
  sport and entertainments   164
  standards   166–8, 183
  taste and decency   143–52
  transcripts   162–3
  see also Australian Broadcasting Tribunal
protected reports, defamation   50–6
public broadcasting   155, 158, 160, 166–83

public controversy   104, 113–16, 118, 122, 166–8, 175
public meetings, defamation   55
public records, defamation   55–6
publication
   broadcasts   121, 160–78
   contempt   102, 106, 122–5, 140–1
   copyright   84
   defamation   26–9, 58
   offensive   147–9
   restrictions on   136–9, 149, 153, 203–5
puffery   62–3, 72, 211–12
Punch case   14, 24–5
pyramid selling   236, 242–3

qualified privilege   36–44, 55
   see also privilege
quality claims in advertising   221–2

radio
   copyright   78, 80, 81, 83, 87, 89, 95
   interception   187, 191–2, 195–6
   law   5
   see also broadcasting
rebroadcasting   88
recordings, copyright   79, 80, 81–2, 83, 90–3, 95–7
records of broadcasts   162–3
references   6
referral selling   236, 242–3
religion
   blasphemy   145–7
   broadcasting   178
remedies in defamation   58–60
replies to attacks, defamation   38–9
reporters
   see journalists
reputation
   business   18, 32, 61–75
   location   69–71, 75
   personal   7–8, 10–13, 136
   professional   13–15
   subsistence   69–71
research, copyright   94
retraction, defamation   59
reviews
   copyright   94–5
ridicule   16–17, 131, 135

Rigby case   114–16
royal commissions
   contempt by   126–7
   contempt of   104–5, 108, 117
   defamation   54
   disclosure of sources to   192–3

sales promotions   236–43
   bait advertising   236–9
   inertia selling   236, 240–2
   prizes   239
   pyramid selling   236, 242–3
   trading stamps   236, 239–40
   see also advertisements
'scandalizing' courts   129–34
scripts, copyright   78
sedition   152–4
self-regulatory codes
   advertisements   232–4
   broadcasting   64–6, 174–5, 177
   disparaging advertisements   61–6
slander   10
songs, copyright   92
sound recordings   75, 79, 82–3, 87
sources
   copyright, acknowledgement   94–5
   defamation   9–10, 29, 50–3
   journalists   192–3
Special Broadcasting Service   87, 156–63, 164–6, 172, 179–80, 199
speeches, copyright   77, 85
sponsorship
   broadcasting   172–5
   falsely claimed   224–5
sporting broadcasts   164, 175
Spycatcher case   195
'stop' writs   118–20
study, copying for   94
sub judice publications   99–128
   'atmospheric' prejudice   112, 116
   broadcasting   99–104, 106, 116–17, 121–5
   commencement of proceedings   120–1
   parties   110–11
   prejudice, essence of   99–120
   punishment   122–5
   termination of proceedings   121–2
   tribunals   125–8

witnesses 101, 104, 111–13, 127–8
Sunday Times case 102, 103–4, 110–11, 117–18, 120, 122
suppression of names 136–8
Supreme Courts 3–4

Taco Bill case 70, 75
Talbot's case 191
tapes, copyright 78–9, 87
Telecommunications regulations 152, 196
television 155–85
 copyright 79, 80
 mock-ups in advertising 221–2
 sporting events 164, 175
 see also broadcasting, and programmes
terminology, legal 5–6
test results in advertising 220–1
testimonials in advertising 219–20
thalidomide case
 see Sunday Times case
2HD case 181
Timor documents case 86–7, 93–5, 193–4
titles
 copyright 78, 93
 passing off 66–75
trade practices
 advertising 211–35, 247
 copyright actions 96–8
 criminal actions 212–14, 230–2
 defences 231–2
 passing-off actions 71–5
 penalties 230
 private litigants 214
 see also advertisements
Trade Practices Act 4–5, 7, 62, 71–5, 96–8, 126, 139, 156, 172, 194, 204, 211–30
 penalties under the 230
Trade Practices Commission 194, 204, 214–30, 237
Trade Practices Tribunal 126, 139

trade secrets 188–95
 see confidential information
trading stamps 236, 239–40
translations, copyright 85
tribunals
 contempt of 125–8, 139
 see Administrative Appeals Tribunal, Australian Broadcasting Tribunal, Australian Journalists' Association, Press Council, and Trade Practices Tribunal
triviality, defamation 57–8

United Kingdom courts 3–4
United States legal system 4
Universal Copyright Conventions 95–6
University of New South Wales (copying) case 91

voluntary codes
 advertisements 211–12, 232–5
 Australian Journalists' Association 206–7
 broadcasting 64–6, 174–5, 177
 disparaging advertisements 64–6
 'D' notices 197
 Press Council 208–10

Waterhouse case 107, 117
Willesee case (first) 117, 124–5
Willesee case (second) 115
witnesses
 abuse of 127
 influencing 101, 104, 111–13, 127–8
 intimidating 133
 protecting 135, 136–8
words, defamatory meanings 18–26, 32
World Series Cricket case 216, 224
Wran case 100, 117

Zoo Discotheque case 72, 75